THE ART & SCIENCE OF TRADING

THE ART & SCIENCE OF TRADING

TIMELESS MARKET FUNDAMENTALS

ROHIT KATWAL

AMARYLLIS

AMARYLLIS

An imprint of Manjul Publishing House Pvt. Ltd.
• C-16, Sector 3, Noida, Uttar Pradesh 201301, India
Website: www.manjulindia.com
Registered Office:
• 2nd Floor, Usha Preet Complex, 42 Malviya Nagar, Bhopal 462 003 – India
Distribution Centres
Ahmedabad, Bengaluru, Chennai, Hyderabad, Kochi, Kolkata, Mumbai, Noida, Pune

The Art & Science of Trading by Rohit Katwal

First published in paperback in India in 2025

ISBN 978-93-5543-642-9

Printed and bound in India by Repro India Limited

This book is dedicated to my father, Mr. Krishan Pratap Singh, who taught me what the market is, and is the reason for where and what I am today.

To my mother, Nisha Singh, who endured every hardship and never lost her trust in me.

And most of all, to my wife and loving daughters, who always put a twinkle in my eye.

Disclaimer

This book is for informational and educational purposes only and does not constitute financial advice. The author is not responsible for any losses incurred as a result of information contained herein.

Contents

CHAPTER 1

Introduction

The journey begins

The stock market can be intriguing for someone who has no knowledge of it in the first place. When someone asks me how to "start trading", my answer is that you need to open a demat account, and then you can start trading. And just by saying the phrase "demat account", the conversation is lost.

The easiest way to start is to have someone guide you through the process. For me, it was my father who introduced me to the stock market. By the time I graduated with a degree in computer science, he had already helped me set up my own trading account.

Back then, I didn't have a clue what I wanted to do. I thought about starting a business, but I didn't have any experience. At one point, I even considered learning web design, but I'm glad I didn't.

One afternoon, I was sitting with my dad helping him operate his laptop for trading. He initiated a buy trade on INFY, which was called INFOSYS back then. In 15 minutes, he made a profit of Rs. 55,000 on the trade, and he was done.

That was the exact moment I understood that I loved computers, but not computer science. The possibility of not leaving my hometown, the ability to make decent profit (at the time, Rs. 55,000 was like half a month's salary), being rich, financial freedom, and working with the internet and a laptop was all I ever wanted.

Boy, was I wrong!

Over the next six years, I went through one of the most challenging periods of my life. I 'blew up' my trading account several times, graduated with an MBA, reluctantly took a job I never wanted, and eventually quit after four years and returned to full-time trading once again.

As I look back now, the learning curve was too steep. My father was from a service background. Apart from decent behavior and strong academic performance, I was never groomed for the service sector, or for a business, or entrepreneurship. Today, I wish I could go back in time with the knowledge I have now. I look back at decades of learning and tons of missed opportunities.

With all the information out there, how would I learn trading now? There is too much information out there. Price action, technical analysis, indicators, candle patterns, chart patterns, strategies, and whatnot. I learnt it all at the same time. Everything, everywhere, all at once. My mind took decades of practical trading to create a structure out of it. Why am I writing this book? So that when someone asks me how they can learn trading, rather than thinking about my answer, I can simply refer them to this book and say, "This is how I would learn it all over again."

This book goes beyond just learning patterns, strategies, and indicators. It offers a structured approach to understanding all the essential aspects of successful trading. By the end, you'll gain the clarity and confidence to develop your unique trading framework. You'll learn to critically assess various techniques, including price action, trends, technical analysis, candlestick, chart patterns, timeframes, etc. and apply them strategically in your trading journey.

The objective of this book is to make you an independent trader who can think for yourself without looking for outside advice.

CHAPTER 2

Risk Management and Position Sizing

The most important part of your trading journey. Do not skip this!

Your first profit can blind you to the inherent risks of the stock market. Sometimes, that blindness can last until you've blown your account, depleted your savings, accumulated debt, or gone bankrupt.

The key to success in any business, not just the stock market, lies in managing risk and allocating resources wisely. We do this instinctively in our daily life. The life and health insurance you buy, the skills you learn to stay relevant, taking on a side hustle – these are all ways of managing risk for financial hardship, health concerns, or job security. Yet, when it comes to trading, where real money is on the line, we often get caught up in the potential profits and neglect this instinctive core principle.

And I understand! The stock market is intoxicating and addictive. What other business allows literally anyone with a trading account to earn profit from the comfort of their smartphone during a bus ride or on a lunch break? And that allure, coupled with the blinding effect of early profits, can be catastrophic. I have seen traders with accounts worth crores sliding into bankruptcy, get ridden with debt, or reach the verge of having a mental breakdown, all because they downplay the risks.

How important is risk management and position sizing? Well, I bet if you only understood this chapter and avoided the rest of the book, you would still become a profitable trader. Does that sound like a good starting point?

It is only when you have nothing that you understand who your real friends are.

Money is a resource. This resource is finite. The most important task of a trader is to protect it at any cost. You can only trade in the stock market if you have money. And if you lose your savings, investments, or money, do you think someone will cover for you during hard times? I have seen traders asking their friends, family, and relatives for financial help, taking a loan, or mortgaging an asset, buried so deep in debt that it's impossible to recover. To the point that once they have nothing left, they are finally ready to learn risk management and position sizing. Even if you can somehow recover the money, can you recover the lost time? Is it necessary to endure such hardship, such mental torture, to learn the core principle the hard way?

My point is this: once you have lost your capital, there is no one that can help you. The only way to protect your capital in stock market is to understand risk management and position sizing before anything else.

Understand that trading is the most competitive business in the world. Just because you have the comfort of trading from your smartphone sitting on a bus or in a park doesn't mean it's easy. You are trading against computers who can trade faster than you and people who are more intelligent than you, have more information than you, and have more money than you. Do you think it will be easy? No. That is why risk management and position sizing are at the start of this book, when I have your maximum attention. Learn this now, and the rest of the book will be a breeze.

Risk Management – Coin Toss Experiment

I want you to do an exercise. Suppose you have Rs. 1,00,000. Take a 1- or 5-rupee coin. Take a notebook and a pen. Toss the coin. Every time you get a head, you win Rs. 1000 on a trade. Every time you get a tail, you lose Rs. 500. Do this 100 times. This is a real-world simulation of what happens when you trade based on a chance, but with proper risk management. I did this exercise for you, and the results are in Image 2.1.

1	Head	26	Tail	51	Head	76	Head	
2	Tail	27	Head	52	Tail	77	Tail	
3	Head	28	Tail	53	Tail	78	Tail	
4	Head	29	Head	54	Head	79	Head	
5	Tail	30	Head	55	Head	80	Head	
6	Head	31	Tail	56	Head	81	Head	
7	Head	32	Tail	57	Head	82	Tail	
8	Head	33	Tail	58	Head	83	Head	
9	Head	34	Tail	59	Head	84	Head	
10	Tail	35	Head	60	Head	85	Tail	
11	Tail	36	Tail	61	Tail	86	Head	
12	Head	37	Head	62	Tail	87	Head	
13	Tail	38	Head	63	Head	88	Tail	**Head - 51**
14	Head	39	Tail	64	Tail	89	Head	**Tail - 49**
15	Tail	40	Head	65	Tail	90	Tail	
16	Tail	41	Head	66	Tail	91	Head	
17	Head	42	Tail	67	Head	92	Tail	
18	Head	43	Tail	68	Tail	93	Tail	
19	Tail	44	Head	69	Tail	94	Head	
20	Head	45	Head	70	Tail	95	Tail	
21	Tail	46	Tail	71	Head	96	Tail	
22	Head	47	Tail	72	Head	97	Tail	
23	Tail	48	Tail	73	Head	98	Head	
24	Tail	49	Head	74	Head	99	Tail	
25	Tail	50	Head	75	Tail	100	Tail	

IMAGE 2.1: The result of tossing an unbiased coin 100 times

Here's how the experiment played out.

Scenario 1: Coin toss experiment

Here are the statistics of this random unbiased coin toss experiment.

- **Total capital** = Rs. 1,00,000
- **Total trades** = 100
- **Total heads** = 51
- **Total tails** = 49
- **Profit** = No. of heads * Rs. 1000 = 51 * Rs. 1000 = Rs. 51,000
- **Loss** = No. of tails * Rs. 500 = 49 * Rs. 500 = Rs. 24,500
- **Net Profit** = Profit – Loss = Rs. 51,000 – Rs. 24,500 = Rs. 26,500

But this is not the only information that we got through this experiment.

- **Longest winning streak**: 4 (no. of times heads came consecutively)
- **Longest losing streak**: 4 (no. of times tails came consecutively)
- Our **winning probability** is 51%.
- Our **losing probability** is 49%.
- We are risking Rs. 500 against a potential gain of Rs. 1000. Our **risk/reward ratio** is 500:1000 = 1:2 (generally called RR).

We can see that a random unbiased coin with a 51% chance of winning with a proper RR (risk/reward ratio) has a profitability of 26.5% after 100 trades. Which brings us to another observation.

> *Trading is not about 1 or 10 trades. To validate whether a trading method, strategy, or philosophy will work, we must validate that hypothesis across a large sample of data.*

Here, we are testing that on at least 100 coin tosses. We are net profitable even when we are making a loss 49% of the time by controlling our risk.

In real-world trading, win probabilities rarely sit at a perfect 50/50. Let's explore how the experiment changes with win probabilities between 40% and 60% and a risk/reward of 500:1000. See Table 2.1.

Scenario	Win %	Loss %	Risk	Reward	Profit	Loss	Net P/L	ROI
Scenario 1	51%	49%	500	1000	51,000	24,500	26,500	26.5%
Mod 2	35%	65%	500	1000	35,000	32,500	2500	2.5%
Mod 3	40%	60%	500	1000	40,000	30,000	10,000	10%
Mod 4	60%	40%	500	1000	60,000	20,000	40,000	40%

TABLE 2.1: How ROI changes with various winning probabilities and risk/reward ratios

Table 2.1 shows different modifications, and most important of all is Mod 2 – even when the losing probability is 65%, by controlling how much we lose versus how much we win (RR of 1:2), we are slightly above our breakeven point.

It also demonstrates that by increasing our winning probability by 5% in Mod 3, we increased our net profit to 10%; that is an overall increase of 300% in net profit compared to Mod 2.

Coming to Mod 4, when we increased our winning probability by 9% from Mod 3, which was the original coin toss experiment, we increased our net profit to 40%; an increase in profitability by 50.94%.

This whole experiment is meant to demonstrate how we can make profit in the market with a random method following a strict risk management method with a 1:2 RR, even when our winning probability might just be as low as 40%. This experiment emphasizes the importance of both win probability and risk/reward ratio in achieving profitability. But what happens if a trading strategy has a high or low win probability but not a good risk/reward ratio? Let's explore this scenario.

Scenario 2: Coin toss experiment with risk of Rs. 1000 and reward of Rs. 1000

Let's explore how, with a slight change in risk/reward, the profit-loss matrix changes completely. See Table 2.2.

Scenario	Win %	Loss %	Risk	Reward	Profit	Loss	Net P/L	ROI
Scenario 2	51%	49%	1000	1000	51,000	49,000	2000	**2%**
Mod 2	35%	65%	1000	1000	35,000	65,000	-30,000	**-30%**
Mod 3	40%	60%	1000	1000	40,000	60,000	-20,000	**-20%**
Mod 4	60%	40%	1000	1000	60,000	40,000	20,000	**20%**

TABLE 2.2: The effect of bad RR on profitability

Observe how the statistics have changed drastically by changing just 1 variable – that is, the risk/reward ratio – to 1:1. In Mod 2, we are making a loss of 30%. In Mod 3, we are making a loss of 20%, and in Mod 4, we are making a profit of 20%.

Head back to Scenario 1. In our coin toss experiment in Table 2.1, with the same winning probability of 60% in Mod 4, we were making a profit of 40%, which has now dropped by 50% by just reducing the risk/reward ratio.

Without delving further into complicated calculations, let me share a cheat sheet with you. See Image 2.2.

RR/Win%	30	40	50	60	70
01:01	-40%	-30%	-20%	-10%	0%
01:02	-10%	0%	10%	20%	30%
01:03	20%	30%	40%	50%	60%
01:04	50%	60%	70%	80%	90%
01:05	80%	90%	100%	110%	120%
01:06	110%	120%	130%	140%	150%

IMAGE 2.2: A cheat sheet showing the effect of winning probability and RR on profitability

Image 2.2 shows the risk/reward ratio and win rate at which you can be profitable, at a breakeven, or at a net loss. The next time you think about taking a trade in the market based on any indicator, strategy, pattern, analysis, etc., ask yourself whether you know the winning probability and RR on a sample of at least 100 trades. If the answer is "no", you had better avoid the trade. And if you are already trading but facing challenges becoming consistently profitable, ask yourself whether you know the winning probability and risk/reward ratio of your trading system.

Risk Management =
Optimized (Risk/Reward + Winning Probability)

Position Sizing

Position sizing refers to how much of your trading capital you will deploy on a single trade. Why is that important? Look at the chart of PAYTM. In Image 2.3.

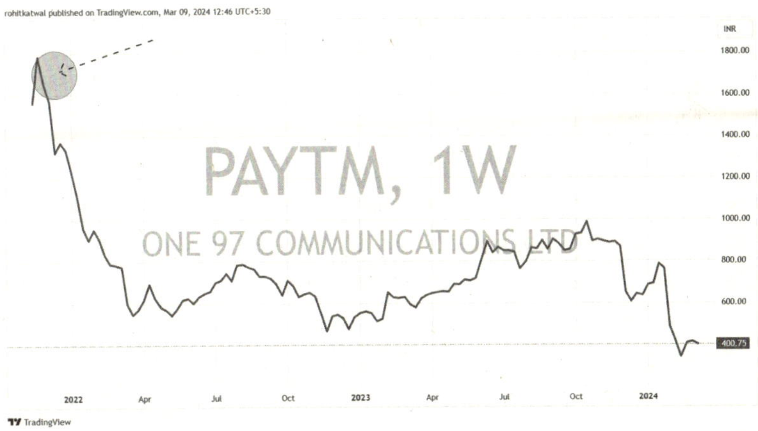

IMAGE 2.3: A PAYTM chart after listing on bourses

Imagine that after PAYTM's listing day, a trader, caught up in the excitement (FOMO – fear of missing out), decides to invest their trading capital, Rs. 1,00,000, into the stock. They purchase 58 shares at the listing price of Rs. 1700 per share.

- **Total investment:** Rs. 1,00,000
  (58 shares * Rs. 1700/share)

Here's the key part. Fast forward to March 2024:

- The current market price of PAYTM is around Rs. 400.
- The total value of their 50 shares today: Rs. 23,200
  (58 shares * Rs. 400/share)

Ouch! Our investor's initial Rs. 1,00,000 investment is now worth only Rs. 23,200. This is a ~78% loss!

I'm not saying this will happen every time, but there's always a possibility.

The revenue beat analyst estimates and future guidance seemed promising, but the stock tanked after you bought it. Why? This could be due to profit-booking by earlier investors, or unexpected government regulation, or even investigation into the company.

These scenarios are out of your control, and if you invest or trade all your capital into one stock, you are one trade away from disaster.

If you invest your entire capital (Rs. 1,00,000) into a single stock like PAYTM, you're one bad trade away from disaster.

Imagine if you had instead only invested 20% of your capital (Rs. 20,000) into PAYTM. With the 80% loss, you'd incur a loss of Rs. 16,000 (80% loss on Rs. 20,000). This translates to a 16% loss on your total capital. But crucially, you'd still be in the game with Rs. 84,000 remaining. This allows you to recover from the loss and potentially make profitable trades in the future.

This example highlights how position sizing can help you limit potential losses and stay in the game even if a trade goes against you.

If you need further convincing why position sizing is essential, refer to Image 2.4.

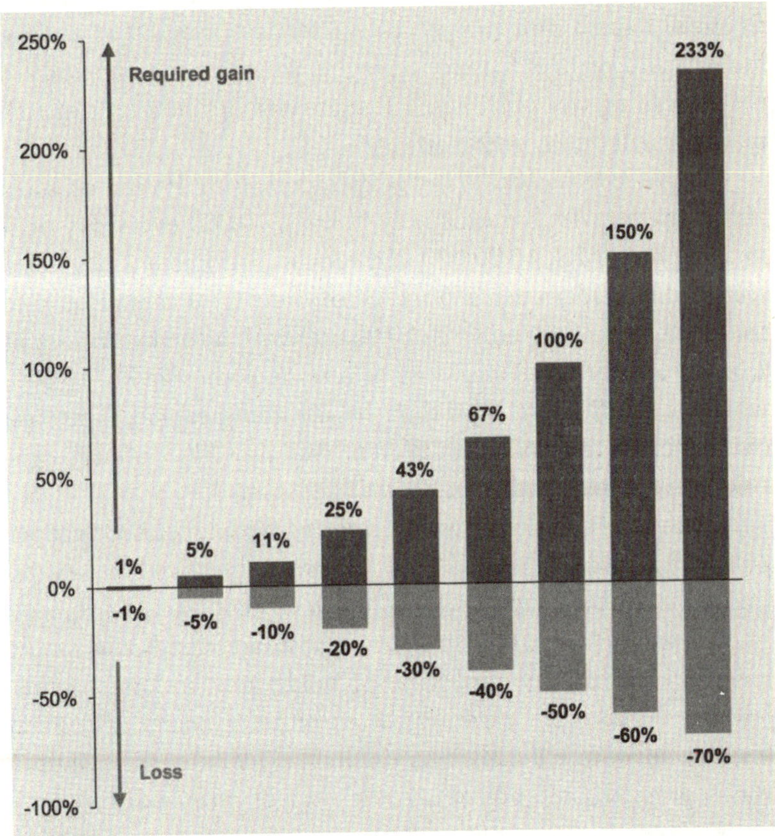

IMAGE 2.4: Percentage gains required for breakeven after loss

If you make a loss of 10%, you need to make profit of 11% on reduced capital to get a breakeven. For 50% loss you have to make profit of 100% from reduced capital to get a breakeven.

Like I said at the start of the chapter:

It is only when you have nothing that you understand who your real friends are.

Before you start trading, you must ask yourself, what if you lose all your capital? Would you be comfortable with even the slight possibility of blowing your trading account or having to face financial hardship or turn to your friends or family, or endure months and years of frustration trying to figure out why you are not becoming net profitable? The answer lies in a lack of risk management and position sizing.

I have seen successful intraday traders using 1% risk on their 100% capital, which means they risk Rs. 10,000 every day on a total capital of Rs. 10,00,000 and remain profitable. I have also seen swing traders using only 4% of their total capital on one trade; i.e., Rs. 40,000 off Rs. 10,00,000 with a total stop-loss of 25% on a trade. 25% stop-loss of a trade comes at Rs. 10,000, which is again only 1% of their total trading capital. They are two different traders with different trading styles and different risk management and position sizing systems.

I learnt all this the hard way. I started trading without proper guidance and knowledge. I blew up my trading account several times. I went bankrupt. I was ridden with debt. I had to do a job I never wanted to in the first place. I lost old friends and family members during my hard times. I made new lifelong friends. I learnt lessons the hard way. I endured 10 years of mental frustration, where during every moment, I wanted to give up, I was depressed, and I pulled my hair out, but I still backtested my trading system at the end of the day while in my job, and then discovered this wisdom through trial and error. Even then, I had no money. You can't trade if you have no capital. Already ridden with debt, I raised money – somehow.

Why am I telling you this? Just to make you understand where this chapter is coming from. This chapter is key to the rest of your trading journey. You will learn new strategies, patterns, trading styles, etc., but the principle that you just learnt in this chapter will remain true forever. I just wish I had someone to teach me this when I was where you are right now.

Going forward, you may want to do any kinds of trading, be it intraday, investment, swing trading, breakouts, momentum, or options buying or selling. The ultimate holy grail of any trading strategy is simply how well you understand risk management and position sizing. Remember, we even made money with a random coin toss.

I urge you to do the coin toss experiment yourself.
It will be a lesson for life.

CHAPTER 3

Understanding Price Action

Just remember: the beginning is always tough!

Price Action

Have you ever noticed how the price of everyday items seems to change over the years? Take Coca-Cola, for example. As a kid, it was a real treat, and my mom always had a crate on hand. Back in the 1970s, a bottle cost just 0.25 paise! By the 1980s, the price had risen to Rs. 1, and in the 90s, it ranged between Rs. 5 and Rs. 8. I remember the family uproar in 1995 when the price jumped another Rs. 2. This price increase wasn't unique to Coca-Cola – it's a common trend we see with many products.

This is where understanding price movements becomes crucial for investors and traders. By plotting these price changes on a chart, we can visually see how prices fluctuate over time.

The price can be summarized over the years in Table 3.1.

Coca-Cola	
Year	Price
1970's	₹ 0.25
1980's	₹ 1
1990's	₹ 5
1995's	₹ 8
2010's	₹ 20
2020's	₹ 36

TABLE 3.1: Tabulated price of a 300 ml Coca-Cola bottle as I remember it

Image 3.1 shows how Coca-Cola prices might appear on a chart, with years on the x-axis (horizontal) and price on the y-axis (vertical).

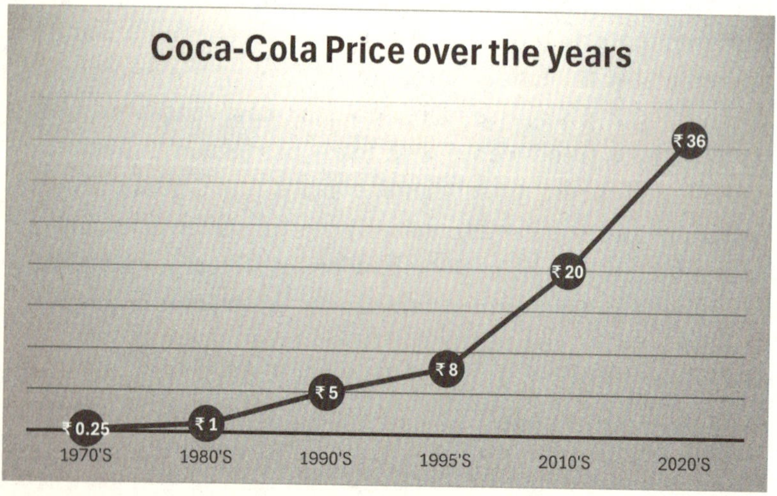

IMAGE 3.1: A chart of the price over time of a 300 ml Coca-Cola bottle

Observe how the price of Coca-Cola has been rising over the years. It's clear that prices aren't always constant – they can trend upwards over time. This is a concept we call a trend. With everyday items like Coca-Cola, inflation often leads to gradually increasing prices.

Let's look at another commodity whose prices fluctuate more dramatically: petrol. Unlike Coca-Cola, petrol prices are influenced by factors like supply and demand, global events, and even national elections. Table 3.2 shows the annual petrol prices in New Delhi from 2003 to 2018.

Petrol prices	
Date	**Delhi**
16-04-2003	₹ 32.49
20-06-2005	₹ 40.49
05-06-2006	₹ 47.51
10-06-2006	₹ 47.51
16-05-2007	₹ 42.85
24-05-2008	₹ 45.56
29-01-2009	₹ 40.62
02-07-2009	₹ 44.72
27-02-2010	₹ 47.43
01-04-2010	₹ 47.93
15-05-2011	₹ 63.37
24-05-2012	₹ 73.18
23-05-2013	₹ 63.09
07-06-2014	₹ 71.51
16-05-2015	₹ 66.29
17-05-2016	₹ 63.02
16-05-2017	₹ 65.32
29-05-2018	₹ 78.43

TABLE 3.2: Petrol prices in Delhi over the years

By plotting this data on a chart (Image 3.2), we can see the ups and downs of petrol prices over time. The price might go up to ₹47 one year and then come back down to ₹42 the next. This is how petrol prices would appear on a chart. There are occasional dips but the overall trend for petrol prices have been upwards in recent years.

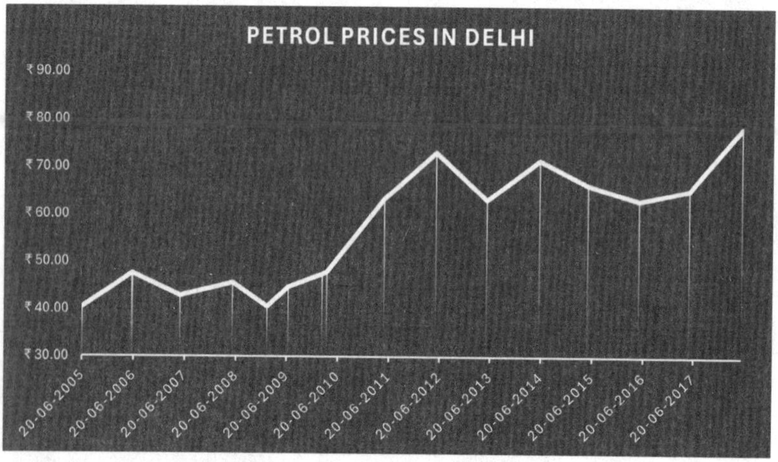

IMAGE 3.2: Chart of petrol prices in Delhi from 2003–2018

Now that we understand how the price fluctuates for commodities like petrol, in the same manner, the price of the stock of a company also fluctuates constantly based on various factors. To understand these price fluctuations, traders, investors, and analysts use a technique called price action analysis.

Price action analysis refers to the identification of trends or potential trading opportunities using historical price movements of a stock visualized on charts.

Price action analysis is widely accepted across the trading community; therefore, it is essentially a reflection of human behavior with respect to the prices of a particular stock. That is why when we analyze chart with price action, we are essentially analyzing the psychological behavior of stock market participants.

Does that make sense? Don't worry. It will become clear as we move forward. For now, let us start with basic analysis.

Types of Charts

Let's analyze the RELIANCE line chart in Image 3.3.

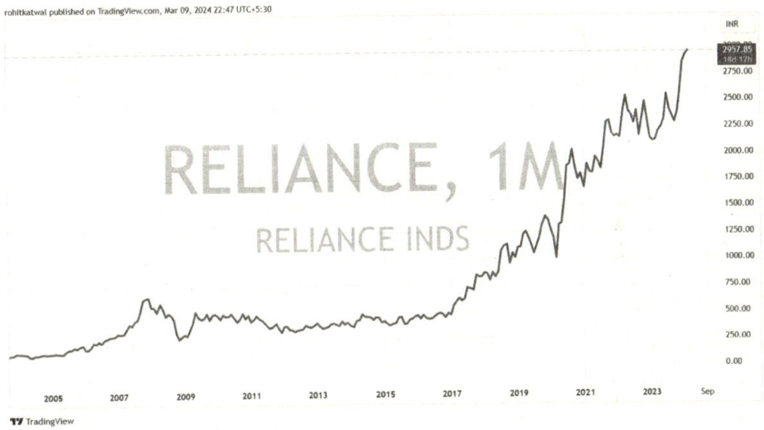

IMAGE 3.3: A monthly line chart of RELIANCE

Line chart

The line chart in Image 3.3 shows the price history of Reliance Industries Limited (RELIANCE) plotted on a monthly timeframe. We can see that the price has experienced a significant upward trend, going from Rs. 120 in August 2004 to Rs. 2900 in February 2024.

Line charts are a fundamental tool for analyzing price movements over extended periods. As we saw with the Coca-Cola and petrol price examples, line charts provide a clear visual representation of trends. In the Reliance chart, we're looking at price movements over a 20-year timeframe.

It's important to note that line charts typically plot only one data point per time period. For example, since the RELIANCE chart is on a monthly timeframe, the charting software plots the closing price of RELIANCE for each month. (The closing price is the price at which the stock last traded on a particular day. This is a common data point used for monthly charts as it provides a snapshot of the stock's price at the end of the trading day.) While the price may have fluctuated throughout the month during trading hours, the line chart focuses on the closing price to represent each month.

But since we are analyzing price action, one data point is not enough for us. Price fluctuations, which are not captured, might be telling a different story. So let's analyze the price data of RELIANCE for the period of Jan '20 to Dec '23 on monthly as well as weekly charts (Images 3.4 and 3.5).

By reducing the timeframe from monthly to weekly charts, we increased the data per month by 4 new data points; i.e., the closing price of RELIANCE for each week on Friday evenings. This adds more details to the price for us to analyze. How will we analyze it? We'll come to that in the subsequent chapters. But understand that the line chart only presents one data point (i.e., the closing price) which may be good to suggest a trend on a big timeframe, but gives no detailed insight into market behavior. That is why we use candlestick charts.

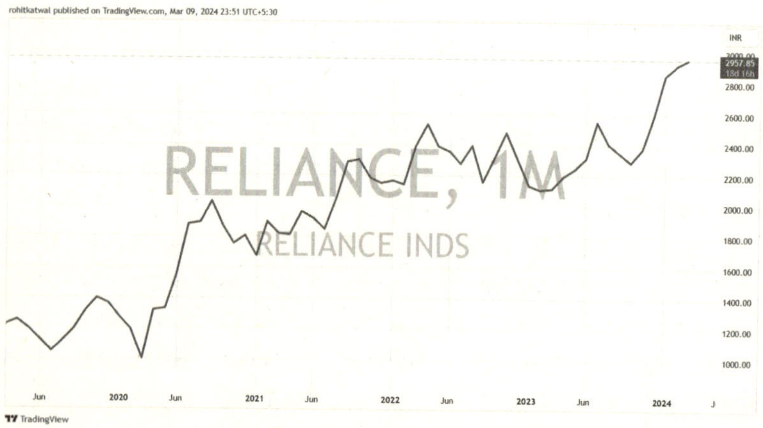

IMAGE 3.4: A monthly chart of RELIANCE (2020-2024)

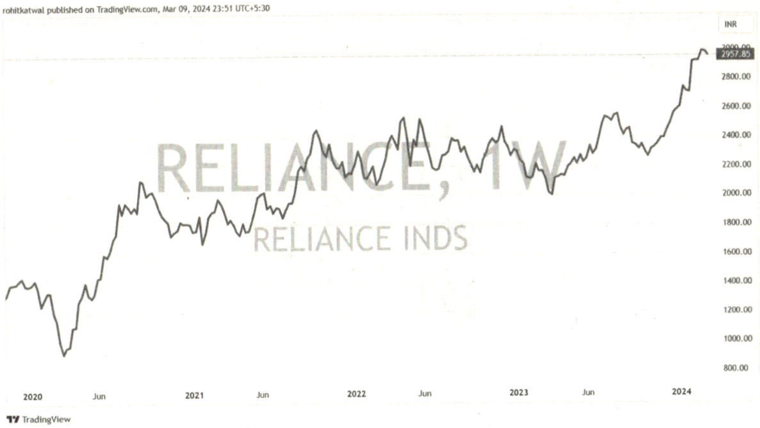

IMAGE 3.5: A weekly chart of RELIANCE (2020-2024)

Candlesticks

Chart candlesticks reflect the price behavior of an asset over a specific timeframe. For example, a daily candlestick chart shows the open, high, low and close prices for a single trading day (typically between 9:15 a.m. and 3:30 p.m.).

O = Open (opening price for the day)

H = High (highest price for the day)

L = Low (lowest price for the day)

C = Close (closing price for the day)

LTP = Used primarily for incomplete timeframes, showing the last traded price at the time of viewing.

It is also called an OHLC chart pattern (for Open, High, Low, Close formation).

Image 3.6 shows what a candlestick looks like.

A green candlestick indicates a bullish day, where the closing price was higher than the opening price. Conversely, a red candlestick signifies a bearish day, where the closing price was lower than the opening price. This color-coding helps us quickly visualize whether buyers or sellers were in control for that particular timeframe.

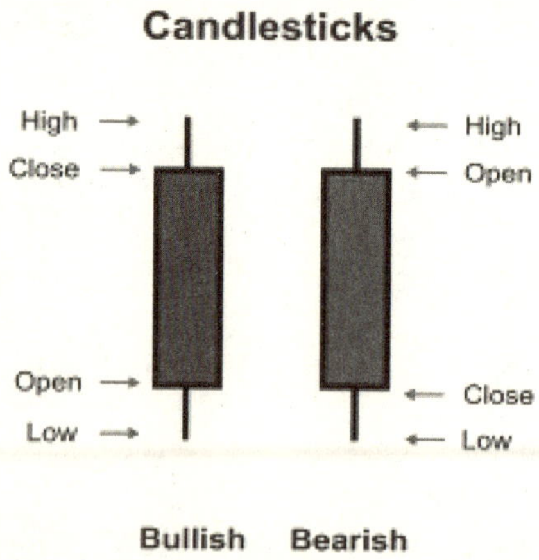

IMAGE 3.6: Candlesticks

A candlestick reflects the price behavior between two different times. Breaking down timeframes:

- **Monthly:** Price behavior between the 1st to 31st of that month.
- **Weekly:** Price behavior between Monday to Friday.
- **Daily:** Price behavior for the day between 9:15 a.m. to 3:30 p.m.
- **Hourly:** Price behavior between 9:15 a.m. to 10:15 a.m., 10:16 a.m. to 11:15 a.m., and so on.

This will make more sense when we put a monthly chart of RELIANCE on line charts and candlestick charts side by side (Images 3.7 and 3.8).

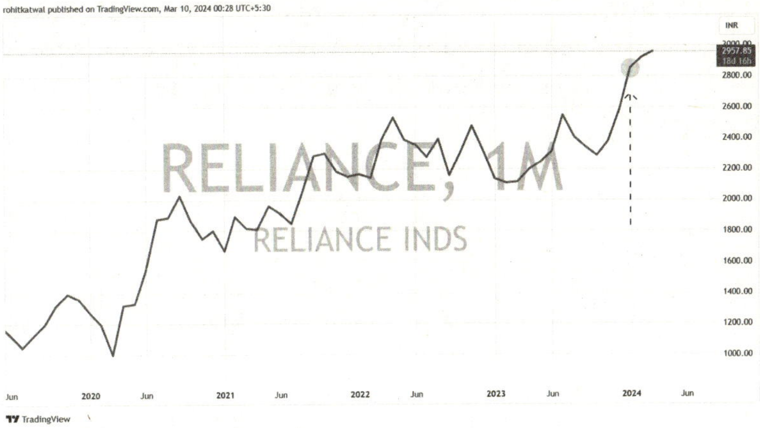

IMAGE 3.7: A RELIANCE monthly line chart

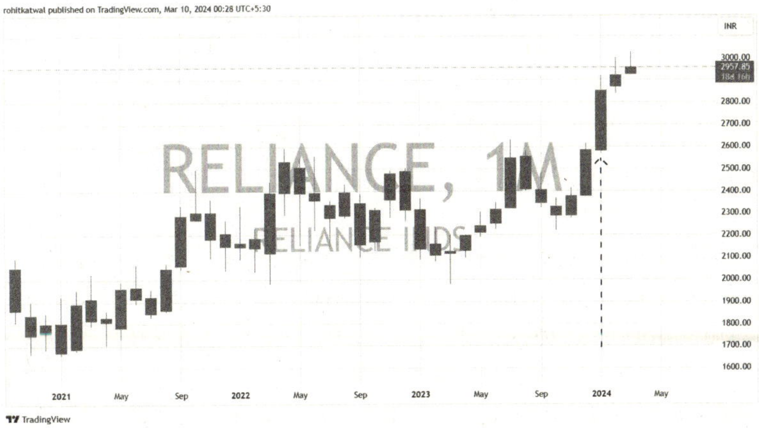

IMAGE 3.8: A RELIANCE monthly candlestick chart

Can you spot the difference? While both charts can tell you that the price is moving up, the candlestick chart has the added distinction of indicating days where the price closed lower than the open with red candles. But the major difference is the information it conveys.

The line chart simply tells us where the price closed at the end of January 2024. But the candlestick chart tells us that on 31 January 2024, the candle price opened at 2580, made a low of 2569, made a high of 3025, and finally closed at 2957 (i.e., approximately 380 points up), which means the price, for most of January 2024, remained bullish. Something like the illustration in Image 3.8.1.

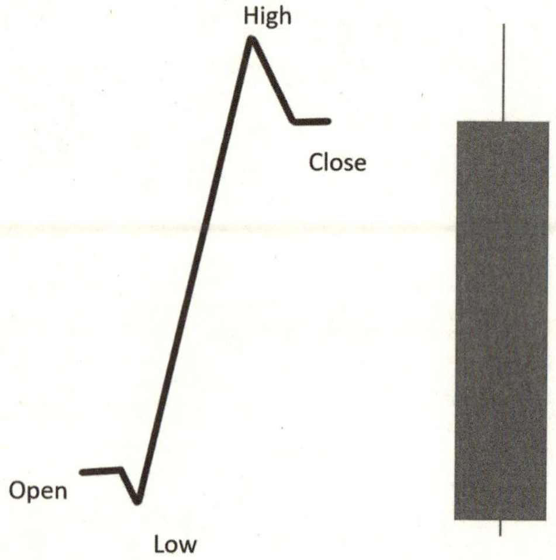

IMAGE 3.8.1: How a candlestick is formed

This data represents human behavior, and we can analyze this as a part of price action analysis to identify trends and trading opportunities.

Why do charts represent human behavior? Since we have established that price action analysis is a widely accepted way of identifying trends and trade identification, a large section of the trading community uses price action for analysis, which is built around largely the same principles. When too many people use the same principles, they tend to form a pattern that becomes visible on price charts. Reading these patterns, formed by human behavior, is called price action analysis. That is why you will sometimes find unusual price patterns that might work because enough traders are giving validation to them through trading, such that it starts reflecting them on the charts.

We will learn more about candlesticks later on. For now, let's move on to understand another basic idea: timeframes.

Timeframes

We know that a line chart represents the last closing price of the selected timeframe. If we are looking at a monthly line chart of RELIANCE until February 2024 (Image 3.9), we can see that the closing price in the month of February for RELIANCE was 2921, but when we switch to candlestick charts., it gives us a bit more information. Rather than telling us where the price closed in the month of February after trading for the full 29 days, it gives us the following information about the month of February '24:

- The opening price on 1 February 2024
- The lowest price traded from 1 February 2024 to 29 February 2024
- The highest price traded from 1 February 2024 to 29 February 2024
- The closing price for the month of February 2024

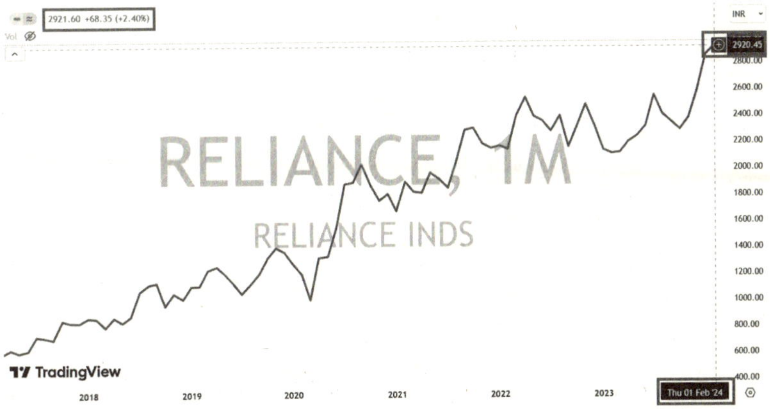

IMAGE 3.9: A line chart showing only the closing price

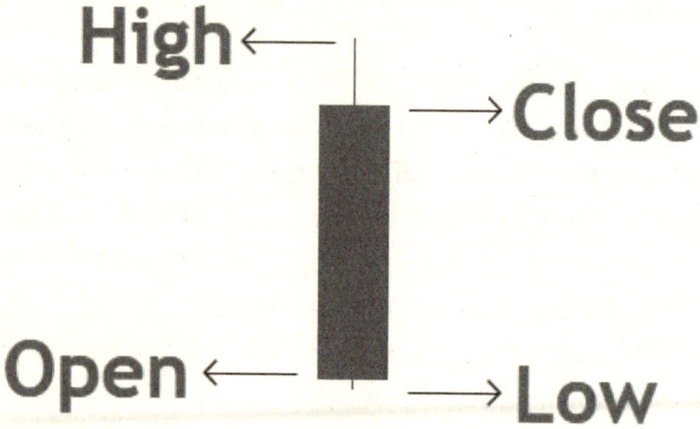

IMAGE 3.10: Depiction of a monthly candlestick for Feb '24

But does that mean prices weren't traded between 1st Feb '24 to 29 Feb '24? If we change our timeframe from monthly to weekly (Image 3.11), we can see 4 weekly candles, and if we go further down, we can see approximately 20 daily candles for RELIANCE in Feb '24 (Image 3.12).

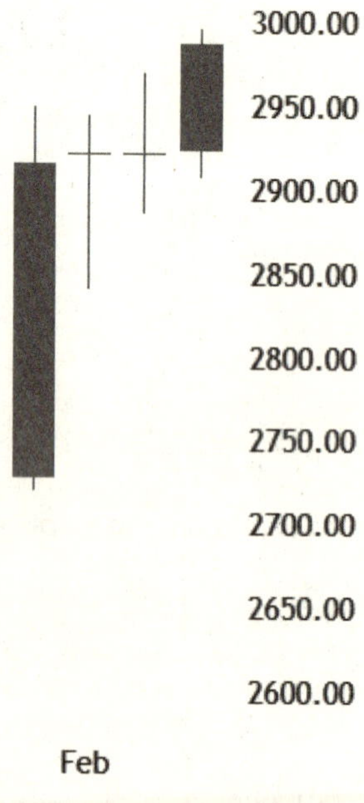

IMAGE 3.11: A weekly chart showing 4 candles for Feb '24

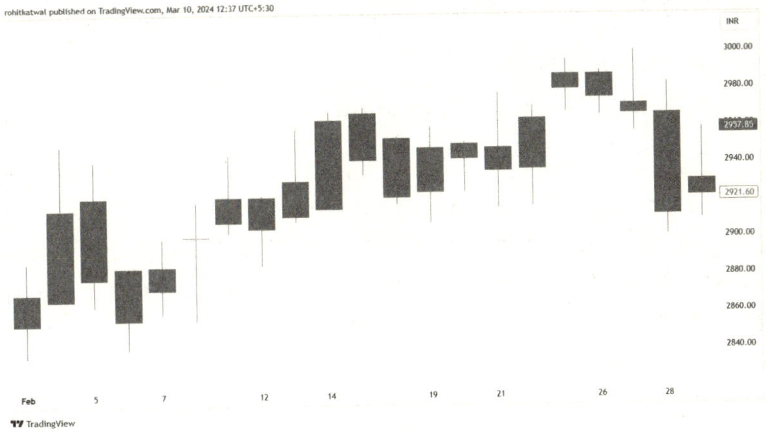

IMAGE 3.12: A daily chart showing 21 candles for Feb '24

And this timeframe can go lower and lower, down to 1 minute, or even 5 seconds. Why? Because when the market is open and stocks are being traded, it's just a price being traded every second of the day as long as the market is open. We have to organize that price into meaningful data to make it easier to take a trading decision.

This will become easier with time, but for now, I have built a handy cheat sheet for you to understand what kind of traders or investors trade on what timeframe. This cheat sheet is according to my understanding, and is not something that's set in stone. Every trader will have a different experience with timeframes based on his learning and experience. See Image 3.13.

	Timeframe	**Holding Period**	**Type of Chart**	
Investors	Monthly	More Than 10 Years	Candlestick	Line
	Weekly	More Than 10 Years	Candlestick	Line
Swing Traders	Weekly	More than 6 Months	Candlestick	Line
	Daily	More than 2 Months	Candlestick	
	2/3/4 Hours	More than 5 days	Candlestick	
Intraday Traders	1/3/5/15 Minutes	No Overnight Positions	Candlestick	Line
		Trades from 09:15 to 03:30 pm		

IMAGE 3.13: A timeframe cheat sheet

But why have different timeframes in the first place?

- To reduce noise; or
- To give more information

Higher timeframes allow us to view data over longer periods, reducing noise and providing clearer insights. If a long-term investor has invested in RELIANCE in 2016, it only makes sense that he wants to check the price on monthly charts to get an overall sense where his investments are. He is not bothered about daily or weekly price fluctuations. Better yet, he can shift to a line chart for a cleaner perspective.

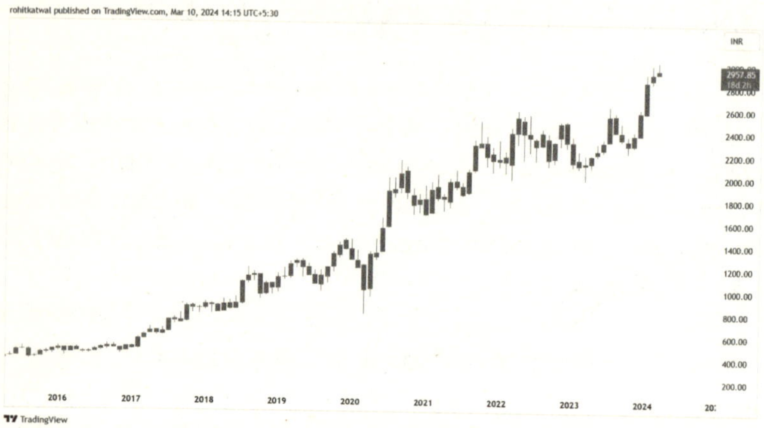

IMAGE 3.14: A RELIANCE monthly candlestick chart

Compare Image 3.14 and Image 3.15. Can you see the difference between a candlestick chart and line chart, and how the noise has been reduced?

But what if you are a short-term swing trader who just wants to analyze the price movement for the next 3-4 months? If we look at the RELIANCE chart on a daily timeframe (Image 3.16), see how the level of noise and detail has increased so much that it can lead to confusion.

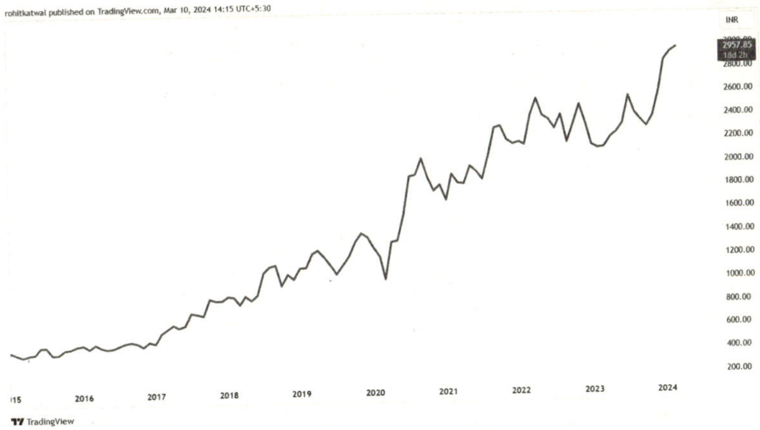

IMAGE 3.15: A RELIANCE monthly line chart

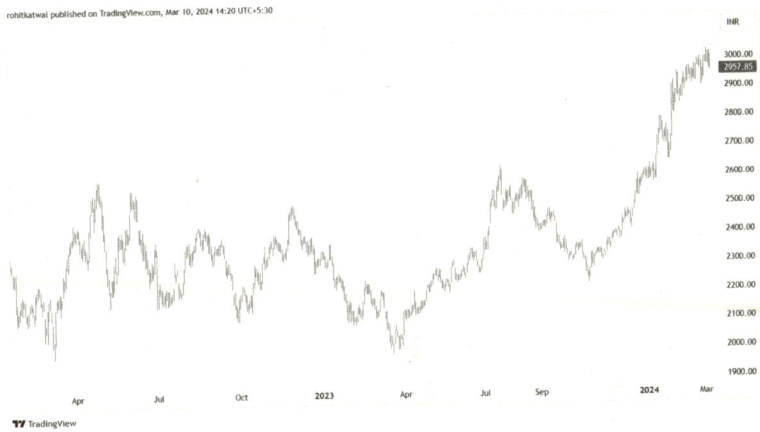

IMAGE 3.16: A RELIANCE daily timeframe chart

Most importantly, understand how our holding period decides the level of information we want to see. When looking at a monthly or weekly chart, it might make sense to choose a 5- to 6-year lookback period. But when trading the daily charts, we might only need 1 year of data to take a decision.

Understanding the significance of different timeframes is crucial for tailoring trading strategies to specific objectives, which will come with practice and experience. Candlesticks are not the only chart type. There are more chart types, like bar, Heikin-Ashi, Renko, point and figure, etc., but right now, candlesticks are enough to get you started. Once you gain some experience, you can delve deeper into other chart types, too. For now, let's cover another important topic before we start understanding price action: short selling.

Short Selling

The idea behind price action analysis is to try and find trends and identify probable trades. The price can go up or down, and both these directions can be predicted from price action analysis. When it is about buying a stock and selling it at a higher price, it makes sense. But what if I tell you that you can sell a stock and buy it later at a lower price and make a profit? Don't get confused. Images 3.17.1 and 3.17.2 will remove your confusion.

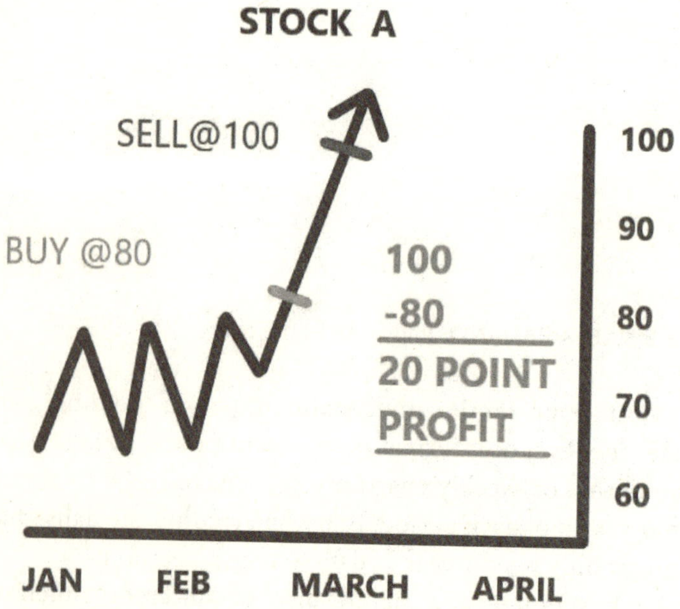

IMAGE 3.17.1: How we profit from a bullish buy trade

In stock A, when the price is rising, we buy the stock at Rs. 80, and when the price rises to Rs. 100, we sell it. Thus, we make a profit of 100 - 80 = Rs. 20 per share.

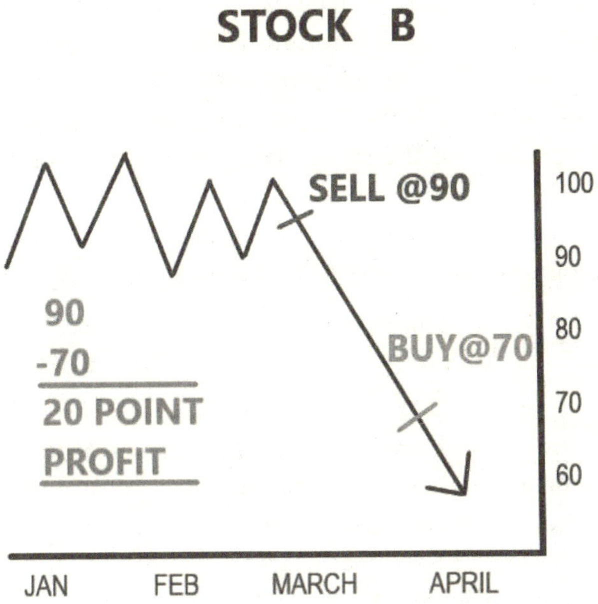

IMAGE 3.17.2: How we profit from a bearish short sell trade

In stock B, when the price is falling, we sell the stock at Rs. 90, and when the price falls to Rs. 70, we buy it. Thus, we make a profit of 90 - 70 = Rs. 20 per share.

Whether you buy a stock or sell a borrowed stock, you'll eventually need to square off your position. Squaring off simply means closing your trade by buying or selling shares to bring your net quantity back to zero. The concept is similar to how you bought shares at Rs. 80 (positive 100 shares) and then sold them at Rs. 100 (negative 100 shares), resulting in a net quantity of zero.

We understand the math. We are making Rs. 20 profit in both scenarios. In stock A, we bought a share and sold it at a higher price. But in stock B, how can we sell a share when we haven't purchased it? Let's understand this.

Let's say you own a property you want to sell for Rs. 10 lakhs, but you can't find a buyer. A realtor approaches you with an interesting proposition. They can find a buyer for Rs. 10 lakhs, but if they manage to sell it for more, they'll keep the difference as their commission. Imagine they sell it for Rs. 11 lakhs and give you your Rs. 10 lakhs, keeping Rs. 1 lakhs as their profit.

Short selling in the stock market works in a similar way. Normally, when you buy a stock, the broker uses your money to purchase shares and delivers them to your account. You can then hold those shares or sell them later for a profit (if the price goes up).

But with short selling, it's like selling a property you don't own. Here's how it works:

1. **Borrow shares:** You borrow shares of a stock you believe will decline in price from your broker.
2. **Sell borrowed shares:** The broker immediately sells these borrowed shares in the market at the current price.
3. **Repurchase shares later:** You wait for the stock price to fall (ideally). Then, you repurchase the same number of shares at the lower price.
4. **Return borrowed shares:** You return the borrowed shares to your broker.
5. **Profit potential:** If the price did go down as you expected, you profit from the difference between the selling price (higher) and the repurchase price (lower).

It's important to remember that there's a risk involved in short selling. Unlike the property example, where the price can only go up to a certain point, the stock market price can go up infinitely. This means if your prediction is wrong and the price goes up, you could lose money. We'll explore these risks and other short selling considerations in more detail later.

Short selling can be a tempting strategy, especially when you believe a stock's price is headed downwards. However, it's crucial to understand the significant risks involved, particularly for retail investors in India.

Unlike some other markets, the ease of borrowing shares for short selling in the Indian stock market can be unpredictable for retail investors. Your broker might not always have the shares available to lend, and failing to deliver borrowed shares can result in hefty penalties from the exchange. This situation, where you are unable to deliver the borrowed shares during short selling, is called short delivery.

Here's a breakdown of the potential consequences of short delivery:

- **Auction penalty:** The exchange conducts an auction to locate shares for delivery. The difference between the original selling price and the higher auction price is charged as a penalty to the seller who failed to deliver (you, in this case). This can be a significant cost if the stock price has gone up between the time you sold it and the auction.
- **Exposure to potential price increase:** Since you haven't repurchased the shares yet, you're exposed to the risk of the stock price increasing. If you're unable to deliver the shares during the auction and the price goes up significantly, you'll need to buy them back at a higher price to return them to your broker, leading to a larger loss.
- **Brokerage penalties:** Your broker might impose additional penalties for failing to fulfil your delivery obligations.

Therefore, for most retail investors in India, it's advisable to avoid short selling in the cash market, given the potential for short delivery and its associated penalties.

However, this doesn't mean short selling opportunities

don't exist in India. Experienced traders can explore short selling strategies in derivative markets like futures & options (F&O), commodities, or forex markets, subject to specific regulations. We'll delve deeper into these advanced strategies later in the book.

Understanding short selling and its risks is essential before attempting this strategy, especially for beginners.

Now let's move to one more important concept before we start with our price action analysis.

Stop-loss

Remember the investor who bought PAYTM at Rs. 2000 and is now facing an 80% loss? Stop-loss orders are designed to help prevent such situations.

When you buy a stock, you're hoping the price will rise. But stock prices can also fall, and there's no guarantee any stock is immune to a decline. This is where stop-loss orders come in. A stop-loss order is an instruction you give to your broker through a trading platform to automatically sell a security if the price falls below a certain level you set (your stop-loss price). This helps you limit potential losses if the market moves against you.

Let's revisit the example of PAYTM. Once the stock listed, you purchased 58 shares @ 1700, amounting to Rs. 1,00,000. Since you were a cautious investor, you decided that if the price comes below its listing price, near Rs. 1,534, you will consider this investment or trade a failure and stop further erosion of your capital, and will look for better trading opportunities. This is explained in Image 3.18.

Once we have set the stop-loss on our trading system, as soon as the price hits the stop-loss level, the broker will automatically exit the trade. In our PAYTM example, this would result in a loss of Rs. 166 per share, totalling Rs. 9,048 for the 58 shares we purchased. While seeing a stop-loss trigger can be discouraging, it's important to remember that it limits potential losses and helps you move on to your next trade.

IMAGE 3.18: A stop-loss explanation using a PAYTM chart

Where you should place a stop-loss order and what an ideal stop-loss is for you – that comes down to the optimal combination of risk management, position sizing, and trading strategies that align with your psychology and mindset. The idea of telling you about stop-losses right now is to make you understand that such a system exists where you can limit your losses as soon as you buy something.

A stop-loss can be also used on short selling trades. See Image 3.19 for an example with ITC. Please note that for the rest of this book, we will be using candlestick charts. For the ease of understanding this concept, I am using line charts. On a daily timeframe, ITC triggered a sell at 444. This trade was shared by me live during one of my *Economic Times* livestreams. We sell the stock at 444 and, per my analysis, I believe if ITC's price goes to 457, my analysis is wrong and I should cut my losses and look for another trading opportunity, hence I will put my stop-loss at 457. If the price goes down, we buy it back at a lower price. If it negates the bearish trend, we will be out with a 13-point loss at 457.

This is a stop-loss in simple language. In real trading, traders get creative with stop-losses, and they can be used for two purposes:

- Booking loss at a certain price
- Booking profit at a certain price

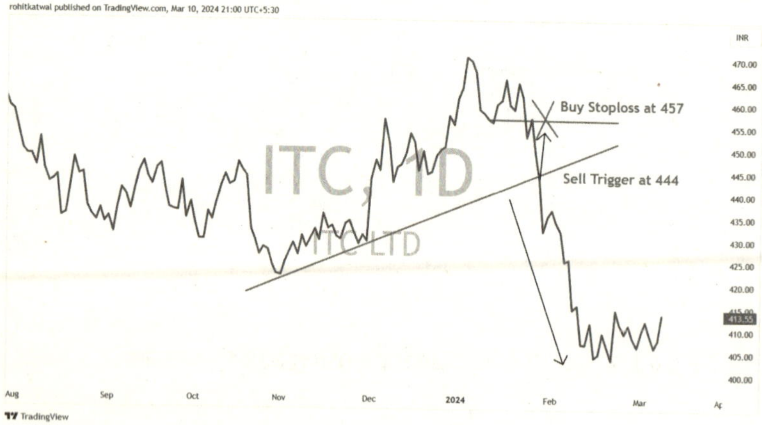

IMAGE 3.19: A line chart of ITC with a stop-loss

Remember when we bought PAYTM at Rs. 1,700 and placed our stop-loss at 1534? We just don't give a stop-loss order to our trading system. In fact, we decide from two available option types to define what kind of stop-loss we want to put in our trading system.

- Stop-loss limit order (SL-L)
- Stop-loss market order (SL-M)

Limit orders are ones which execute a buy or sell order at the price that we specify. If I specify PAYTM to be bought at 1700, the trading system will not buy PAYTM till the time the price trades at 1700. If you place a buy order for PAYTM on the market, your trading system will attempt to buy PAYTM at the current best available market price, which in this case is 1640.

When we set a stop-loss order at 1534 for PAYTM, what happens is that when the price goes below 1534, it triggers an event – the stop-loss is triggered. Based on this trigger, the trading system sells the stock at whatever price is being traded at 1534. If the next buyer is willing to buy at 1532, the trading system will square off the stock at 1532 and you will incur a loss of 168 points against the intended 166 points. That is a 2-point slippage, or extra loss, you have to incur. But what if the next buyer after 1532 was available at 1500, or 1400? That would have meant an extra loss of 34 or 134 points. That is why the trading system gives us an option between choosing a stop-loss limit or stop-loss market order.

In a stop-loss limit order, we give a stop-loss trigger point at 1534 but also define a limit below which the stock is not to be sold (Image 3.20). If the stop-loss is triggered, the broker can only sell the stock within the specified limit. If my trigger price is 1534 and limit price is 1530, then the trading system can only sell the stock if a buyer is available between 1530-1534. If the limit is 1500, then the trading system can sell the stock at the best price available between 1500-1534.

In a stop-loss market order, we give the stop-loss trigger point, and the limit for such a stop-loss order is whatever price is currently being traded in the market. If the immediate price below 1534 is 1530, then stocks will be squared off at 1530, and if the immediate buyer is at 1510, then stocks will be squared off at 1510 (Image 3.21).

Before putting stop-loss orders, it is important to understand the distinction between the two.

Stop-loss orders create a price range around your purchase price where your broker will automatically buy or sell a security to limit your potential loss. We can understand stop-loss orders with the illustration in Image 3.20.

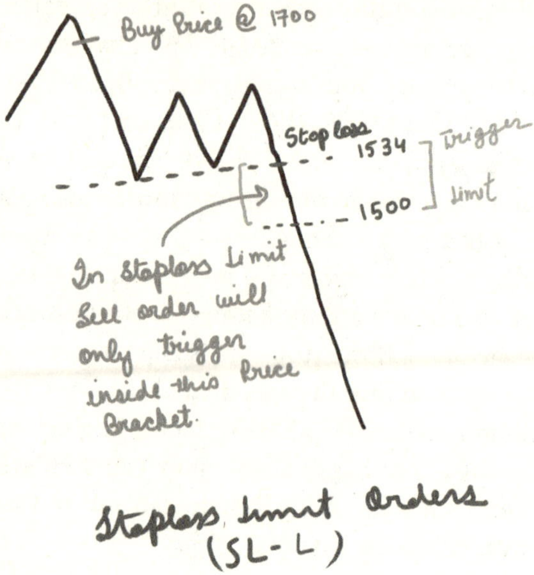

IMAGE 3.20: A stop-loss limit order

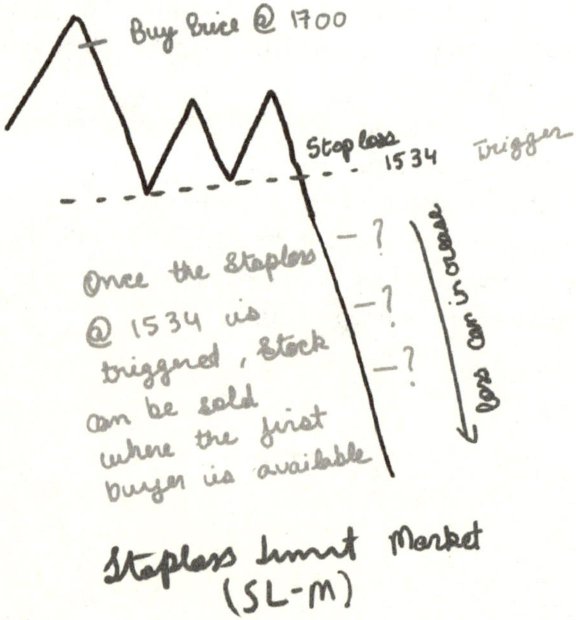

IMAGE 3.21: A stop-loss market order

If the order type is stop-loss market (SL-M), then refer to Image 3.21 to see what you can expect the order execution to be like. Once the stop-loss is triggered, the stock can exit wherever the first buyer is available.

This is how stop-loss limit and stop-loss market orders work. It is imperative that you understand the difference between two. Most of the stocks that trade in the stock exchange are liquid, so putting in SL-M orders is not a problem, as we get best of the prices available. But SL-M orders can pose serious slippage if the stock or option that we trade is illiquid or volumes are quite less for the stock that we are trading.

Trailing stop-loss is a method of locking in profits in trending markets. Once you're in a winning trade with the price moving in your favor, how do you protect those profits? This is where the concept of a trailing stop-loss comes in. Trailing stop-losses are used to ride big trends after taking an initial risk in the trade.

Once your trade has started winning, we can use a trailing stop-loss to protect our profits. This can best be understood from Image 3.21A.

1. We buy the stock at 359 and put our initial stop-loss at 327. The risk on the trade is 32 points.
2. The stock moves from 359 to 425, and we shift our stop-loss from 327 to 377. At this point, we are locking in our profit. The price of any security can drop at any time regardless of technical analysis. By shifting our stop-loss higher, we are protecting some part of our gains. If the stock price drops below 377, we will be stopped out of the trade with minor profit against our initial stop-loss.
3. The price moves up from 425 to 525, and we move our stop-loss to 425.
4. The price moves up to 525, and we shift our trailing stop-loss to 470, and so on.

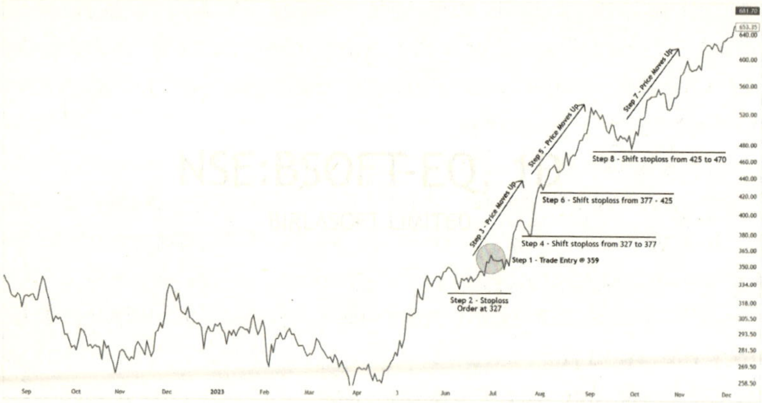

IMAGE 3.21A: Trailing stop-loss explained

The method used here to trail the stop-loss is called trailing stop-loss using an HH-HL structure, which we will study in further detail later in this chapter. Technical indicators can also be used for trailing indicators, which we will cover in later chapters.

Benefits of a trailing stop-loss

- **Locks in profits**: By adjusting the stop-loss as the price moves in our favor, we can capture a larger portion of potential profits in a trending market.
- **Limits losses**: Even with a trailing stop-loss, we still have a safety net in place to prevent excessive losses if the market turns against us.
- **Improves risk/reward ratio**: Trailing stop-loss helps tilt the risk/reward ratio in our favor by potentially capturing more significant gains while limiting potential losses.

Now that we have covered all the basic concepts that would be needed later on, we can move towards understanding the various concepts of price action analysis.

Supply and Demand

Like all markets, the stock market is driven by the principles of supply and demand. Stock prices fluctuate based on the balance between these two forces.

This concept of bid and ask prices translates directly to the stock market. Imagine you're in a marketplace and want to buy a jacket listed at Rs. 3000. The shopkeeper's asking price is Rs. 3000, but you're willing to offer Rs. 2800. In this scenario, your Rs. 2800 offer is the bid price, and the shopkeeper's Rs. 3000 asking price is the ask price. Unless a buyer and seller agree on a price (bid and ask prices meet), the trade won't be executed. If another customer comes in and offers Rs. 2900, that becomes the new bid price. The seller may then be willing to sell at this higher price, causing the price of the jacket to rise.

Similarly, in the stock market, buyers compete by raising their bids to purchase shares, and sellers compete by lowering their ask prices to sell shares. When there's high demand for a particular stock, with more buyers than sellers, buyers tend to raise their bids, pushing the price up. Conversely, when there's an abundance of supply (more sellers than buyers), sellers may need to reduce their asking prices to attract buyers, which can cause the price to fall.

By analyzing this supply and demand imbalance, price action traders attempt to forecast where prices might be headed in a given timeframe.

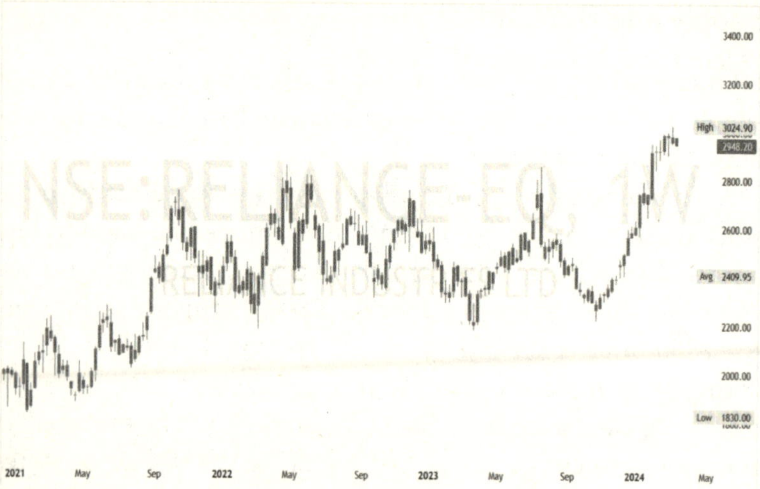

IMAGE 3.22: A RELIANCE chart on a daily timeframe

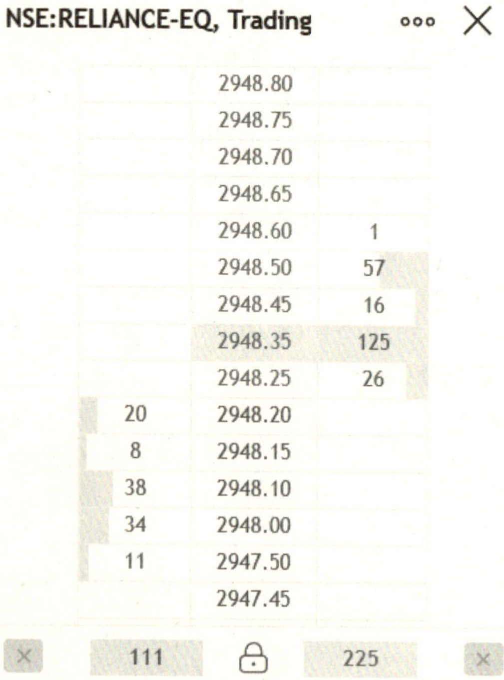

Bid	Price	Ask
	2948.80	
	2948.75	
	2948.70	
	2948.65	
	2948.60	1
	2948.50	57
	2948.45	16
	2948.35	125
	2948.25	26
20	2948.20	
8	2948.15	
38	2948.10	
34	2948.00	
11	2947.50	
	2947.45	

IMAGE 3.23: Market depth of RELIANCE

Let's understand bid-ask using the chart of RELIANCE and its market depth (Images 3.22 and 3.23).

This market depth data will help you understand how bid-ask helps determine the market price. The price of RELIANCE is trading at 2948.20 on the left side, and we can see the corresponding market depth of how buyers and sellers are placed around that price.

On the left side of market depth are bid offers by buyers at different prices. On the right side of market depth are ask offers by sellers at different prices. A trader is bidding to buy 20 shares of RELIANCE at 2948.20, and another trader is offering to sell 26 shares of RELIANCE at 2948.25. This difference of 0.05 paise in the bid offer is called the spread size. When a buyer's bid price meets a seller's ask price, the trade is executed, and the price is reflected on the chart. For liquid stocks, where the volume of shares traded is high, the bid-offer spreads are low – up to 0.05. If the stock is traded less, then the spread size can be big.

But what difference does bid-ask spread make? Bid-ask can also be understood this way. The ask is the price where you can immediately buy a stock. The bid is the price where you can immediately sell a stock.

Suppose a stock is trading at Rs. 110. You want to buy 1000 shares. The bid price is 109 and the ask price is 111. The stock is not liquid enough. If you must immediately buy and sell the stock, you will be essentially buying it at Rs. 111 and selling it at Rs. 109, which is an immediate loss of Rs. 2. This is just for an example. Remember in our PAYTM trade how our stop-loss was 1534, but with a limit stop-loss at 1530, we were selling the stock 4 points below our loss level? In case of PAYTM, where we are holding only 58 shares, this Rs. 4 might make an extra loss of 4 * 58 shares = Rs. 238, but in this case, it's a loss of 2 * 1000 = Rs. 2000, which is 1.9% of the capital. The spread size determines this additional cost that we will incur during trading. If the stock price that we are trading is highly liquid, then these additional costs can be reduced.

Therefore, bid-ask price helps:

1. Formation of the market.
2. Determine spread size for the trade.
3. Identify the supply-demand imbalance.

In Image 3.22, bid-ask tells us that at that time, there is more sell-side supply in the market compared to buy, since the sell-side quantity is 225 and the buy-side quantity is 111. This figure keeps on changing because traders from different parts of the country can be trading the stock.

In the stock market, supply and demand can be affected by various factors. These factors could be good quarterly results, regulatory action in favor of or against a company, the national budget, war breaking out, etc. They can cause fear or euphoria in the market. When there is fear, the stock prices fall. When there is euphoria, the stock prices rise. Various analysts, traders, investors, etc. try to speculate on the effect of these factors on stock prices. But in the end, it's just the price that matters. The real gauge of whether a particular factor was in favor of or against the stock price always comes down to whether the stock rises or falls after the factors were in the public domain. The price is the ultimate winner.

Volumes

Apart from the last traded price, the most important data that we get from charts is volumes. Without volumes, the price movement is meaningless. It has no context. Volume provides context to the price action.

Volume indicates how many shares have changed hands at any given timeframe. There are two types of trading entities in stock market: retail traders and institutions. Retail traders are traders with less money, whereas institutions are big corporations, fund houses, banks, foreign and domestic institutional investors, mutual funds, insurance companies, etc. Institutions invest heavily in stock markets. When there is a sudden surge in volumes in a specific stock, it is the institutions that are buying or selling the stock. Retail traders can leverage high volumes to make informed decisions. Because a significant sum of money is invested by these institutions, we assume that when they take a trading decision, it is backed by more research, analysis, non-public information, etc., and such news is not available to retail traders. That is why volumes are important. When prices move up or down with big volumes, it can be an indication of institutions stepping in. Retail traders can use this information to further validate their analysis and trade the opportunity with a slightly higher winning probability.

Volume is what fuels stock price movements. If the volumes are less, then it probably means the stock price is not moving much in either direction. But when volume starts to increase, it is a sign that a move in either direction might be building up. Which direction? We can analyze that with additional price action methods.

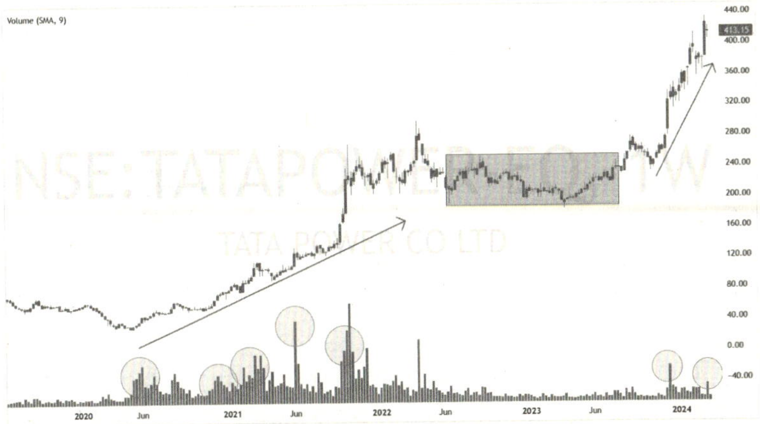

IMAGE 3.24: A weekly chart of TATAPOWER indicating correlation between price and volume

Observe the weekly chart of TATAPOWER in Image 3.24. Red and green bars along the x-axis are the volume for the week. In Jun '20, the price was at Rs. 35 and volumes increased significantly, which is an indication that institutional buying is coming. The stock price in the next 2 years touched 240; i.e., a 7-fold increase in price. From Jun '22 to Jun '23, there were low volumes, and the price traded between Rs. 200 to Rs. 240. As soon as the volumes started picking up in Nov'23, the stock price again doubled from Rs. 220 to Rs. 430.

Let us observe another chart of INFIBEAM (Image 3.25). From Jan '22 to Jul '23, INFIBEAM was trading between Rs. 15 to Rs. 22. In Aug '23, volumes increased, followed by a rising stock price. INFIBEAM stock price started rising from Rs. 14 and touched Rs. 40.

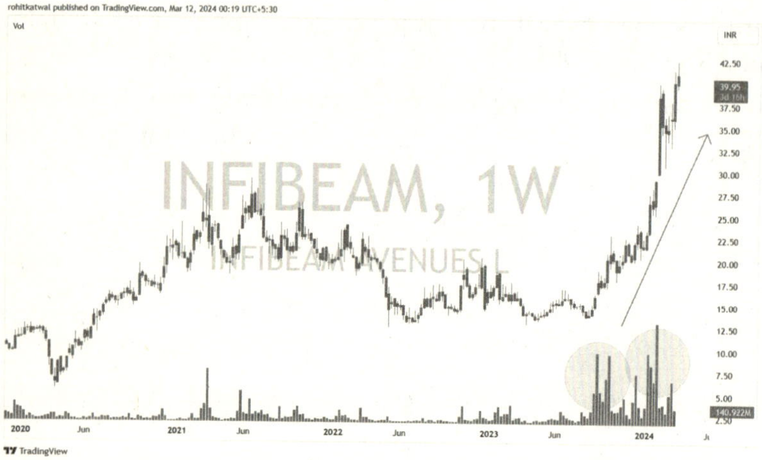

IMAGE 3.25: A weekly chart of INFIBEAM indicating correlation between volume and price

The effect of volume is visible in both strong and weak markets. See Image 3.26 for a weekly chart of NAVINFLUOR. From Feb '20 to Sep '22, the stock price was rising, backed by heavy volumes. In Sep '23, there was big drop in the price with heavy volumes, and the stock price has been falling since then.

This demonstrates how volumes are an important metric when we analyze price action on a stock.

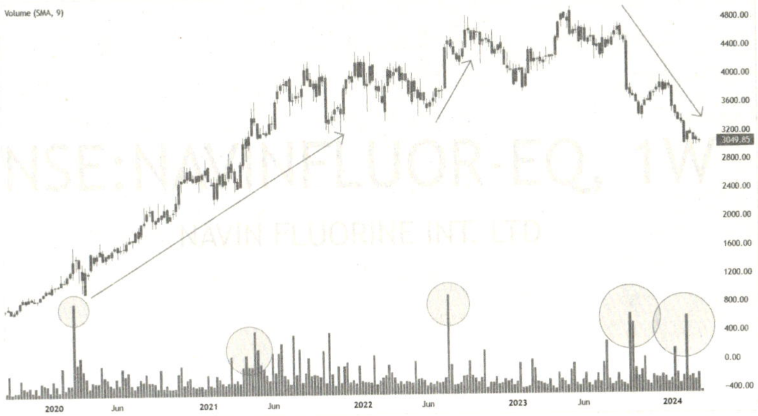

IMAGE 3.26: A weekly chart of NAVINFLUOR illustrating the correlation between price and volume

There is a correlation between price and volume, as summarized in Table 3.3.

Price	Volume	Market Outlook
Rising	Up	Strong Market
Rising	Down	Weak Market
Falling	Up	Weak Market
Falling	Down	Strong Market

TABLE 3.3: Price and volume interpretation

Let's understand these 4 market conditions:

1. *Price Rising, Volume Up*

When a stock price is rising and the volume is rising with it, it is a sign of a strong market. Prices going up backed by rising volume means more and more buyers want to buy the stock at higher price, which means the demand is genuine and the stock price is expected to move further up. Remember that we are not a doing candlestick-to-candlestick analysis at this stage. We are just looking at broader market sentiment. Some traders confuse this information with candlesticks and their respective volume analyses. Here, we look at the general trend of the market.

Look at another chart of COALINDIA in Image 3.28. Observe how prices for COALINDIA were stagnant and started rising with rising volumes, indicating a bullish or strong market.

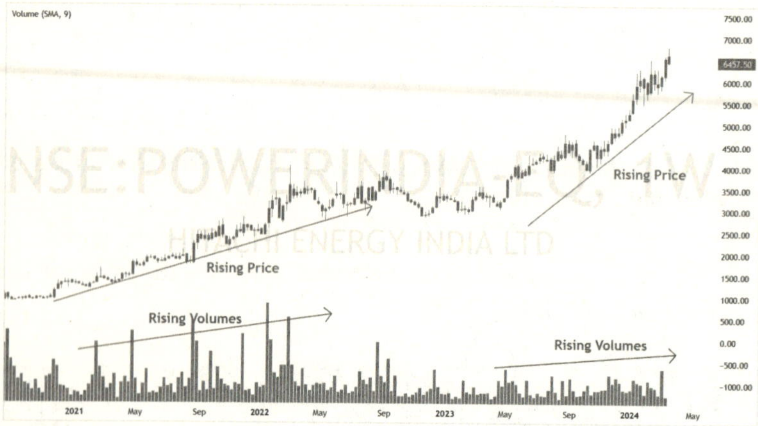

IMAGE 3.27: A POWERINDIA weekly chart demonstrating how the price is rising with rising volumes, indicating a strong or a bullish market

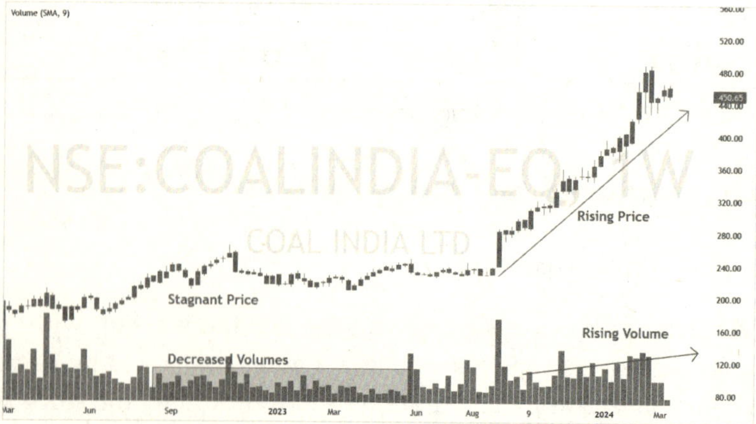

IMAGE 3.28: A weekly chart of COALINDIA showing sideways price

movement when volumes are less, and a strong market when volumes and price starts rising

2. Price Rising, Volume Down

When prices are going up but volumes are not high or are less, it is a sign of a weak market. A weak market means that it lacks strength. It means the move is not backed by institutional money. Either the volumes will increase, confirming a further price rise, or it could be a probable top forming in the market. Let's observe the chart of ITC on a weekly timeframe in Image 3.29. When the price was rising between Mar '23 and Aug '23, the volumes were less. ITC went sideways for 4 months after that. In Jan '24, ITC started falling, backed by rising volumes, suggesting a weak or a bearish price structure.

IMAGE 3.29: ITC showing signs of a weak market, first with rising price and low volume, and then with falling price and rising volumes

3. Price Falling, Volume Rising

When prices fall with increasing volumes, it represents a weak or a bearish market. This is a selling capitulation phase where there is panic in the market. High volumes highlights offloading of shares by big institutions, and sometimes retail traders also follow suit. Such selling capitulation may be triggered by negative government action, company results, inflation, etc. While falling prices with high volume can indicate weakness. further confirmation (e.g., technical indicators) is recommended; sometimes, a specific big institution might be booking profit, or an investor might be exiting with a block deal, there must be inclusion or exclusion of a stock from the index, and sometimes there might not be a reason at all (some big institution or public might just be booking profit after a bull run). We might need more triggers or analysis to trade a short trade on the stock, but falling prices and increasing volume does gives us an early heads-up that we are into a weak market structure. ITC in Image 3.29 is an example of price falling with increasing volume.

Look at another example of DELTACORP (Image 3.30). Between Sep '23 and Oct '23, DELTACORP was slapped with multiple GST notices of Rs. 23,000 crores by the government, and the stock price started falling with increased volume. In 2022, we witnessed the same phenomenon, when the price of DELTACORP fell off highs with rising volume and never recovered.

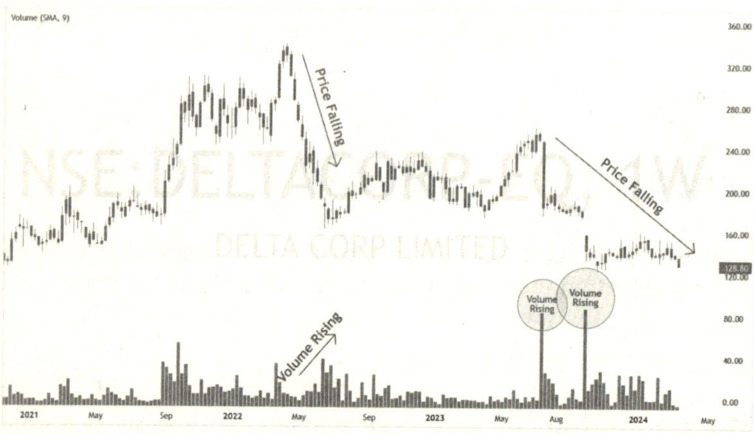

IMAGE 3.30: The price of DELTACORP falling with rising volumes

When we started learning volumes, I said big institutions have access to more information and have done more research. All factors unknown to retail traders are reflected in the price of a stock if we monitor the volumes closely, thus leading us to the old saying, "Price is King", or "Bhaav Bhagwan Che". If you use Google and refer to Images 3.30 or 3.31, you will see that around Jan '22, there was no negative news floating about DELTACORP yet. Problems started for DELTACORP in Sep '23, yet the prices of DELTACORP fell with increasing volumes. Can we thus say that information regarding troubles at DELTACORP was already building in the stock price, or, more precisely, that this is a good example of human behavior: where someone with undisclosed public information knew some bad news was brewing for DELTACORP, and booked out his profits? I leave this to your interpretation.

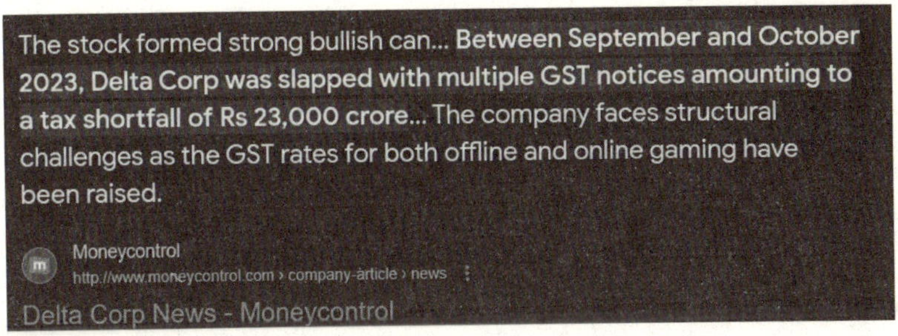
The stock formed strong bullish can... **Between September and October 2023, Delta Corp was slapped with multiple GST notices amounting to a tax shortfall of Rs 23,000 crore...** The company faces structural challenges as the GST rates for both offline and online gaming have been raised.

Moneycontrol
http://www.moneycontrol.com › company-article › news

Delta Corp News - Moneycontrol

IMAGE 3.31: News of DELTACORP being slapped with multiple GST notices

In my humble opinion, I do believe there are people who have access to information that a retailer does not have and that, from time to time, lawfully, they take benefit of such information. Why are volumes important? Because these big institutions or big volume traders can hide their trades or be secretive about them, but one thing they cannot hide is their trading volume. And if we are able to understand this activity of what the big money is doing, we have access to information that they have – albeit not in the truest sense.

4. Price Falling, Volume Falling

In a bear market, when prices are falling but volumes are not rising, it might be a sign of a strong market, or the end of a bearish market, or what we call the 'bottoming out' phase. This suggests a potential buying opportunity because at lower prices, the supply of stock is not coming. Traders are not selling any more. This might be a sign that the selling phase might be coming to an end and buy-side demand might soon arrive come at any time. Observe BOMDYEING in Image 3.32. See how prices were falling, but volumes were hardly increasing. This potentially signalled a buying opportunity. The stock bottomed out in April 2023 with rising prices and rising volumes, confirming the buying pressure.

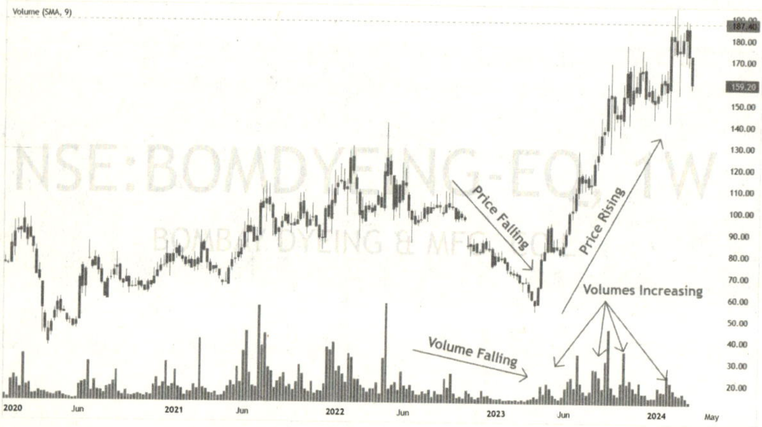

IMAGE 3.32: BOMDYEING on weekly charts with falling on low volumes and bottoming out of increasing prices and increasing volumes

Stock Liquidity: Buying and Selling with Ease

Liquidity refers to how easily and quickly you can buy or sell a stock at a fair price, with a minimal spread between the bid and ask prices. This spread can significantly impact your entry and exit points, especially in low-liquidity stocks.

Imagine you want to buy 100 shares of a stock, but the order book shows limited sell orders at your desired price. You might have to pay a higher price (ask price) to get your order filled immediately. Conversely, selling at the bid price might result in a lower return than expected. This highlights the importance of stock liquidity.

Highly Liquid vs. Low Liquidity Stocks

Highly liquid stocks, like those in the NSE 1000 or NSE 500, typically have a tight bid-ask spread and high trading volume. This allows investors to enter and exit positions quickly with minimal impact on the price and lower transaction costs.

On the other hand, low-liquidity stocks have a wider bid-ask spread and lower trading volume. This can make it challenging to buy or sell at your desired price, potentially leading to higher transaction costs and difficulty exiting a position if needed. The chart of CUPID (Image 3.33) exemplifies low liquidity, where limited volume can cause significant price movements and trading halts.

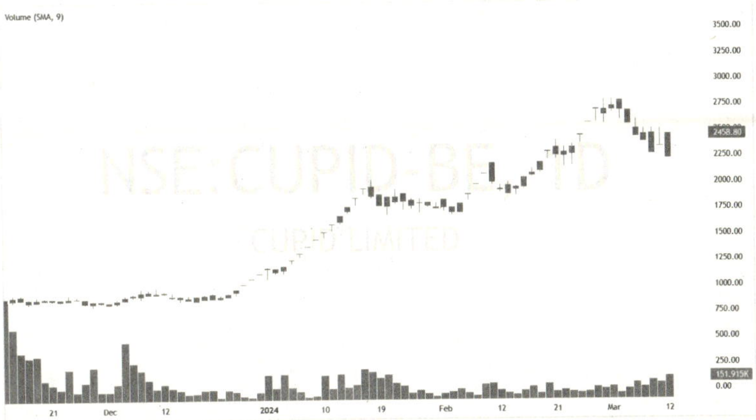

IMAGE 3.33: A daily chart of CUPID going up with low volumes, showcasing less liquidity

As a trader or investor, prioritizing stocks with high liquidity can help you avoid high transaction costs and ensure smoother entry and exit from positions. The NSE 1000 or NSE 500 can be a good starting point for finding liquid stocks.

This is how we read volumes with respect to price to understand the direction and increase winning probability of our expected trade. Volume analysis is a valuable tool, but it's important to use it in conjunction with other technical indicators, chart and candlestick patterns, etc., for a more comprehensive trading strategy, which we will learn in more depth in later chapters.

The Market Cycle

Prices rise and fall in cycles, and this concept isn't unique to the stock market. We experience it in our daily lives!

1. **Think about gold jewellery:** Your wife knows prices tend to be lower in the first half of the year due to less demand. As the festive season approaches, prices go up.
2. **Seasonal fruits and vegetables:** Off-season produce is more expensive because it's less available.
3. **Weekend vacations:** Prices for flights and hotels are often higher on weekends due to higher demand.

These same principles of supply and demand that affect everyday items also apply to the stock market. Stock prices move through cycles of accumulation, markup, distribution, and markdown. By understanding these cycles, traders can potentially identify buying opportunities during periods of lower prices, and selling opportunities when prices are higher.

In the stock market, the market cycle means the upward or downward trend that a stock or overall market experiences over time. These movements could be driven by a variety of factors like economic conditions, supply and demand, investor psychology, company performance, etc., but the bottom line is that prices tends to move up and down, and there is a cycle to it. By understanding these market cycles, a trader or investor can understand which market cycle he is in and can use that information to buy when the prices are lower and sell when the prices are higher.

Analyzing market cycles is not a method to perfectly predict future price movement, but it increases the probability of our trading decision being successful. It is crucial to use other forms of analysis alongside understanding the market cycle. The market cycle has 4 stages:

1. Accumulation phase
2. Markup phase
3. Distribution phase
4. Markdown phase

Image 3.34 shows the structure of a market cycle, otherwise called the stages of the market.

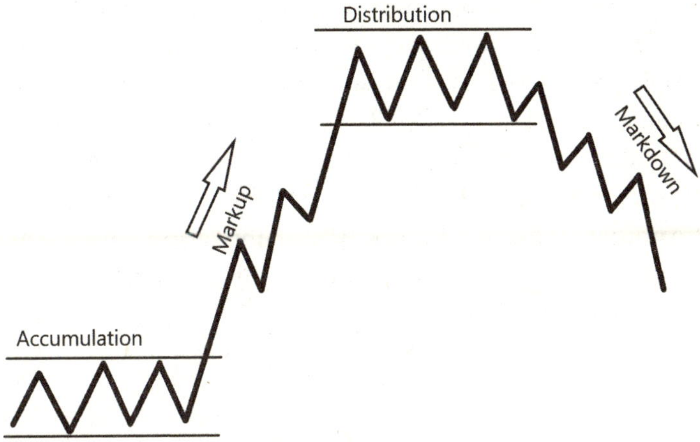

IMAGE 3.34: The market cycle, or the stages of the market

This is a typical example of a market cycle, or stages of the market, which you will see the in market many times.

Accumulation Phase

The accumulation phase is the first stage of the market. The following are essential ingredients of a accumulation phase:

1. Accumulation happens after an existing uptrend or downtrend (markup or markdown).
2. In the accumulation phase, the stock price fluctuates in a narrow to small price range.
3. Volumes are less in accumulation phase.
4. Volumes tend to increase when the accumulation phase is about to finish and the markup phase is about to start.
5. If the price breaks into an uptrend or markup phase from range, it's usually an accumulation phase.

The accumulation phase is also called the consolidation phase, or the base formation period, or the basing phase.

In Image 3.35, the stock price witnessed a downtrend, and the accumulation started. You can see how the price was fluctuating between price points 730-800. Volumes were extremely less in this narrow range. Volumes only increased when the price broke out of this narrow range to start the markup phase.

Another understanding of the accumulation zone is that it is a zone where large investors build their positions. It is where big institutions buy the stocks.

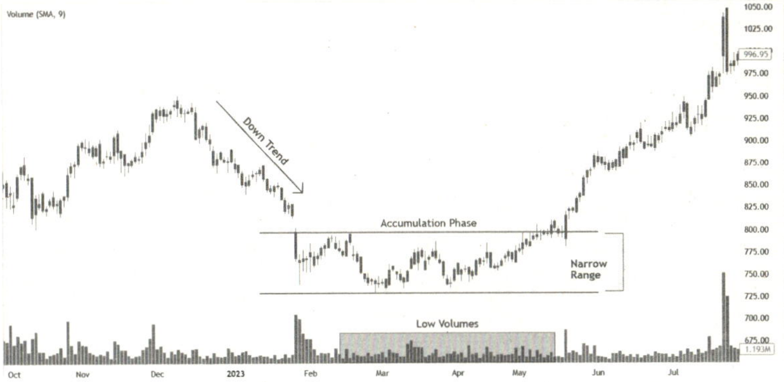

IMAGE 3.35: The accumulation phase in MCDOWELL-N

They have access to more capital to invest in the stock market, but that can be a problem for them. Unlike retail traders, large investors can't buy all the shares they want at once, because it might significantly affect the price. Hence, the accumulation phase is the zone where large investors buy the stock in small quantities in a narrow zone to hide their volumes and reduce their slippage. Once they have collected the quantity of stock they intend to buy, the price starts coming out of the accumulation zone. If big institutions and large investors are really buying the stock, it will eventually start its markup phase. As a retailer, you have to understand that it is the big money that moves the market, not the retail traders. As I said in the previous chapter, large investors have more information, more news, and have done more research, hence they are the early buyers if the stock is good. There is a saying in the stock market:

We cannot direct the wind, but we can adjust our sails.

In the stock market, we trade in the direction of the big money, not against it. That is why I said that unless the price starts coming out of the accumulation phase into the markup phase, we can never know whether it was big money buying the stock or selling it.

Markup Phase

The markup phase is when the price breaks up from the accumulation phase and starts rising (an uptrend). The breakout of the price from the accumulation phase into the markup phase is with increased volume. Once the price starts trading outside the accumulation phase, the price starts showing strength and moves higher, and more traders are now bullish on the stock price.

When prices are going up, we call it a bullish market. When prices are going down, we call it a bearish market. These terms are famous in the trading world. Imagine a bull and a bear. A bull attacks by thrusting its horns upwards, while a bear swats its paw downwards. In the stock market, we use these animals to represent opposing outlooks on future prices.

A breakout is when the price starts trading out from a range. E.g., if a price is trading between Rs. 90 and Rs. 100 for the last three months and starts trading at Rs. 101, it is called a breakout. A breakdown is when the price starts trading below Rs. 90, at Rs. 89.

The following are essential ingredients of a markup phase:

1. At this point, the price makes a clear uptrend in the market.
2. Trading volumes increase with the increasing stock price as more traders are showing interest in buying the stock.
3. While not always the case, the markup phase is often accompanied by strong company performance, like positive earning reports. Remember, the price has all the information about company.
4. The price starts to make a higher highs and higher lows formation, which is an uptrend identification pattern. We will discuss this further in later chapters.

Understanding the psychology of volumes and large investors is of utmost importance here. If the price breaks out of the accumulation zone with volume and the price is increasing with volume, then how is it that large investors and big institutions were buying the stock in the accumulation phase? You can understand this with the help of a hypothetical situation. Suppose I am a large investor who wants to invest 100 crores into a company. I will slowly and steadily buy the stock of Rs. 80-90 crores when the price is in its accumulation phase. Once I have collected 90% of the stock I want and I am reaching the end of my accumulation phase (accumulation also means collection), I can now use the rest of the 10 crores to create a breakout from the accumulation phase with a big volume. Since the trading community uses the same analysis techniques, once they spot that the price is breaking out of the accumulation phase with volume and is starting its markup phase, more and more traders start buying the stock, which builds the demand for further markup. At this point, the wider market, which sails in the direction of the wind, starts participating, and this is how a markup phase starts. This concept can be understood from Image 3.36.

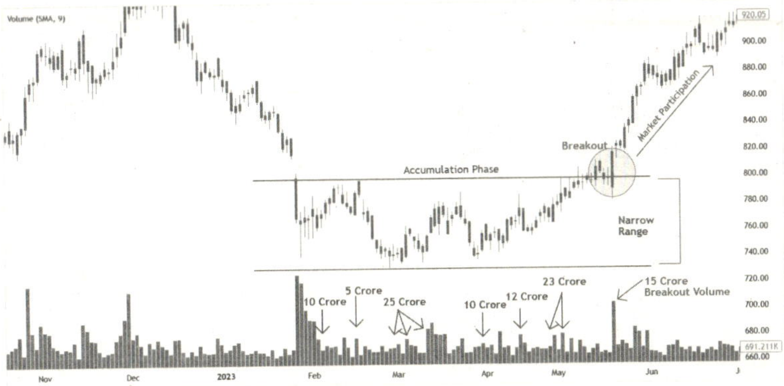

IMAGE 3.36: How large investors accumulate and cause a breakout into a markup zone

It is important to understand the psychology of the investors here. In an accumulation phase, by collecting the majority of the shares at lower levels, a scarcity of shares is created, which pushes the demand of the stock by other investors higher, thus pushing the prices higher. The market participants get greedy and don't want to miss the trend. Hence the price starts to move up.

Distribution Phase

The distribution phase follows the markup phase and signifies a shift in investor sentiment. Early investors who bought during accumulation often start booking profits by exiting their positions. Prices have risen to an extent that there's an uneasiness in the market, causing traders and investors to turn cautious about fresh buying. The following are essential ingredients of a distribution phase:

1. Like the accumulation phase, the distribution phase occurs after a markup phase.
2. After creating a price top, the price starts fluctuating in a narrow to small price range.
3. Trading volumes are less in the distribution phase.
4. Volume tends to increase when the distribution phase is about to start, and the price starts breaking into a markdown phase.
5. If the price breaks down from the range, it is usually a distribution phase.

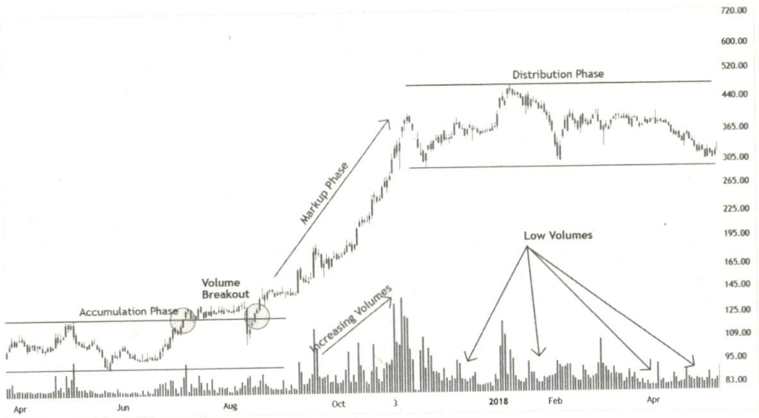

IMAGE 3.37: Example of a distribution phase in RAIN

There can be some confusion about when the distribution phase actually starts. Here are two situations to keep in mind:

1. **Downward move after accumulation:** Imagine the price goes down after a downtrend, then enters a period where it seems to be going sideways (like accumulation). But instead of breaking upwards (like a true markup phase), it breaks downwards again. This doesn't mean a new accumulation phase happened. It just means the original markdown phase (downtrend) is continuing at lower levels. The key point is a real distribution phase only happens after a markup phase (uptrend).
2. **Upward move after markup:** Similarly, imagine the price goes up after an uptrend, then enters a period where it seems to be going sideways (like distribution). But instead of breaking downwards (like a true markdown phase), it breaks upwards again. This doesn't mean a new distribution phase happened. It just means the original markup phase (uptrend) is continuing with even more buying pressure. The key point is a real distribution phase only happens after a strong uptrend.

I know this can be a bit tricky, so remember: a true distribution phase comes after a markup phase (uptrend), and a true accumulation phase comes after a markdown phase (downtrend).

In a distribution phase, large investors tend to book profits, which cannot be achieved in a single order. It's something similar to how they purchased stock in the accumulation zone. That is why volumes start to diminish in the distribution zone. Large investors start selling their shares in small quantities without creating any fear regarding prospects of the stock price. This is when overpriced shares are offloaded to the general public. Once large investors have sold the majority of their shares without major fluctuation to the price, the volumes start increasing and the price starts breaking down into the markdown phase.

Markdown Phase

The markdown phase starts when the price breaks down with volumes from the distribution zone and starts trading at lower prices, creating a downtrend. At this point, most people are bearish on the stock or the market. The following are essential ingredients of a markdown phase:

1. At this point, the price makes a clear downtrend in the market.
2. Trading volumes increase with the declining prices which means traders and investors are bearish on the stock or market.
3. While not always the case, the markdown phase can also start due to expected poor company performance, adverse government regulations, etc.
4. The price starts to make a lower highs and lower lows formation, which is a downtrend identification pattern we will discuss in detail in later chapters.

Image 3.38 shows a markdown phase in RAIN. The price entered a distribution zone, followed by low volumes of distribution. The price broke the range with heavy volumes and started its markdown phase.

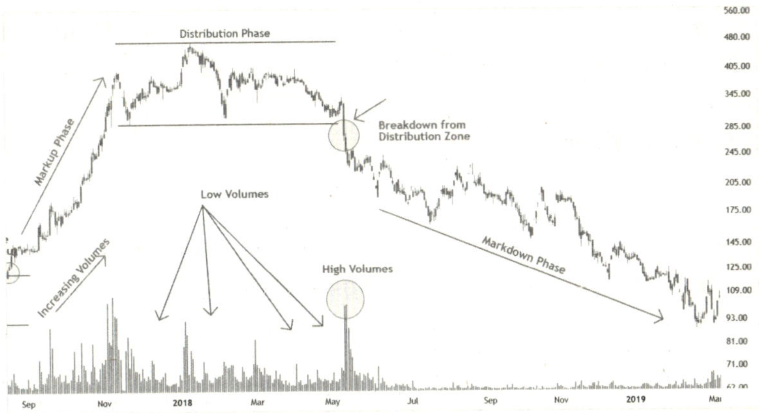

IMAGE 3.38: A markdown phase in RAIN

The markdown phase is the reverse of a trend from an existing uptrend, but it is different from the term 'reversal'. Reversal is a slightly different term used in trading, which we will discuss in detail in later chapters.

In the distribution zone, large investors have offloaded shares. Once the offloading of the shares is done, the last sell order with volumes creates fear in the market. Traders and investors who bought the shares in large quantities are staring at losses, and once the markdown phase starts, the fear induces the buyers at the top to start selling their stocks in fear, thus increasing the supply of the stock price and hence causing the markdown phase.

In the end, it's the game of supply and demand, which a trader or investor must understand.

Trend

The trend refers to the broader direction in which the overall market or a stock price is moving over a specific period. If the price on a particular timeframe is moving upwards, it's called an uptrend. Conversely, if the price is moving downwards, it's called a downtrend. Finally, if the prices fluctuate within a narrow range without any clear upward or downward direction, it's called a sideways or range-bound market. Therefore, at any given time, the market or a stock can be in either a trending or sideways movement.

Trending Market

There is an old adage in the stock market:

The trend is your friend.
Always trade in the direction of the trend.

This adage highlights the importance of aligning your trading decisions with the prevailing market direction. The vast amounts of money flowing through global markets can significantly impact stock prices. As a retail trader, we cannot fight against the sheer force. However, we can potentially react more quickly to market changes due to our smaller trading sizes.

It is like the advice The Ancient One gave to Dr. Strange:

You cannot beat a river into submission. You have to surrender to its current and use its power as your own.

Large institutions, such as fund houses, mutual funds, and banks, often accumulate stocks at lower prices during a specific market phase. Their significant capital can cause price spikes and slippage if they buy large quantities at once. To avoid this, they spread their buying activity over a longer period. While this might be necessary for them, retail traders can potentially capitalize on trends more quickly due to their smaller order sizes. The best way to achieve this is by following the direction of the trend while conducting your own market analysis.

But how do you identify trends? As a layman, a simple way to identify trends is this:

If the price on a chart is in the top-right corner, it is in an uptrend. If the price on the chart is in the bottom-right corner, it is in a downtrend.

Look at the chart of BHARTIARTL on a weekly timeframe in Image 3.39. In Oct '19, the price of BHARTIARTL was trading at Rs. 330. In Mar '24, the price is trading at 1220. The price is in the top right corner of the chart. If we draw an arrow from the low of Oct '19 to the high of Mar '24, we can clearly see that the price has been rising up, depicting a clear uptrend.

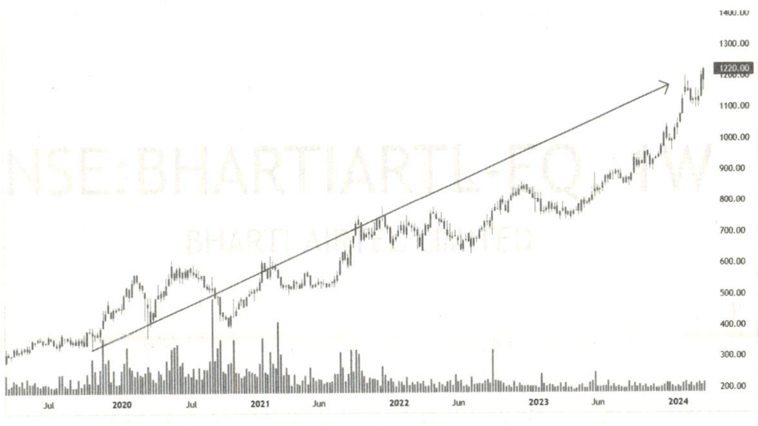

IMAGE 3.39: A BHARTIARTL chart on a weekly timeframe in an uptrend

Now look at the weekly chart of UPL in Image 3.40. In Jun '21, the price of UPL was Rs. 850. As of Mar '24, the price at Rs. 475 is in the bottom right corner, showing a clear downtrend on UPL over the last three years.

IMAGE 3.40: A UPL chart on a weekly timeframe in a downtrend

It's important to remember that this is a basic starting point, and other factors should be considered for confirmation. On a lighter note, if you squint a bit at the chart, the overall direction of the price movement (up or down) might become more evident.

While the general location of the price on a chart can give you a basic idea of the trend, for more precise identification, especially for trading decisions, we can delve into technical analysis tools. One common belief is that prices trend only about 30% of the time, with the remaining 70% spent in sideways ranges (consolidation). This emphasizes the importance of accurately identifying trends to capture those profitable price movements.

Higher Highs, Higher Lows & Lower Lows, Lower Highs

Uptrends can be identified using a specific price pattern called Higher Highs, Higher Lows (see the HH-HL structure in Image 3.41). This pattern reflects the underlying strength of an uptrend.

The following are essential ingredients of an HH-HL structure:

IMAGE 3.41: An uptrend

1. During an uptrend, the price makes a series of higher highs (HH). Each new high is higher than the previous high.
1. After reaching a high, the price might experience a pullback, which is a temporary decline. However, the pullback doesn't fall below the previous low point.
2. Following the pullback, the price creates a higher low (HL) compared to the previous low. This shows buying pressure is still present, pushing the price up again.
3. This sequence of higher highs and higher lows continues throughout the uptrend.

The HH-HL pattern can form on any timeframe, from short-term charts like daily charts to long-term charts like monthly charts. The more frequent the HH-HL formation, the stronger the uptrend might be.

Downtrends reflect a decline in price momentum. We can identify them using the Lower Lows, Lower Highs (LL-

LH) pattern, which highlights the selling pressure pushing prices down.

The following are essential ingredients of an LH-LL structure:

1. During a downtrend, the price creates a series of lower lows (LL). Each new low is lower than the previous low.
2. After reaching a low, the price might experience a temporary bounce or rally. However, this rally doesn't surpass the previous high point.
3. Following the rally, the price creates a lower high (LH) compared to the previous high. This indicates continued selling pressure, pushing the price lower again.
4. This sequence of lower lows and lower highs persists throughout the downtrend.

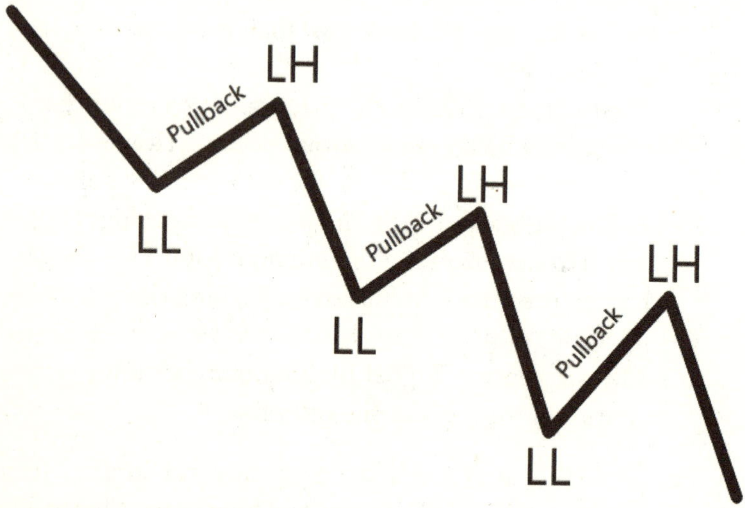

IMAGE 3.42: A downtrend

Similar to uptrends, the LL-LH pattern can form on any timeframe. The more frequent the LL-LH formation, the stronger the downtrend might be.

Let's look at some stock charts to understand how HH-HL and LH-LL structures form in the real world. Image 3.43 is a weekly chart of ABBOTINDIA. The stock price was in accumulation phase from Jun '20 to Jun '22. The stock price tried to start an uptrend in Jul '21, but failed. The stock price again started an uptrend in Jun '22 by making an HH-HL formation.

IMAGE 3.43: An uptrend on an ABBOTINDIA weekly chart (HH-HL structure)

In the real world, chart patterns have to be interpreted, and they are as not obvious as the illustrations in Images 3.41 and 3.42. ABBOTINDIA is showcasing all the characteristics of an HH-HL structure.

If we look at UPL on a weekly chart in Image 3.44, we can observe how the price broke its distribution phase in Jul '23 and has been forming a LH-LL structure, indicating a clear downtrend.

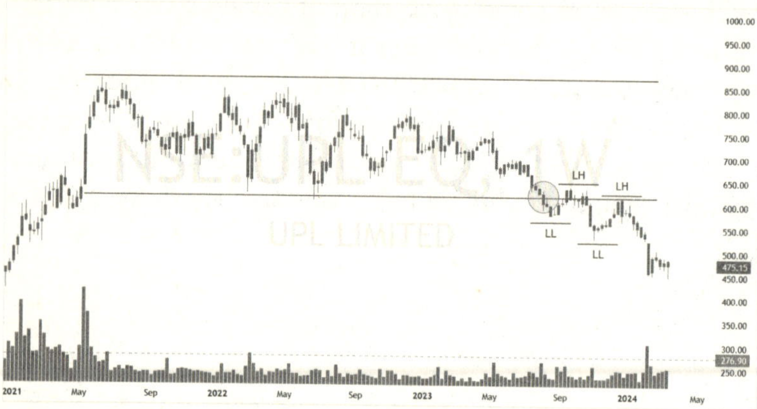

IMAGE 3.44: An downtrend on a UPL weekly chart (LH-LL structure)

HH-HL and LH-LL structures are also used in price action for trailing stop-loss purposes to lock in profit and ride big trends. In an uptrend, every time the price makes a new higher high, stop-losses are shifted to the recent higher low. Conversely, in a downtrend, every time price makes a lower low, the stop-loss is shifted to the recent lower high.

Horizontal Lines: The Building Blocks of Trend Analysis

Before we delve into more advanced tools, understanding horizontal price levels is crucial in technical analysis. Here's why:

Price movement is step-by-step: Picture a price chart like a climbing a stair. You can only reach higher points step by step (horizontal price levels in Image 3.45) below. Similarly, on a chart, the price moves up or down by breaking through these horizontal levels one by one.

The Bank Nifty example: Look at the Bank Nifty chart on a daily timeframe in Image 3.45. We see gridlines marking horizontal price intervals. The current price is at 46,694.70.

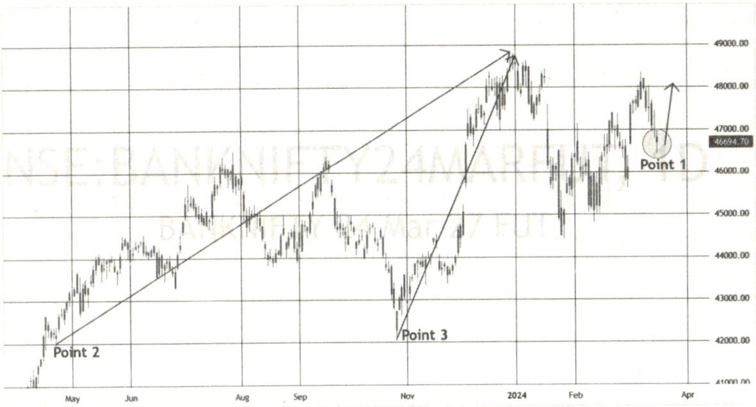

IMAGE 3.45: The difference between a horizontal and a slanting trendline

Think about these points:

1. **Price moves level by level:** If the price needs to climb to 48,000, it must first overcome the hurdle at 47,000. It can't simply jump directly to 48,000 without 'conquering' that level in between.
2. **Price rises over time:** Consider the price movement of Bank Nifty from April '23 to December '23. It rose from 42,000 to 48,700. This increase happened by surpassing numerous horizontal price levels, one after another, over those six months. Same price point was achieved at point 3 in a 2-month time period.

The key takeaway is that price action is all about these horizontal levels. Even if a trendline suggests an upward slope, the actual movement happens through these individual price points. The price climbs or falls by overcoming or succumbing to the buying and selling pressure at each horizontal level.

By understanding this core concept, you can build a solid foundation for further technical analysis. We'll explore additional tools like trendlines later, but for now, just remember that price movement is a step-by-step process through horizontal price levels.

Sideways Market

While uptrends and downtrends offer clear directional moves for potential profits, sideways markets, also known as ranging markets or chop zones, can be a different story for traders. These periods can be frustrating for traders looking to capitalize on strong trends. Image 3.46 shows what a sideways market looks like.

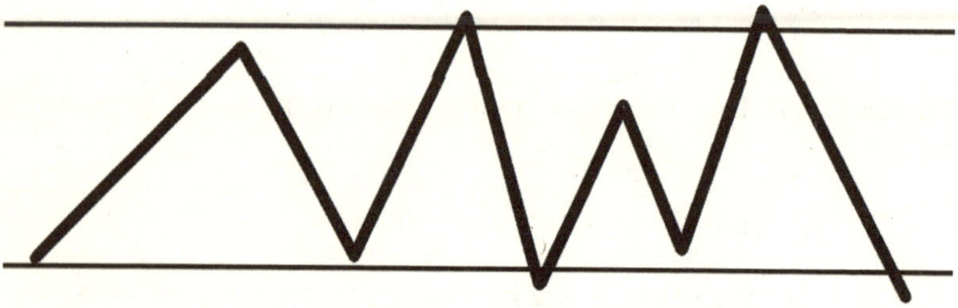

IMAGE 3.46: A sideways market

The following are the main ingredients of a sideways market:

1. The price starts consolidating or fluctuating between a price range. This price range can be narrow or wide, but there is clear absence of an uptrend or downtrend on the current timeframe.
2. The stock price witnesses selling pressure on the upper price zone and buying interest on the lower price zone.
3. There might be multiple attempts by the stock price to trade above the upper or below the lower price range, but every time, selling pressure or buying interest brings the price back into consolidation mode.

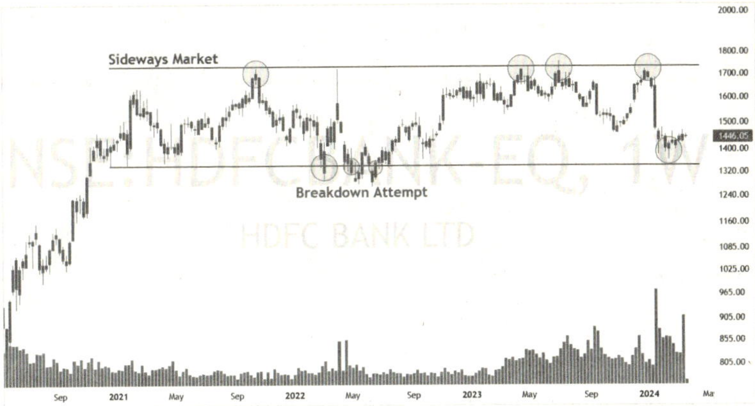

IMAGE 3.47: HDFCBANK in a sideways zone on weekly charts

In Image 3.47, HDFCBANK on a weekly chart has been in a consolidation phase for the last 3 years, from Jan '21 to Mar '24. At 1730, the price witnesses selling pressure, and at 1340 buying interest. For 3 years, the price is trading between the range of 390 points. We can see that in Feb, May, and Jun '22, the price briefly broke the lower price point and immediately witnessed buying interest and a bounce back into the consolidation zone.

This is where the important concept of support and resistance comes into play.

Support and Resistance Zones

When, at a certain price level (1340 for HDFCBANK in Image 3.47), the stock price witnesses buying interest again and again, it's called a support zone, or simply a support. A support is where market participants expect buying pressure to come and the price to bounce from this level. Therefore, the support becomes an important reference point for traders and investors. Inversely, when, at a certain price level, the stock price witnesses selling pressure again and again (1730 for HDFCBANK in Image 3.47), it's called a resistance zone, or simply a resistance.

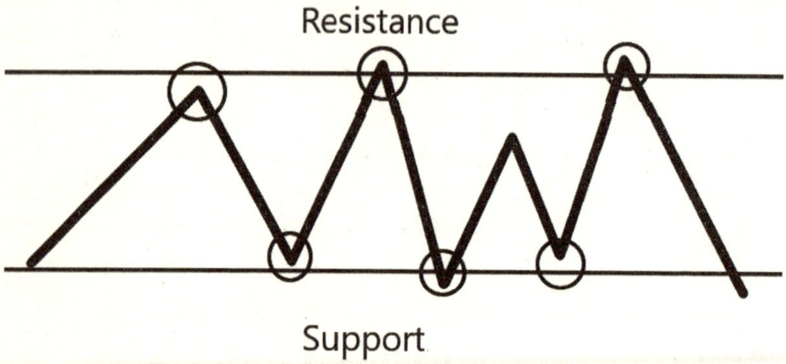

IMAGE 3.48: An example of support and resistance

There are three reasons for a sideways market:

1. Accumulation
2. Distribution
3. Indecision

In an accumulation phase, institutional investors might be quietly scooping up shares. They believe the stock is a good buy at a certain price range. When the price dips to their sweet spot, these big investors jump in, creating buying pressure that pushes the price back up. But they're not willing to pay more than a certain point. Once that price is reached, the buying dries up, and the stock falls back into the trading zone. This back-and-forth buying and selling keeps happening until the big guys have all the shares they want. These big investors have bought the majority of shares; coupled with a breakout into the markup zone, participation of retail traders and investors, and no major supply of shares, the stock price starts moving up due to FOMO and demand.

Conversely, in a distribution phase, big money wants to book profit and are silently distributing shares at an inflated price. They have a certain price target which is achieved. Every time the price goes up, they have a sell order waiting, which creates a supply, and the price starts drifting down. Once this supply is over, buying pressure comes from late investors or traders, which takes price higher again. This back and forth selling and buying keeps happening until the big investors have sold all their shares at a profit. Once they've sold all their shares at a profit, there's no more upward pressure from the big money. This, coupled with fear of losses, can induce a final push down as investors and traders sell their holdings, starting a markdown phase.

But how do you explain this accumulation and distribution happening for 3 years in HDFCBANK (Image 3.47)? Because if a sideways market extends for a long duration, then it's no longer accumulation or distribution, but indecision. Investors and traders are not sure of the company's prospects above and below that price range. This is where the concept of support and resistance comes in. When there is indecision in the market, traders and investors may identify supports and resistances to either trade reversals within the zone or find trends on lower timeframes.

These advanced analysis techniques will be covered later in a dedicated chapter.

Now let's explore support and resistance in a little more detail.

Support and Resistance

While we previously encountered support and resistance in sideways markets, they are also crucial concepts in trending markets.

In the previous section, we knew the characteristics of a sideways market and we knew that the price is in a range; therefore, the low of the range is where the buying is expected, and the high of the range is where the selling is expected. Based on these characteristics, we may identify it.

But what if the market is trending? How do we identify the support and resistance in a trend?

In trading, the support is a price point on the chart where buyers may step in, and the resistance is a price point on the chart where sellers may step in. This might pause the short-term trend for the time being.

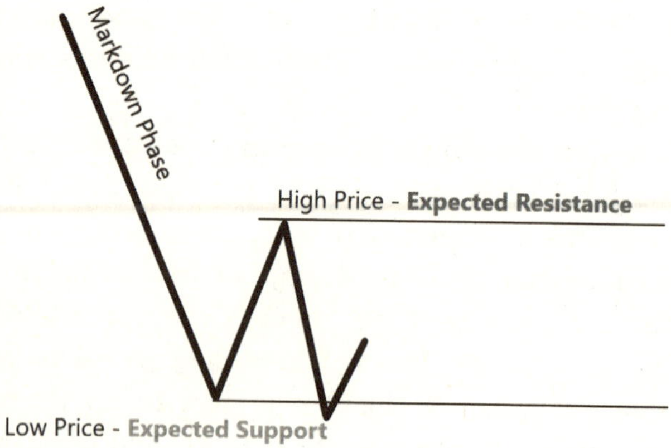

IMAGE 3.49: Expectation of support and resistance when a sideways moment starts

The following are essential ingredients of supports and resistances:

1. The higher price point of the sideways market is called a resistance point. The lowest price point of a sideways market is called a support point. When support and resistance levels cluster around the same price zone, it's called a support and resistance zone.
2. When the support is broken and the price starts a downtrend, the previous support level often becomes resistance. Conversely, when the resistance is broken and the price starts an uptrend, the previous resistance level becomes a support. See Images 3.51 and 3.52.
3. In an uptrend, higher lows act as support points, while higher highs act as resistance points (Image 3.53). In a downtrend, the opposite is true: lower highs act as resistance, and lower lows act as support points.

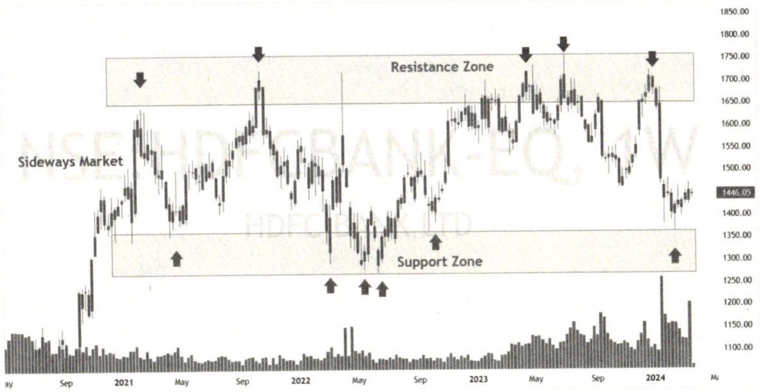

IMAGE 3.50: Support and resistance zones in HDFCBANK

IMAGE 3.51: Resistance turning into support

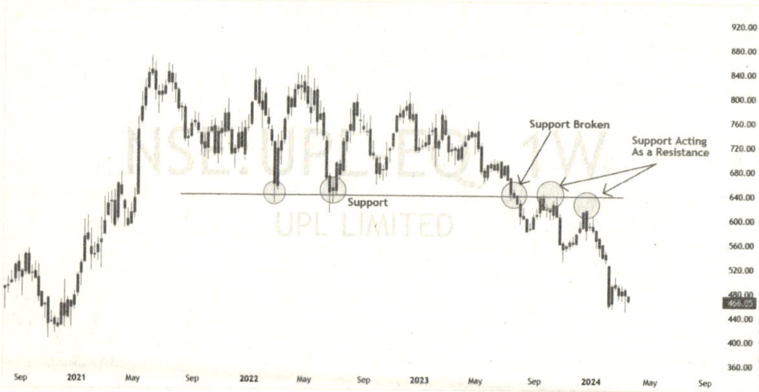

IMAGE 3.52: Support turning into resistance

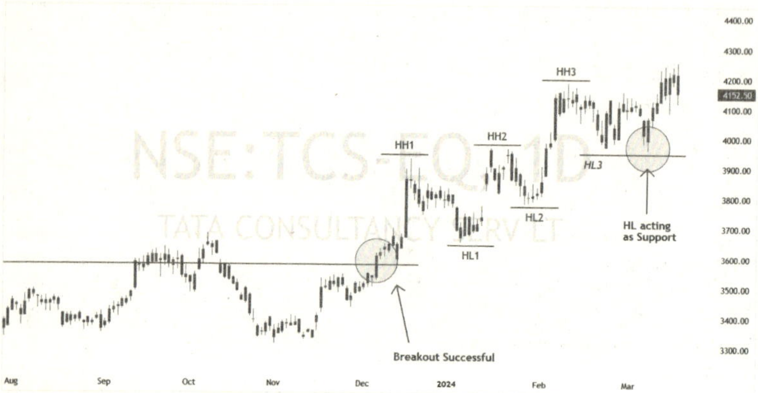

IMAGE 3.53: Higher low becomes a support in an uptrend

Let's observe Image 3.53 of TCS on daily charts. The price of TCS broke out of an accumulation phase and started forming a higher highs, higher lows (HH-HL) structure. Every HH is a resistance which must be broken for the price to continue the uptrend. Every HL acts as a support from where the price can bounce. Once HH3 and HL3 are created, the price started coming down as sellers got active, but at HL3, buyers stepped in, and that price point acted as a support.

4. A chart on any given timeframe can have multiple support and resistance points. Any previous high/low or psychological round number where the price has witnessed selling pressure in the past can become a resistance. Conversely, any price point where significant buying interest has previously emerged can turn into a support.

Observe the chart of IndusInd Bank on a daily timeframe in Image 3.54. The price initially broke the support at 1450. Following that, we see a support zone between 1340-1390, and finally the support zone 3 at 1265. All these price points represent areas where buying interest has come in the past, and may come again.

IMAGE 3.54: Multiple supports on INDUSINDBK on a daily timeframe

IMAGE 3.55: Multiple resistances on IDFCFIRSTB on a daily timeframe

Similarly in Image 3.55, we can see the multiple resistance on IDFCFIRSTB.

While we previously encountered support and resistance in sideways markets, these concepts are also crucial in trending markets. We've seen how breakouts of support and resistance can change their roles. But why do these past price points seem to hold significance in the present market? Support and resistance zones can be explained by market psychology. If a large number of traders are using similar technical analysis and identify the same support or resistance levels, their buying and selling decisions can influence price action around those zones.

Think of it like traffic rules. When you are driving on the road, like everyone else, you are expected to follow specific rules – drive on the designated side, slow down at speed bumps, stop at red lights, and give way to emergency vehicles. These rules work because everyone follows them, creating an orderly flow of traffic. Similarly, in the stock market, if a large number of traders identify the same support or resistance level, their combined buying or selling activity can create a 'yield sign' or 'caution zone' for the price around that level. Trendlines add another layer of confirmation to these zones, helping us identify the overall direction of the trend.

Trendlines

Apart from traditional methods of identifying trending or sideways markets, trendlines are the most basic tool, used extensively in technical analysis to identify trends, support and resistance points, chart patterns, and advanced methods of confluence trading.

Trendlines are diagonal lines drawn by connecting the significant high points or low points on the chart.

But why do we use trendlines in the first place?

1. The stock price is a reflection of human behavior. Since the stock price reflects human behavior, trendlines help us visualize the prevailing trend – uptrend, downtrend, or sideways – by connecting significant highs or lows.
2. Trendlines can sometimes provide a clearer picture of the trend compared to just using higher highs (HH) and lower lows (HL).
3. Trendlines can act as potential support or resistance zones, which can be helpful in identifying entry and exit points for trades.

However, it's important to remember that no technical indicator is perfect, and prices can sometimes break through trendlines.

Let's look at the daily chart of MCDOWELL-N in Image 3.56. If points A, B, and C are connected on a straight line, it forms a diagonal trendline. Observe how the price witnesses a support at point D and bounces back.

IMAGE 3.56: A chart of MCDOWELL-N on a daily timeframe with a trendline

It might be a coincidence on a smaller timeframe, or we might be using selective data on the chart to make the trendline, but what about DMART on a weekly timeframe in Image 3.57?

IMAGE 3.57: A chart of DMART on weekly timeframe with a trendline

IMAGE 3.58: A chart of UPL on a weekly timeframe with a trendline showing a downtrend

IMAGE 3.59: A chart of JINDALSTEL on a weekly timeframe with a trendline showing an uptrend

Trendlines can sometimes provide a clearer picture of the trend and act as potential support or resistance zones. But always remember that key to successful trading is:

Always trade in the direction of the trend.

With trendlines, we can identify a resistance in an uptrend, which can be a caution point for buying. Similarly, in a downtrend, we can use a support to identify potential selling opportunities. Identifying and trading potential trend reversals is a more advanced strategy that we'll explore later. For now, focusing on trendlines helps us understand the overall trend direction and potential support/resistance zones within that trend.

IMAGE 3.60: SBICARD in a downtrend on a daily timeframe

The chart of SBICARD in Image 3.60 is a good example of how a downtrend can be confirmed by a trendline. In downtrends, we generally look for selling opportunities near the trendline as the support gets tested.

Trendlines are a valuable tool for beginners in technical analysis. They provide a simple yet effective way to visualize trends and potential support/resistance zones. By understanding trendlines, you'll be well-equipped to identify the overall market direction and make informed trading decisions. Sooner or later, every trader understands the value of K.I.S.S. in trading, which means:

Keep It Simple, Stupid!

Never underestimate simple. Some of the best traders and investors use simple tools to earn big profits.

In the following chapters, we'll explore more advanced tools for identifying trends and delve deeper into various technical analysis concepts to enhance your trading skills.

Now that we have our basics complete, let's explore candlestick patterns in the next chapter.

CHAPTER 4

Candlestick Patterns

Candlestick patterns are the footprints of money flow in the market

Price is just a point on the XY-axis where a transaction occurred – where someone bought or sold a certain volume of shares. Plotting this data for every second over a given time period quickly generates a massive amount of information.

Candlestick charts present price data in a simple pictorial form over a given time period. For example, by looking at the chart for a stock over one trading day, you can easily find out:

- The **o**pening price
- The **h**igh price
- The **l**ow price
- The **c**losing price

All for the given day.

Image 4.1 shows a line chart of how a JINDALSTEL future traded on a 1-minute timeframe.

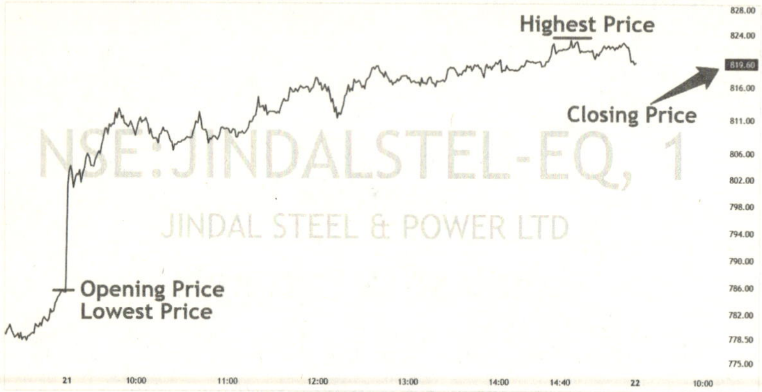

IMAGE 4.1: Line chart of JINDALSTEL on a 1-minute timeframe

The stock price of JINDALSTEL is in an uptrend. The price jumped at the opening and remained in an uptrend throughout the day.

IMAGE 4.2: A candlestick representing the price of JINDALSTEL on a daily timeframe

A candlestick will show the same data for the day, as you can see in Image 4.2.

A few observations: the line chart shows that stock price of JINDALSTEL remained bullish throughout the trading day, whereas the candlestick shows that the price opened at 798.10 and made a low of 778.10 (down 20 points), made a high of 823.40, and closed at 821.55. Also:

1. The stock price, after opening, fell 20 points (i.e., -2.50%) before the buying interest came.
2. From 778.10, the price made a high of 823.40 (i.e., +5.8%), which means the demand overwhelmed the supply.
3. The stock price closed near the highest price point at 821.55, which means that by the closing bell, demand for the stock was still strong.

Additionally, it also tells us that there was an effort by sellers at the opening to take the price down, but this was negated by buyers.

While a daily candlestick provides valuable insights, it cannot capture every twist and turn of the market throughout the day. To gain a more granular understanding of price movement and the psychology behind it, we can break down the daily timeframe into smaller chunks.

By analyzing candlesticks with shorter timeframes, such as 6-hour intervals, we can see how the battle between buyers and sellers unfolded throughout the trading day. For example, in the previous daily candlestick for JINDALSTEL, we observed a strong closing price despite a dip at the open. Analyzing the 6-hour candles could reveal details about the selling pressure at the opening and the subsequent buying pressure that pushed the price higher.

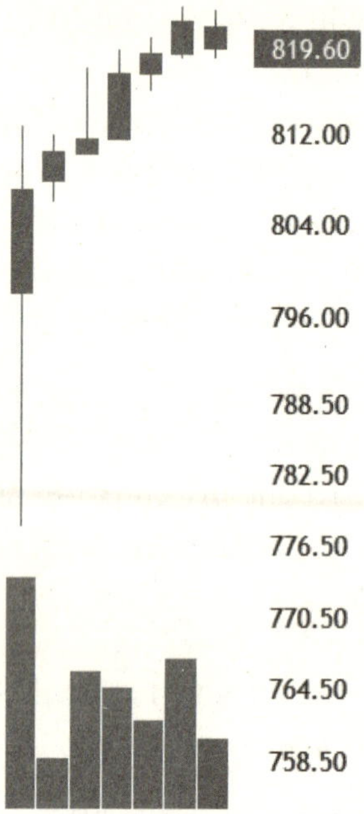

IMAGE 4.3: A candlestick chart of JINDALSTEL on an hourly timeframe for the day, with volumes

Let's analyze the 7 candles showed in Image 4.3 (6 hourly candles and 1 candle at the end, representing the last 15 minutes).

1. In the first candle, we can observe that the price opened at 798 and witnessed selling pressure, but demand from buyers pushed the stock price up above the open price. The price touched a high of 812 and closed at 807 in the first candle. This strong buying pressure confirms the buying pressure from the first candle.
2. The second hourly candle is very small. Volumes are the lowest for the day. The price made a high of 812 and low of 806. Lower volumes mean low demand. But the price did not fall, which means no supply, either. The price remained below the previous candle's high, which means the demand is not yet there.

3. In the third hourly candle, the price touched a high of 817.80 but again closed at 811.60. Volumes increased in this candle, which justifies the positive closing and price creating a new high, but observe how the price closed near the previous candle close, which suggests buyers tried to mark up the price, but somewhere, selling pressure forced the price to close near the previous close, but still above the opening price of the candle. We can even break down this third hourly candle into smaller timeframes, like four 15-minute candles, to understand the exact point at which sellers became active.
4. In the fourth hourly candle, volumes increased, and demand pushed the stock higher. In this hour, buyers decisively closed the price higher, near 817.30, showing the buyers' resolve and their victory over the sellers, who pushed the price down in the previous candle.
5. In the fifth candle, volumes are still higher, but the price did not move much, resulting in a small-bodied candle. The price closed further up at 819.10.
6. In the sixth candle, volumes increased as we approached the closing hour. The price touched a high of 823.05 to close at 822 near the day's high.

From these 6 candles, one thing is clear: throughout the day, it was the buyers who controlled the price of JINDALSTEL. Sellers tried to push the price down twice but were overwhelmed by the buyers.

This was just an example to show how candlestick charts can reveal the behavior and psychology of market participants. The different types of candles, combined with chart patterns, volumes, etc., can give us valuable information that helps us identify trends or potential trading opportunities. Let's now understand bullish and bearish candles.

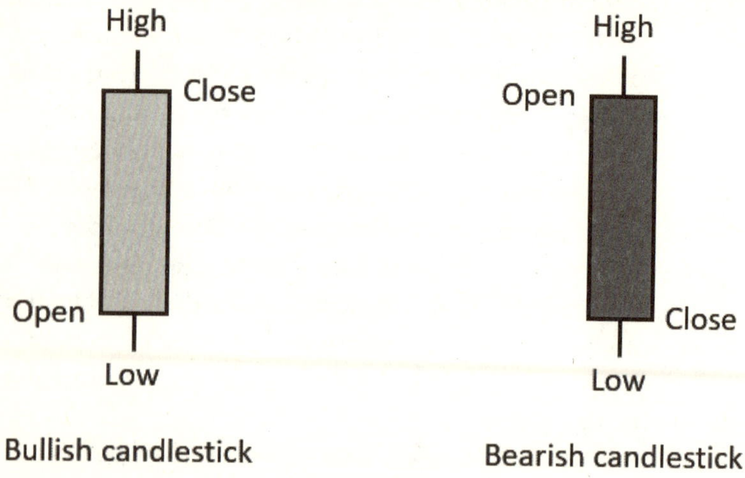

IMAGE 4.4: A bullish and bearish candle

Think of the stock market as a game of tug-of-war!

Bullish Candle (Buyers Win)

1. The bullish candle in Image 4.4 shows a thick rectangle with a green body.
2. The thick body means the closing price was higher than the opening price (buyers pulled the price up).
3. The line above the rectangle (the upper wick) shows how high the price went during the day before buyers and sellers reached a temporary balance.
4. The shorter the line below the rectangle (the lower wick), the less the sellers were able to pull the price down.
5. This candle suggests buyers (bulls) were stronger throughout the day, and managed to push the price up.

Bearish Candle (Sellers Win)

1. The bearish candle in Image 4.4 shows a thick rectangle with a red body.
2. The thick body means the closing price was lower than the opening price (sellers pulled the price down).
3. The line below the rectangle (the lower wick) shows how low the price went during the day before buyers and sellers reached a temporary balance.
4. The shorter the line above the rectangle (the upper wick), the less the buyers were able to pull the price up.
5. This candle suggests sellers (bears) were stronger throughout the day and managed to push the price down.

Okay, we now understand how bullish and bearish candles describe buying and selling pressure throughout the day. By looking at many candles together, we can start to see recurring patterns. These patterns can act like signals that might hint at where the price could be headed next.

Think of it as a language. By learning the different candlestick patterns, we can start to understand the 'language' of the market and make more informed decisions.

Before we continue, you must understand that candlestick patterns, and any other types of analysis, for that matter, are not 100% accurate and cannot give a definitive direction of where the market is heading. We are trying to understand human behavior and increasing our winning probability by understanding the market structure. We may do all kinds of analysis and identify a bullish trend, and the next day, a large investor or an institution could sell a big chunk of their holdings, driving the price down and rendering our analysis meaningless. Candlestick patterns are just a tool to understand price behavior to increase the probability of our trading decision being successful.

Types of Candlestick Patterns

There are more than 50 to 100 candlestick patterns out there – enough to fill an encyclopedia! But after years of trading, I've come to rely on a core set of around fifteen that have proven most helpful. We can categorize them into two main types:

1. Trend reversal patterns
2. Trend continuation patterns

Candlestick patterns are visual representations of price movements over a specific timeframe. By analyzing the body size, wick length, and open-close relationship within each candle, *we can gain valuable insights into market psychology*. These patterns don't predict the future with certainty, but they can highlight areas of potential trend shifts or continuations based on the buying and selling pressure they represent.

Just like a traffic sign's meaning can vary depending on the location and surrounding conditions, *the interpretation of a candlestick pattern depends heavily on the context of the chart*. The existing trend, confirmation from other technical indicators, and the pattern's location all play a crucial role in understanding its true significance.

By delving into specific candlestick patterns and understanding how they appear in different chart scenarios, we can start to decipher the story the market is telling us. Now that we understand the basics of candlesticks and the importance of context, let's explore some common candlestick patterns and how they can be interpreted.

Marubozu (Bearish and Bullish)

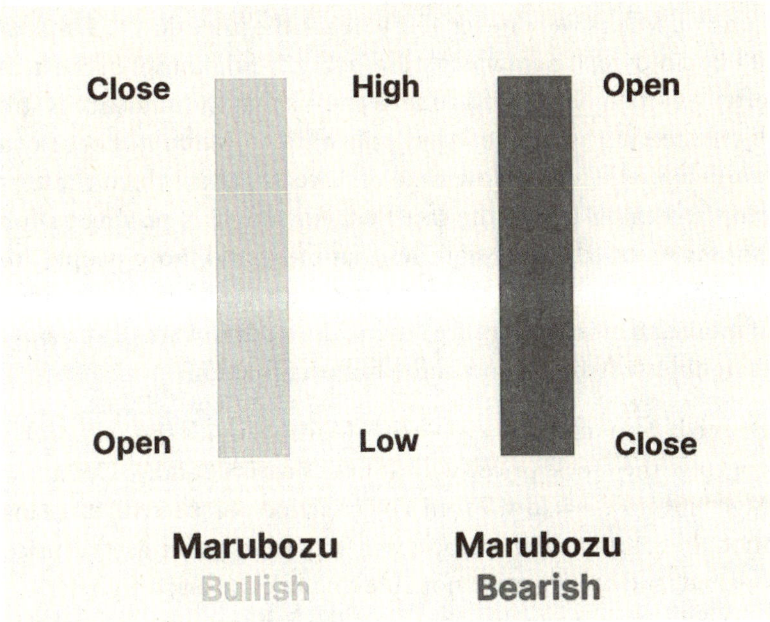

IMAGE 4.5: Marubozu bullish and bearish candles

Marubozu is a trend reversal or trend continuation candle. Marubozu is a Japanese word which means 'close-cropped' or 'bald'. The following are the characteristics of a Marubozu candle:

1. They have a long body.
2. They have small or no wicks.
3. Higher volumes on a Marubozu candle signify a strong signal.

Bullish Marubozu: Marubozu is a dominance candle. It shows the intent of buyers or sellers. Marubozu has either very small or no wicks, which means open ~= close. From a price action perspective, it means for that particular timeframe, as soon as the price opened, buyers dominated the sellers. The demand from the buyers was such that the sellers were not even able to mark the price lower.

Similarly, high ~= close means the closing price was at the highest price point. Until the end of the candle, buyers were in control. Sellers were never able to mark the price down. Think of it like a movie. If a movie is still playing to full houses in theaters after a certain period of a time, it means that the audience is still interested in the movie. They still want to watch it. Let's say a normal movie has a show time of 3 weeks, after which theaters stop screening it, but the fact that *this* movie is playing to full houses in its 4th week signifies that more and more people are coming to watch it. It's the same case with the Marubozu candle. If more and more buyers are buying the stock towards its closing, it signifies a strong trend in the bullish direction.

Bearish Marubozu: In a bearish Marubozu, it's the seller who controls the stock price, with a long bearish candle. Open ~= high and close ~= low. From a price action perspective, it means that the supply of the stock was higher as soon as the price opened, and buyers were not able to mark the price higher.

The Marubozu has its own limitations. The Marubozu candlestick pattern itself is neither definitively a trend reversal nor a trend continuation pattern. It depends on the context in which it appears. It's recommended to look for confirmation from other technical indicators, like volume or price action, in the following days. A Marubozu can sometimes be a false signal, especially if it appears after a period of consolidation. Increased volume on the next candle following the Marubozu can provide additional insights into the strength of the signal. Image 4.6 demonstrates what a Marubozu candlestick pattern looks like on a chart. As you can see, it's a very basic candle; therefore, it needs the help of extra analysis or indicators to decipher the market activity.

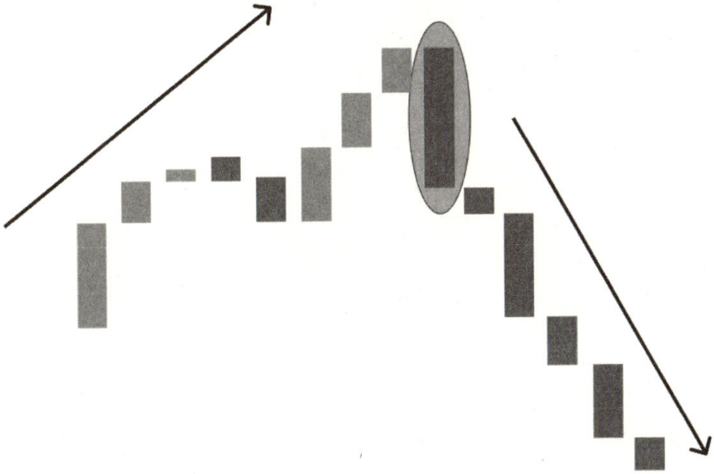

IMAGE 4.6: A Marubozu pattern

Hammer and Hanging Man

As the name suggests, the hammer pattern looks like a hammer. Image 4.7 shows what a hammer pattern looks like.

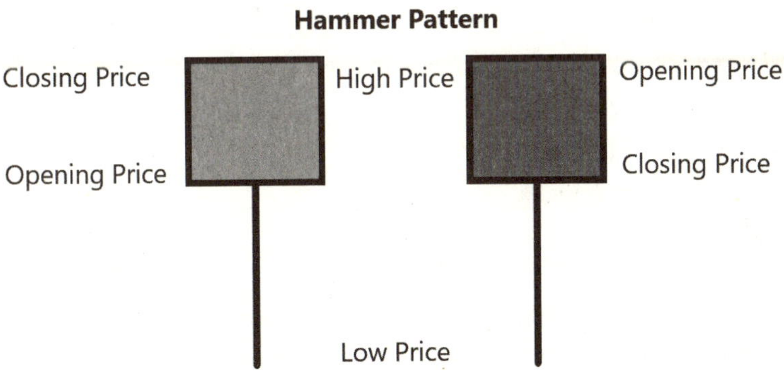

IMAGE 4.7: The hammer pattern

Below are the characteristics of the hammer pattern:

1. It has a small body on the upper side.
2. It has a small or no upper wick.
3. It has a long lower wick.

Incidentally, the hanging man pattern also looks like the hammer pattern. It has the same ingredients; i.e., a small body on the upper side, a small or no upper wick, and a long lower wick. The key difference between them lies in where they appear within the trend. Image 4.8 shows what a hanging man pattern looks like.

The hammer or hanging man pattern suggests a price opening at a relatively high point within the timeframe, followed by sellers attempting to drive the price lower. But by the end of the day, buyers take control of the stock price, and the price closes higher than where it opened.

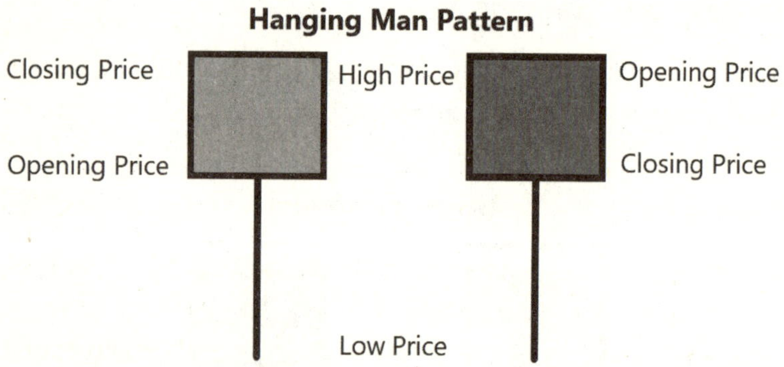

IMAGE 4.8: The hanging man pattern

Apart from the context of where the pattern forms, there is no distinction between both the patterns. A hammer pattern forms in a downtrend, hinting at a reversal, whereas a hanging man pattern forms in an uptrend, hinting at a reversal. But does that mean they are absolute – that a pattern formed in a downtrend will always be a reversal, or vice versa?

Let's look at the INFY weekly chart in Image 4.9. Observe how a hammer pattern formed at the support near the neckline in a downtrend and resulted in an immediate reversal, and the price started moving up. So, in this case, the hammer pattern worked.

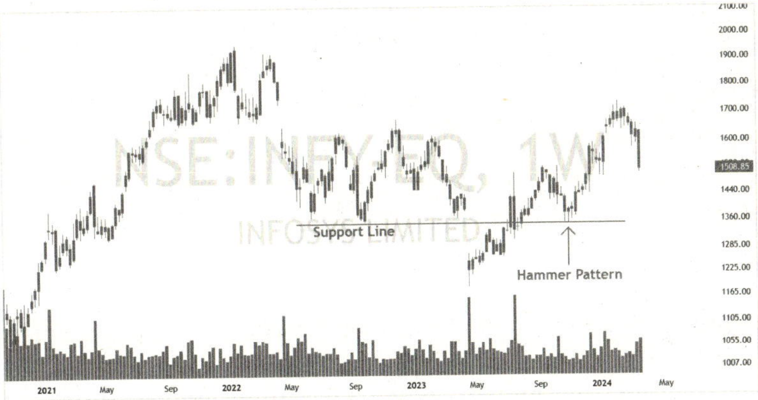

IMAGE 4.9: A weekly chart of INFY with a hammer pattern

And now let's look at the LTTS chart in Image 4.10, in which a hanging man pattern formed at an uptrend and resulted in an immediate reversal and the stock price falling.

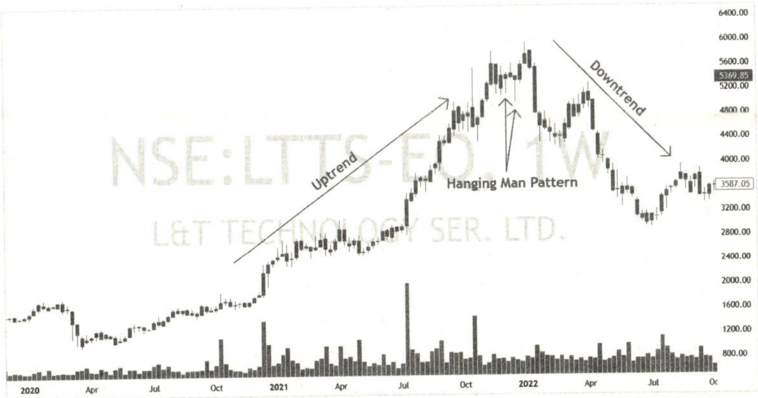

IMAGE 4.10: A weekly chart of LTTS with a hanging man pattern

But then let's look at the daily chart of TATAPOWER in Image 4.11, where the stock price, in an uptrend, made multiple hanging man patterns, and yet the price kept moving up.

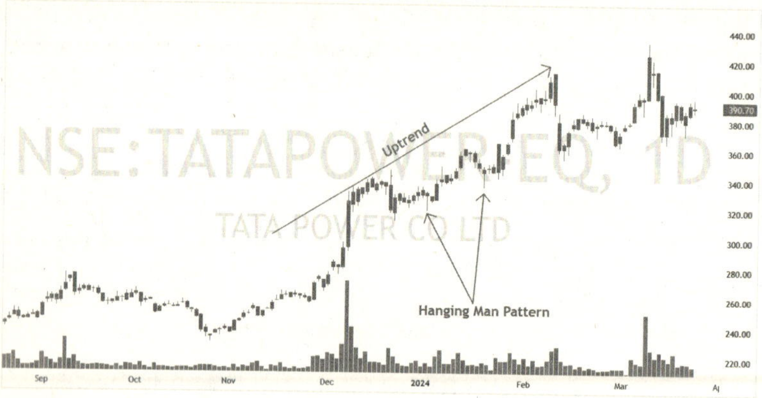

IMAGE 4.11: A daily chart of TATAPOWER with a hanging man pattern

And look at the weekly chart of UPL in Image 4.12. The price kept falling after the formation of the hammer pattern.

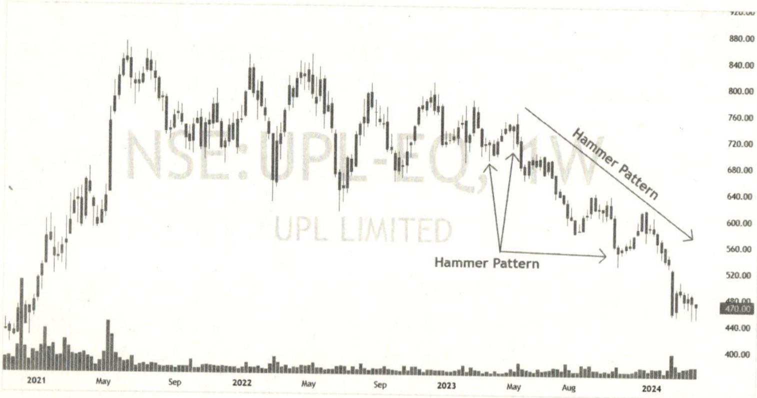

IMAGE 4.12: A weekly chart of UPL with a hammer pattern

Now I understand that every pattern can fail, but why did I go to such lengths to successfully prove, and disprove, a pattern? Because the pattern *itself* is useful, more than just the *name* of the pattern.

The hammer and hanging man patterns offer valuable insight into market psychology. Imagine a negotiation over the price throughout the trading session. The long lower wick suggests sellers initially pushed the price down significantly. However, by the close, buyers stepped in and drove the price back up near the opening level. This closing action indicates stronger buying pressure at the end of the timeframe. This buying pressure at different points in the chart can be construed in a different manner.

Uptrend

An uptrend is characterized by a series of higher highs and higher lows (a HH-HL structure). This pattern often resembles a staircase, with the price going up on increased buying volume, followed by periods of consolidation or pullbacks due to profit-taking by some traders or temporary loss of momentum.

During these pullbacks, sellers may try to push the price down. However, if the underlying buying pressure remains strong, buyers will step in and defend the support level, resulting in the price moving back up towards the end of the timeframe. This price action can sometimes lead to the formation of a hammer pattern on the chart.

The hammer pattern, in an uptrend, can be a potential buying opportunity, suggesting that buyers may be regaining control after a pullback. However, confirmation from other technical indicators or price action is crucial before entering a trade.

While the hammer suggests a potential buying opportunity in an uptrend, the hanging man pattern raises a cautionary flag. It appears during an uptrend but has a long lower wick, indicating emerging selling pressure. This could signal a loss of momentum or, if the uptrend is nearing its end (as identified by other technical indicators or weakening momentum), a potential bearish reversal.

Let's look at the chart of NHPC on a weekly timeframe shown in Image 4.13.

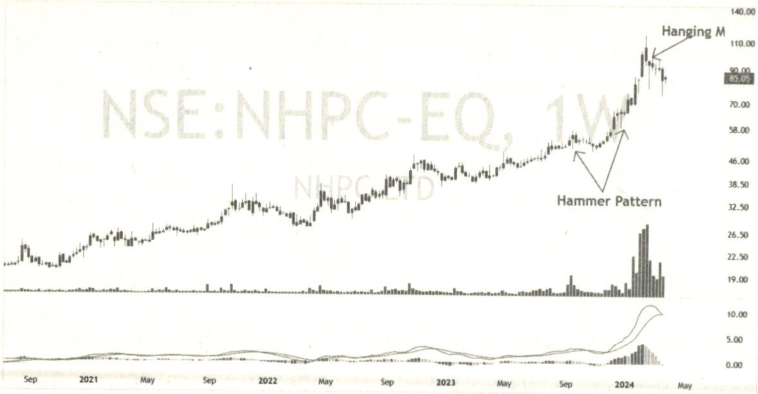

IMAGE 4.13: A weekly chart of NHPC, in an uptrend

MACD is a technical indicator which we will study in the next chapter, but this suggests that the trend is coming to its maturity in NHPC. During an uptrend, a hammer pattern presented buying opportunities. Once the trend matured, a hanging man pattern formed, raising a warning for further buying, followed by a fall in the stock price.

Downtrend

The fundamental idea of trading is to trade with the trend. In trading, we never try to catch a falling knife. If we have to trade reversals, they have to be backed by proper analysis and risk management. That is why buying in a downtrend just because of a candlestick pattern is never a good idea. With that said, a hammer pattern forming at a support can hint at a possible reversal, which might need further confirmation from other technical indicators. Support zones are price points where investors look for buying in a consolidation area. During a downtrend, once the price has hit the support level, the formation of a hammer pattern might suggest that buying interest is returning to the stock. Refer to the weekly INFY chart in Image 4.9, which shows the formation of a hammer pattern at a support.

While hammer and hanging man patterns can be useful reversal signals, they aren't perfect indicators, and should be used in conjunction with other technical analysis tools.

You might be wondering why I went to such lengths when explaining hammer and hanging man patterns. It's because at the end of day, patterns are just human behavior – where the price opened, the low and high it made, and, finally, where it closed. The purpose of this explanation is to help you understand how this information fits into the current context of the chart. The same pattern at different points on the chart can mean different things, and it's up to us to connect the dots. Think of it like this. Say a person regularly gets up in the morning and goes for a walk, and always comes back home in half an hour. One day, he doesn't come back for a full hour, and now his family members are worried. If he took a phone with him, they might call him, but if he didn't, they might take the path he followed for his walk and try to understand where he went. It's the same thing with charts. In an uptrend or downtrend, a pattern might disclose what the market participants are thinking. That is what this whole exercise is about.

Inverted Hammer and Shooting Star

Visually, an inverted hammer and a shooting star look the same. The following are the characteristics of an inverted hammer and a shooting star:

1. The real body is small and positioned near the bottom of the trading range.
2. The upper wick is long, which means the price opened at lower level, made a high, and then came back down.
3. The lower wick is small or negligible, which means that after opening, the price did not drift further lower.

Distinctions between inverted hammer and shooting star patterns:

1. An inverted hammer has a green body, whereas a shooting star has a red body.
2. An inverted hammer is a bullish reversal signal at the bottom of a downtrend, whereas a shooting star is a bearish reversal signal at the maturity of an uptrend.

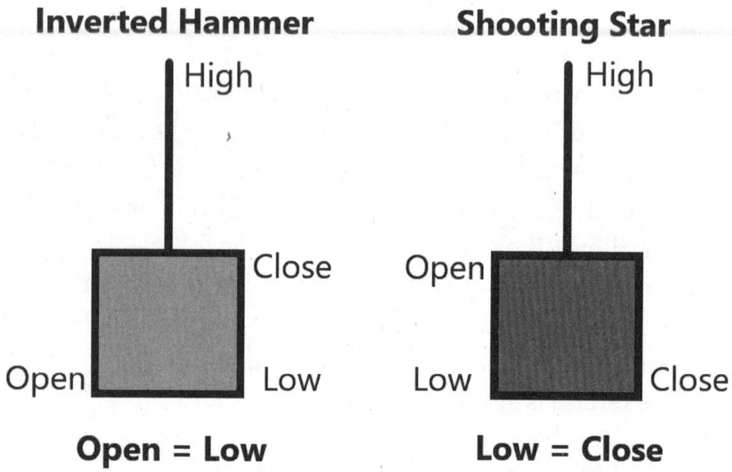

IMAGE 4.14: An inverted hammer and a shooting star

As you can observe in Image 4.14, in an inverted hammer, open ~= low, which means that as soon as the price opened, sellers were never able to mark the price down, and buyers took control. In a downtrend, at a support, an inverted hammer is a strong bullish reversal pattern, regardless of volumes. If the volumes are high, that means there's buying interest. If the volumes are low, that means a strong market according to price action theory. Remember, prices falling in the absence of volume signifies a strong market because it signifies an absence of supply, which means buyers can jump in any time.

Inversely, in a shooting star, close ~= low, which signifies that the price opened higher and buyers were able to mark the price higher, but in the end, sellers controlled the market and the price closed nearest to the low, which means that till the end, supply for the stock was there, which is a bearish signal. High volumes with a shooting star can hint at a potential reversal signal.

The above explanation for inverted hammers and shooting stars is true in most cases, but based on chart context and volumes, the interpretation can change. For example:

1. A shooting star in a downtrend with a high volume might mean further bearishness. The price failing and rising volume is a sign of a weak market.
2. An inverted hammer in an uptrend with a high volume might mean a bullish trend. The same inverted hammer with a low volume can be a bearish reversal.

Therefore, some interpretations depend on the context of the chart.

Doji Candles and Their Types

A doji candle signifies indecision in the market. The following are the characteristics of the doji candle:

1. A small or absent body, which means open ~= close.
2. Long lower and upper wicks.

A doji candle appears when market participants are undecided about the direction of the market. It is not a decisive direction candle. The only significance of a doji is to understand the price action. The stock opens at a particular price, makes a high and low, and then closes near the same price point where it opened, resulting in an indecision candle and hence a small or no body. It is like a draw between buyers and sellers where neither is able to take control of the direction. In a price action context, this does not mean direction, but merely reflects the state of indecision of the market participants. Image 4.15 shows a doji candle.

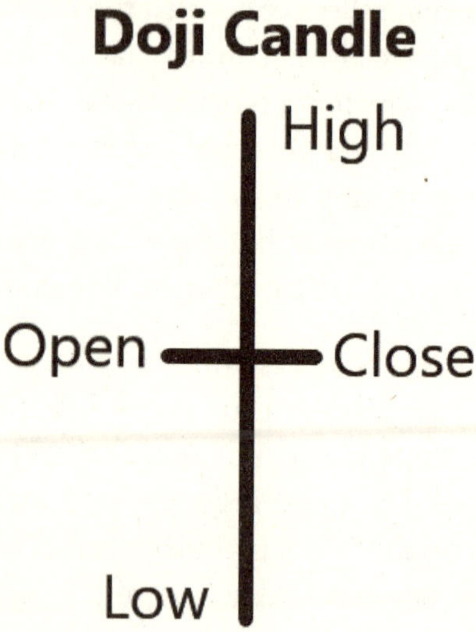

IMAGE 4.15: A doji candle

A doji is the most common candle that you will ever spot on the chart. Apart from indecision, it can hint at consolidation, price slowdown, or a reversal depending on the context of where it appears in chart.

Doji patterns indicate market indecision, but their outcome can vary depending on the specific stock. Just like observing someone's behavior over time allows you to predict their future actions with some degree of accuracy, analyzing a stock's historical price movements (price action) can help you develop an intuition for how it might react to a doji pattern. This understanding of individual stock behavior is crucial for interpreting technical indicators effectively.

If you pick any chart, dojis will be the most repeated candle pattern. Look at the EICHERMOT daily chart shown in Image 4.16 and you can see the number of doji candles that have formed.

IMAGE 4.16: A daily chart of EICHERMOT highlighting a doji pattern

There are 4 types of doji candles:

1. Classic doji
2. Dragonfly doji
3. Gravestone doji
4. Long-legged doji

We have already discussed the classic doji. Let's understand the other doji types.

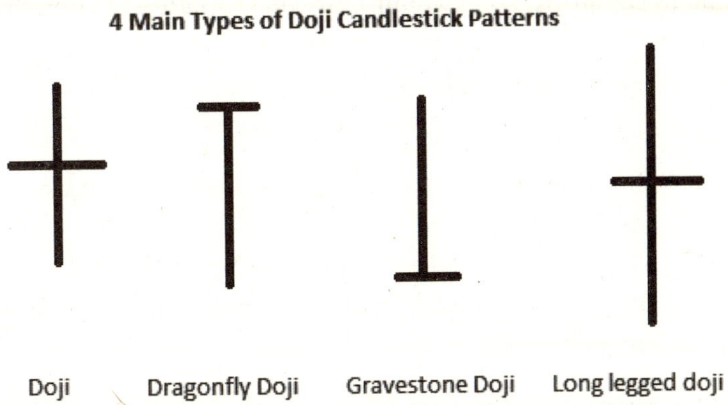

IMAGE 4.17: The four main types of doji candles

Image 4.17 illustrates the different kind of doji candles.

A dragonfly doji looks like a 'T' and can be mistaken for a hammer. A hammer has some real body, which is either green or red, whereas a dragonfly has a very small real body. A hammer is a strong bullish signal, whereas a dragonfly is a bullish (average) signal. The rest of the interpretation is same as that of a hammer.

A gravestone doji looks like an inverted 'T' and can be mistaken for a shooting star. A gravestone doji has a negligible body compared to a shooting star and might hint at a bearish reversal signal.

A long-legged doji is an indecision candle with a long lower and upper wick, which suggests that price volatility in the stock has increased. It means that the price is going up or down abnormally and beyond the normal trading range. This presents a double-edged sword to traders. Increased trading range means traders can extract more profit due to volatility. Inversely, it can also increase losses by incessant stop-loss hunting or bigger stop-losses getting hit. A long-legged doji doesn't necessarily mean a trend change; just increased volatility.

Bullish Engulfing

Bullish engulfing is a bullish reversal pattern. Engulfing means to cover or surround something. The following are the characteristics of a bullish engulfing:

1. It is a two-candle pattern.
2. It requires a preceding red or bearish candlestick in a downtrend.
3. The current candle completely engulfs the real body of the preceding candle covering its lower and higher wick.

It means the current candle opens below or near the previous day's low and closes above the previous day's high in a downtrend, completely engulfing the previous day candle.

Engulfing is a strong bullish reversal signal. If the engulfing is backed by high volume, it further strengthens the bullish reversal analysis. This suggests that after a downtrend, buyers completely dominated the sellers. The strength of the signal may depend on other factors like volume, size of the candle, and the context of the chart (support levels).

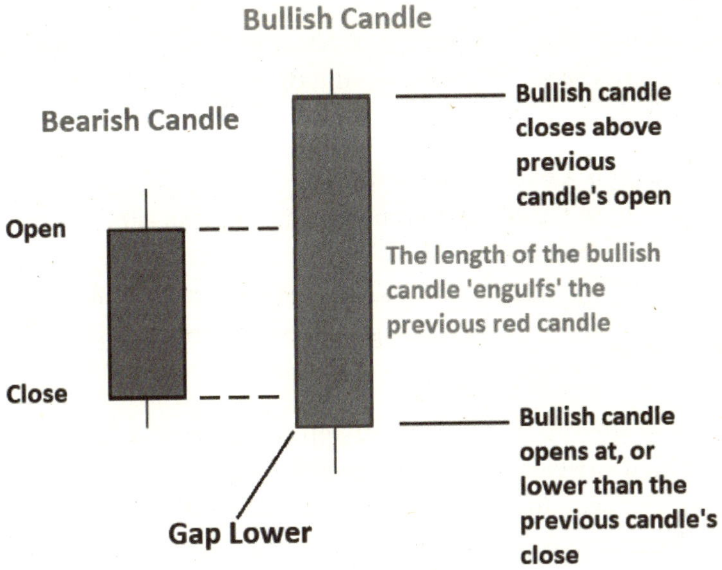

IMAGE 4.18: A bullish engulfing

IMAGE 4.19: A daily chart of ALKEM with bullish engulfing

Observe the chart of ALKEM on a daily timeframe forming a bullish engulfing in Image 4.19. At a support line, the price has formed a bullish engulfing with low volumes. Whether the price bounces or not is yet to be seen.

Bearish Engulfing

Bearish engulfing is a bearish reversal pattern. It is opposite to bullish engulfing. Following are the characteristics of the bearish engulfing:

1. It is a two-candle pattern.
2. It requires a preceding green or bullish candlestick in an uptrend.
3. The current candle completely engulfs the real body of the preceding candle covering its higher to lower wick.

It means the current candle opens above or near the previous day's high and closes below the previous day's low in an uptrend, completely engulfing the previous day's candle.

Engulfing is a strong bearish reversal signal. If the engulfing is backed by volume, it gives further strength to the bearish reversal analysis. It suggests that after an uptrend, sellers completely dominated the buyers. The strength of the signal may depend on other factors like volume, size of the candle, and the context of the chart (support). Bearish engulfing often suggests profit-booking in the market, or it could just be a reaction to any bad news.

Like other technical analysis patterns, bullish engulfing patterns can appear in unexpected places, and their interpretation depends on the overall chart context.

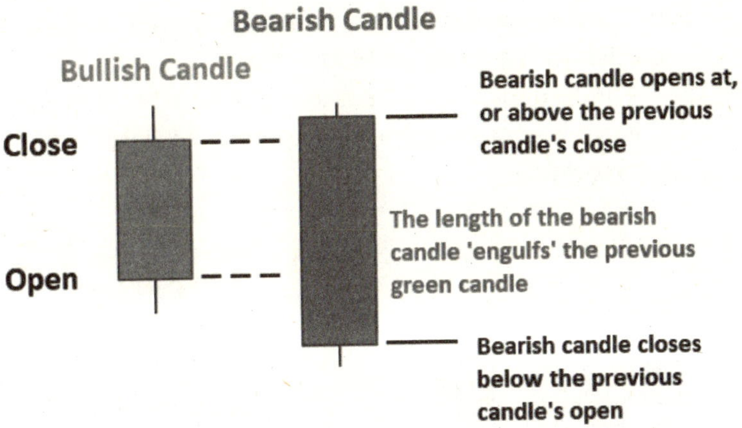

IMAGE 4.20: A bearish engulfing

IMAGE 4.21: A daily chart of BHARATFORG with bearish engulfing

The chart of BHARATFORG in Image 4.21 clearly shows bearish engulfing at a rising resistance line.

Bullish Harami

Bullish harami is a bullish reversal pattern. The following are the essential ingredients of a bullish harami:

1. Bullish harami is a two-candlestick pattern.
2. The first candlestick is typically a large red candlestick establishing an existing downtrend.
3. The second candlestick is a small-bodied green candle entirely contained within the open and close of the first candle.

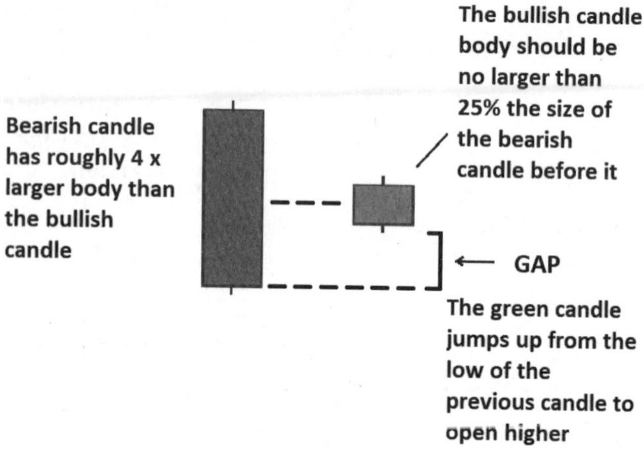

IMAGE 4.22: A bullish harami pattern

For a proper bullish harami, the first candlestick has to be 4 times the size of the second candlestick. Harami patterns suggest a temporary pause or indecision in the prevailing trend. The large first candle reflects the trend's strength, while the small second candle indicates a temporary halt in the momentum, wherein buyers show their willingness to defy an existing downtrend and close the price higher than where it opened, making a green candle.

Bearish Harami

Bearish harami is a bearish reversal pattern, and is the opposite of a bullish harami. The following are the characteristics of a bearish harami:

1. Bearish harami is a two-candlestick pattern.
2. The first candlestick is typically a large green candlestick establishing an existing downtrend.
3. The second candlestick is a small-bodied red candle entirely contained within the open and close of the first candle.

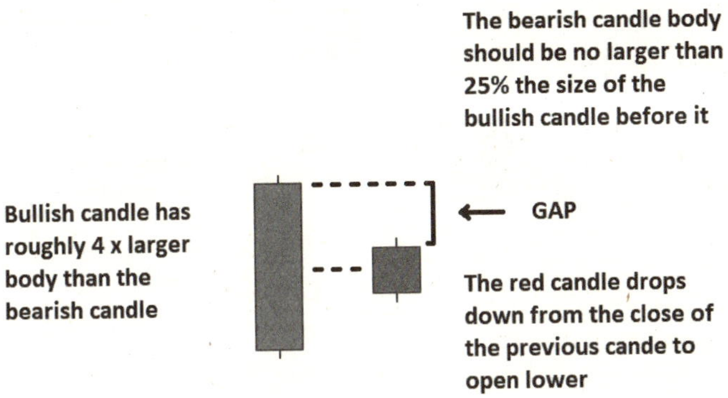

IMAGE 4.23: A bearish harami

For a bearish harami, the first candlestick has to be 4 times the size of the second candlestick. A bearish harami suggests a pause in the uptrend. In the first candle, buyers pushed the price higher. But in the second candle, the price opened lower than the previous close, displaying the intent of sellers at the open. Failure of buyers to push the price any further suggests a temporary pause and trend reversal.

A harami (bullish or bearish) is often confused with an inside bar. The difference between a harami and an inside bar lies in a) the fact that the body of the first candle in a harami is approximately 4 times the size of second candle, making it a special type of inside bar, and b) the difference in color of the second candle. No such size condition exists for an inside bar. An inside bar can be a candle of any size; it just has to be inside the body of the preceding candle, suggesting indecision and a sideways price movement.

Dark Cloud Cover

Dark Cloud Cover is a bearish reversal pattern that signifies the end of an uptrend.

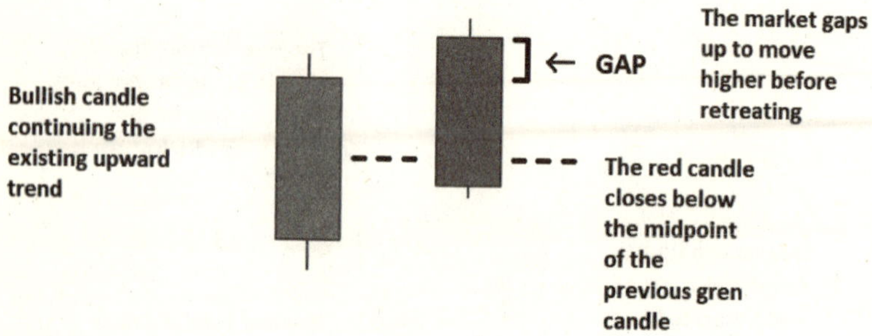

IMAGE 4.24: A Dark Cloud Cover pattern

The following are the characteristics of a Dark Cloud Cover pattern:

1. It is a two-candlestick pattern in which the first candlestick is a large green candle that shows a continuous existing uptrend.
2. The second candlestick opens with a gap-up, tries to move higher, but closes below the body of the first candlestick by at least 50%.
3. The entire body of the second candlestick is within the real body of the first candle.

A Dark Cloud Cover suggests a potential shift in momentum from bullish to bearish. The large first candle reflects the uptrend's strength, but the gap-up and subsequent decline in the second candle indicate a weakening in buying pressure and a potential reversal. High trading volume on the second candle, especially selling volume, can strengthen the bearish reversal signal, as it suggests sellers are actively taking control.

Piercing Line

A piercing line pattern is the opposite of a Dark Cloud Cover, and it signifies a bullish reversal in an existing downtrend.

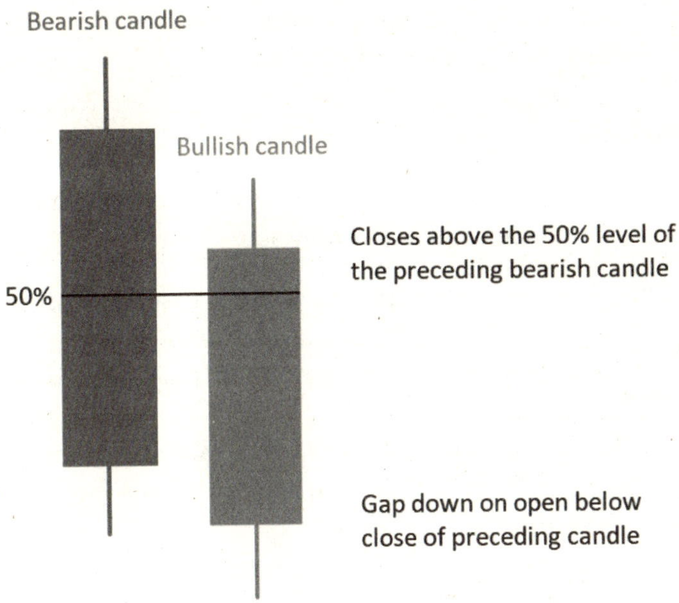

IMAGE 4.25: A piercing line pattern

The following are the characteristics of a piercing line pattern:

1. It is a two-candlestick pattern in which the first candlestick is large red candle that shows a continuous existing downtrend.
2. The second candlestick opens with a gap-down, tries to move lower, but closes above the body of the first candlestick by at least 50%.
3. The entire body of the second candlestick is within the real body of the first candle.

A piercing line suggests a potential shift in momentum from bearish to bullish. The large first candle reflects the downtrend's strength, but the gap-down and subsequent rise in the second candle indicates strength in buying pressure and a potential reversal. High trading volume on the second candle, especially buying volume, can strengthen the bearish reversal signal, as it suggests sellers are actively taking control.

Evening Star

An evening star is a bearish reversal pattern. The following are the essential ingredients of an evening star:

1. It is a three-candle pattern, with the first candlestick being a bearish candle appearing in an uptrend.
2. The second candlestick opens slightly gap-up and is a doji candle.
3. The third candlestick opens with a gap-down, and the price closes 50% below the body of the first candlestick.

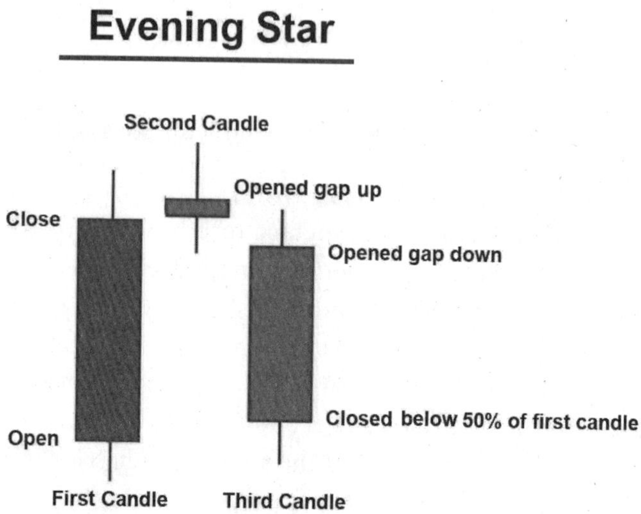

IMAGE 4.26: An evening star pattern

An evening star signifies a halt in the bullish trend. In the first candlestick, buyers pushed the market higher. In the second candlestick, indecision kicked in among market participants. In the third candlestick, sellers dominated the market, hinting at the changed market sentiment. The pattern becomes more significant if it appears at a resistance zone and presents a very good trading opportunity with a smaller stop-loss.

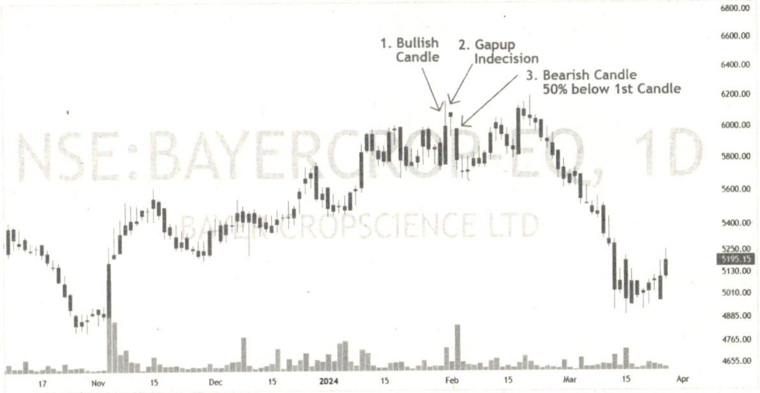

IMAGE 4.27: A daily chart of BAYERCROP with an evening star pattern

An evening star is a 3-candle pattern. The higher the number of candles involved in decision-making, the higher the probability that the pattern is successful.

We can see an example of an evening star on the BAYERCROP daily chart shown in Image 4.27. The price formed a bullish candle, followed by an indecision candle, followed by a gap-down bearish candle which closed 50% below the body of the first candle, and the price fell after that.

Morning Star

A morning star is a bullish reversal pattern. It resembles a rising sun.

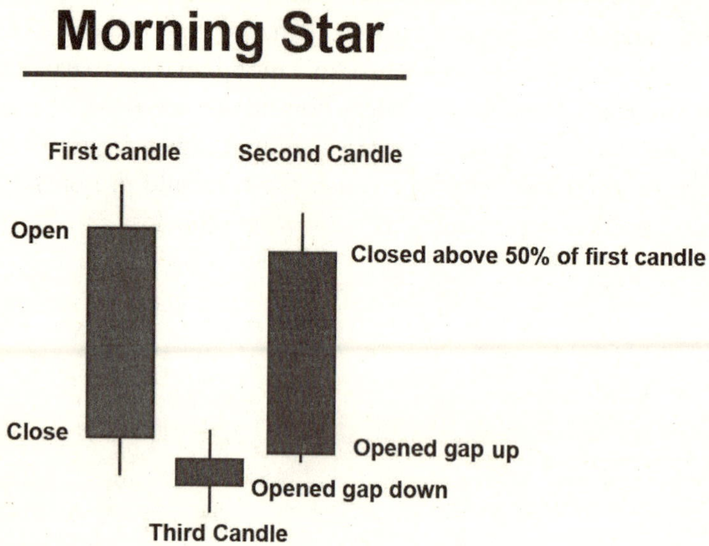

IMAGE 4.28: A morning star pattern

The following are the essential ingredients of a morning star pattern:

1. It is a three-candlestick pattern, with the first candlestick being a bearish candlestick appearing in a downtrend.
2. The second candlestick opens slight gap-down and is a doji candle.
3. The third candlestick opens gap-up and closes above 50% of the body of the first candlestick.

A morning star signifies a halt in the downtrend. In the first candlestick, sellers have control of the market, and they push the market down. In the second candlestick, the stock price opens with a gap-down, but there is indecision, resulting in the formation of a doji candlestick. In the third candlestick, buyers take control of the market from the start by opening the price higher than the previous day's close, further closing it above 50% of the body of the first candlestick, which suggests that buyers are ready to take control. The pattern becomes more significant if it appears at a support zone on charts.

Three White Soldiers

Of all the candlestick patterns, three white soldiers and its counterpart, three black crows, are my favorite patterns. Three white soldiers is a bullish reversal pattern in a downtrend.

IMAGE 4.28.1: A three white soldiers pattern

The following are the characteristics of a three white soldiers pattern:

1. The first candle is a large green candle, reflecting a break from the downtrend and a potential shift in momentum.
2. The second candle is another large green candle, opening higher than the first candle's close and ideally with a small or no upper shadow. This signifies continued buying pressure.
3. The third candle is the strongest of the three – typically a large green candle that opens higher than the second candle's close and closes significantly

higher than the first candle's body. This strong bullish close emphasizes buying dominance.

While the three white soldiers pattern is significant on its own, higher trading volume on each candle, particularly the third candle, strengthens the bullish reversal signal. This increased volume indicates strong buying activity, suggesting a greater conviction among buyers and a higher probability of the uptrend continuing.

In a downtrend with low volume, the three white soldiers pattern suggests that even a modest increase in buying pressure can overwhelm weak selling pressure and reverse the trend. This is because a lack of selling creates less resistance for buyers to push prices higher.

Even in a downtrend with high volume, the three white soldiers pattern can be a strong bullish signal, potentially indicating a short squeeze. A short squeeze occurs when a significant number of short sellers are forced to buy back shares to cover their positions as the price rises against their bets on a continued decline. This surge in buying due to short covering can further accelerate the uptrend, especially when the three white soldiers pattern appears near resistance zones, as a breakout above resistance can trigger stop-loss orders from short sellers, adding more fuel to the buying pressure.

Look at the chart of FINPIPE on a daily timeframe in Image 4.29 and observe how the three white soldiers at the bottom resulted in an uptrend.

IMAGE 4.29: A chart of FINPIPE on a daily timeframe with three white soldiers

This short covering is a very powerful pattern that is synonymous with three white soldiers, and also works in an uptrend. In an existing uptrend, the stock price might witness a severe sell-off, followed by the formation of a three white soldier pattern, and can result in a short covering rally, which pushes the price higher very quickly.

See Image 4.30 for a chart of VADILALIND on a daily timeframe. The stock broke its resistance line. The resistance line turned into a support. From 3800 levels, there was a sell-off, and the price took support at the previous resistance, followed by three white soldiers, and the price again started moving up with buying interest, indicated by heavy volumes. Now one may argue that this is not short covering because the volumes are less and in absence of supply, little demand created a price surge. But the principle remains same. It's either short covering or genuine demand, and three white soldiers works in an uptrend, too.

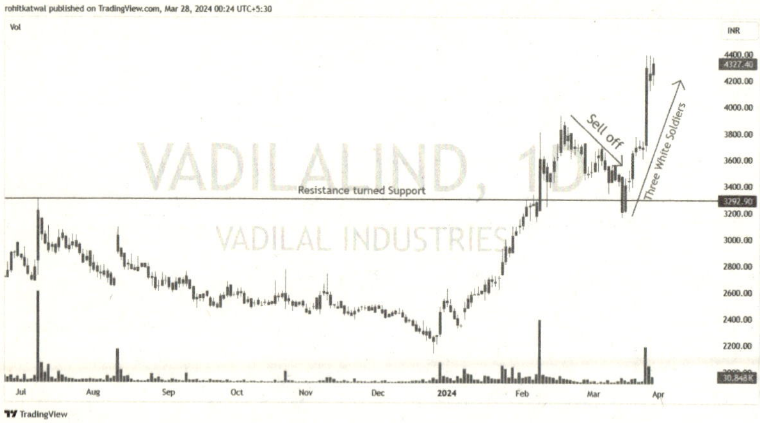

IMAGE 4.30: A VADILALIND chart on a daily timeframe

Three Black Crows

Three black crows is a bearish reversal pattern used in candlestick analysis to signal a potential end to an uptrend and the beginning of a downtrend. It signifies a shift in dominance from buyers to sellers.

The following are the main characteristics of a three black crows pattern:

1. The first candle is a large red candle, reflecting a break from the uptrend and a potential shift in momentum.
2. The second candle is another large red candle, opening lower than the first candle's close and ideally with a small or no lower shadow. This signifies continued selling pressure.
3. The third candle is typically a large red candle that opens lower than the second candle's close and closes significantly lower than the first candle's body. This strong bearish close emphasizes sellers' dominance.

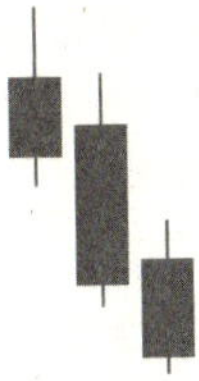

Three Black Crows

IMAGE 4.31: A three black crows pattern

While the three black crows pattern is significant on its own, higher trading volume on each candle, particularly the second and third candles, strengthens the bearish reversal signal. This increased volume suggests strong selling pressure overwhelming buying pressure, adding confirmation to the potential trend reversal.

The three black crows pattern can be seen not only at the end of uptrends but also within existing downtrends, potentially forcing long unwinding. Long unwinding refers to existing buyers exiting their long positions (selling their shares) as the price falls, further accelerating the downtrend.

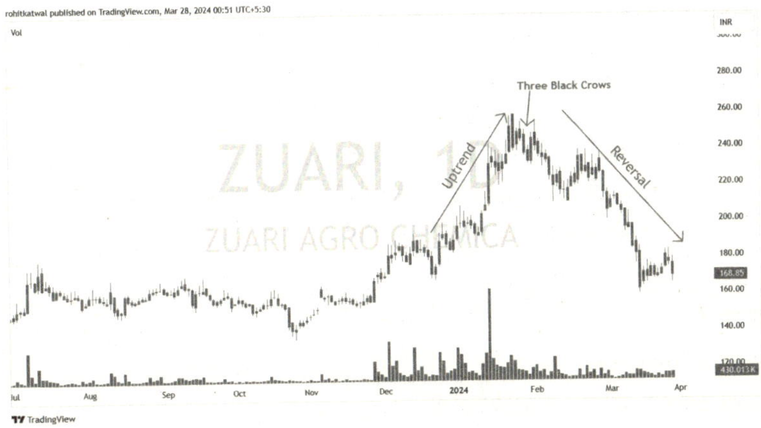

IMAGE 4.32: A ZUARI chart on a daily timeframe with three black crows

The chart of ZUARI on a daily timeframe in Image 4.32 is a good example of the three black crows pattern appearing at the end of an uptrend, followed by a downtrend.

Candle-Volume Relationship

In Chapter 3, Table 3.3 helped us analyze price and volume from a market perspective. Now it is time to expand that analysis from a market to a candlestick perspective. When analyzing candle patterns and volume, we must understand the relationship between them. There are four interpretations of price and volume on a candlestick:

1. **Long build-up**: If the price goes up and the volume goes up, it suggests a long build-up, indicating buyers are actively entering the market and creating buy positions.
2. **Long unwinding**: If the price goes down and the volume goes down, it suggests long unwinding, meaning existing buyers are exiting their long positions (selling their shares).
3. **Short build-up**: If the price goes down and the volume goes up, it suggests short build-up, indicating new short positions are being created by sellers who are betting that the price will continue falling.
4. **Short covering**: If the price goes up and the volume goes down, it suggests short covering, meaning existing short sellers are buying back shares to close out their positions, potentially due to a price increase that goes against their bets.

Do not confuse this interpretation with the interpretation in Table 3.3. In Table 3.3, we were analyzing the overall trend of the market with respect to price direction and volume trading, suggesting at a strong or a weak market.

Here, we are understanding the interpretation of price and volume with respect to buyers and sellers on a single candle, which has to be confirmed with the overall trend of the stock price on the chart and other indicators. It gives us insight into the activity of the various market participants. For example, in Image 4.32, we can deduce that the uptrend was a long build-up because prices were going up on heavy volumes. After the three black crows pattern formed, prices came down with the average volume; i.e., price down, volume down, which means long unwinding.

Price	Volumes	Interpretation
UP	UP	Long Buildup
DOWN	DOWN	Long Unwinding
DOWN	UP	Short Buildup
UP	DOWN	Short Covering

TABLE 4.1: Price-volume interpretation for a candlestick

Advanced Candlestick Analysis

Candlestick patterns are valuable tools for identifying potential trend continuations and reversals. However, candlesticks themselves tell a story beyond these predefined patterns. Each candlestick formed during market hours on a specific timeframe reflects the battle between buyers and sellers throughout that period. By analyzing individual candles, we can gain valuable insights into market psychology.

Imagine each candlestick as a snapshot of the price action within its timeframe (e.g., daily, hourly). The body of the candle represents the difference between the opening and closing prices, while the wicks (or shadows) capture the highs and lows reached during that period.

IMAGE 4.33: Visualization of price inside a candlestick

A large bullish candle with a small upper wick suggests strong buying pressure throughout the timeframe (Image 4.33), with buyers pushing the price higher and overriding any selling attempts. Even if the price action within the timeframe was volatile, the bulls emerged victorious, closing the price at a significantly higher level than it opened. The opposite is true for a bearish candle.

This advanced analysis of interpreting individual candles, along with their relationship to neighboring candles, can provide valuable insights into market psychology. While traditional candlestick patterns offer established reversal or continuation signals, analyzing individual candles can sometimes offer earlier hints about potential shifts in buyer or seller dominance. This analysis, however, should be used in conjunction with other technical indicators for stronger confirmation.

When looking at a price chart, we have to look at how the candlesticks are forming – from one candle to another. We have to interpret the buyers' and sellers' psychology. To understand that psychology, the following characteristics of the candlestick are important:

1. **Size of the body:** A large body suggests strong buying or selling pressure, depending on whether it's a bullish (green) or bearish (red) candle. A large

body with a close significantly higher (bullish) or lower (bearish) than the open strengthens this signal. A small body suggests a balance between buyers and sellers, resulting in minimal price movement. An even narrower body might suggest indecision or even less buying interest.

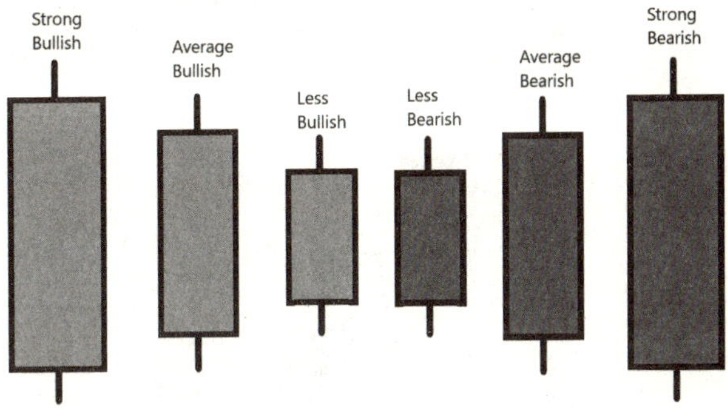

IMAGE 4.34: Size of the candle

If the size of the body is increasing on consecutive candles, it suggests strong momentum in the existing direction of the trend. We can observe this candlestick analysis on the weekly chart of TATAPOWER shown in Image 4.35.

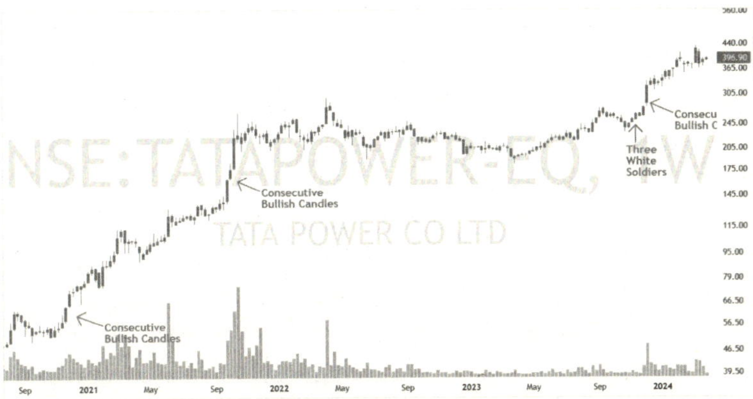

IMAGE 4.35: A weekly chart of TATAPOWER

2. **Length of upper and lower wicks w.r.t. the body:** The length of the wicks matters when trying to understand a candle. A longer lower wick means the buyers dominated the sellers. A longer upper wick means sellers dominated the buyers. See Image 4.36 to understand the behavior of buyers and sellers with respect to the size of the lower and upper wicks.

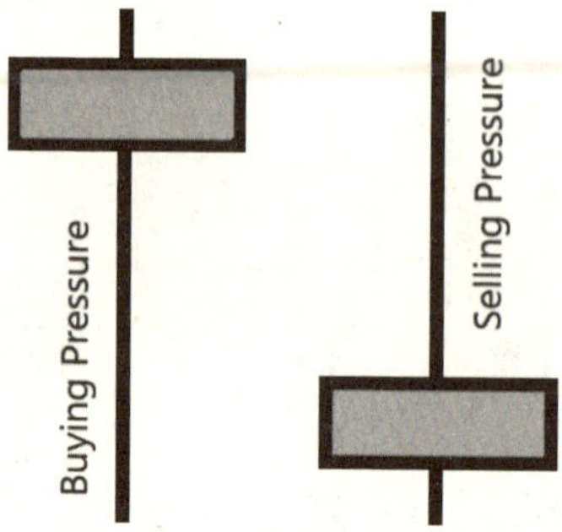

IMAGE 4.36: Interpretation of the size of the lower and upper wick

3. **Opening or closing w.r.t. the previous candle:** The opening and closing prices of a candlestick relative to the previous candle's close offer valuable clues about the trend's strength or potential reversals.

   Uptrend: A candle opening above the previous candle's close and closing even higher suggests a continuation of the uptrend with strong momentum. Conversely, a candle opening below the previous close but still closing higher might indicate a possible trend pause or reversal.

   Downtrend: A candle opening below the previous candle's close and closing even lower suggests a continuation of the downtrend with strong momentum. Conversely, a candle opening above the previous close but still closing lower might indicate a possible trend pause or reversal.

By analyzing these opening/closing relationships in consecutive candles, we can gain valuable insights into the ongoing battle between buyers and sellers and identify potential turning points in the trend.

4. **Volume:** Volume is a crucial factor that complements the signals from candlestick body size and wick lengths. By analyzing volume alongside these candlestick elements, we can gain a more comprehensive understanding of the buying and selling pressure behind a price movement. We have analyzed this relationship in detail in Table 4.1.

For a better understanding, see Image 4.37, which shares a glimpse of how the size and shape of a candle can affect the bearish or bullish perception of the price.

Remember, in trading, it's always best to take a trade once the candle formation is complete on a trading timeframe. It confirms the psychology of market participants for that particular timeframe.

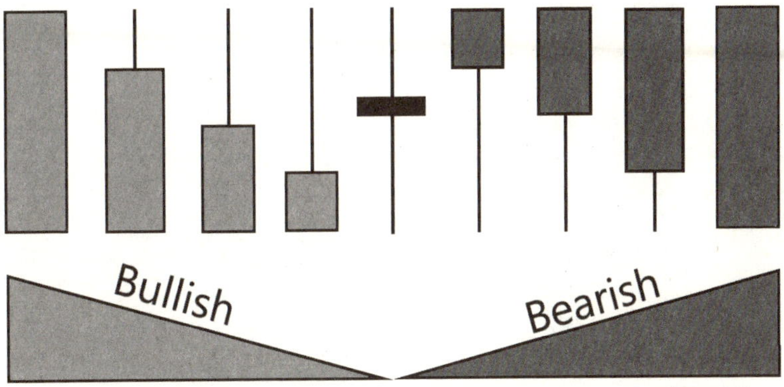

IMAGE 4.37: Different candlesticks and their strengths

With this, we come to an end to candlestick pattern analysis. Before we move to the next chapter, remember that the stock price is not bound to move according to our analysis. Whenever we buy a stock feeling certain in our analysis that the price will go up, there's a seller somewhere else feeling equally certain in their analysis that the price will go on, and both are certain they're right. That is why, ultimately:

Bhaav Bhagwan Che, or *Price is King.*

CHAPTER 5

Chart Patterns

Charts are a way to forecast the future action of markets

Charts are a trader's window into market psychology. While some information might be hidden, price movements on charts reflect the combined actions of all market participants, reacting to news, economic data, and even broader market sentiment. This is why technical analysts have a saying:

News is already built up in the charts.

Chart patterns display human behavior around certain price levels over a period of time. Such human behavior manifests into chart patterns. These chart patterns are one of the most integral parts of technical analysis, helping gauge future price movement.

Before diving into specific chart patterns, it's crucial to understand the concept of timeframes. A timeframe refers to the time interval each candle on a chart represents. Choosing the right timeframe depends on your trading style. If you hold positions throughout the day and exit before the market closes, shorter timeframes of, say, 1/3/5/10/15 minutes might be suitable. For traders holding positions for several days or weeks, daily or weekly timeframes might be more appropriate.

Ultimately, the best timeframe depends on your individual trading style and holding period. Consider experimenting with different timeframes on paper before risking real capital.

Why is the timeframe important?

1. **Holding period**: The timeframe decides your holding period.
2. **Stop-loss and targets**: Timeframe selection can influence the placement of your initial stop-loss orders and potential profit targets.
3. **Historical data**: The chosen timeframe determines the amount of historical data you'll analyze on a chart.

Unlike candlestick patterns, which typically focus on a few candles for potential reversals or continuations, chart patterns can span over days and weeks of candlestick charts.

This book will primarily focus on daily and weekly timeframes for illustrative purposes. In rare cases, we might use 2- or 3-hour timeframes for specific examples.

There are three types of chart patterns:

1. Trend reversal patterns
2. Trend continuation patterns
3. Neutral chart patterns

Trend Reversal Patterns

Trend reversal patterns are those which indicate a reversal to an existing downtrend or uptrend. The most important trend reversal chart patterns are:

1. Double top
2. Double bottom
3. Triple top
4. Triple bottom
5. Rounding top
6. Rounding bottom
7. Head and shoulders
8. Inverted head and shoulders

Double Top Pattern

A double top is a bearish reversal pattern.

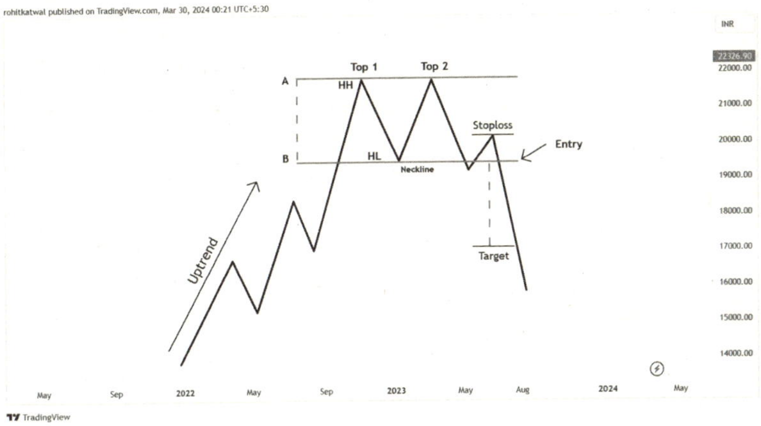

IMAGE 5.1: A double top pattern

A double top pattern looks like a capital M (Image 5.1). After an uptrend, the price reaches a high point (HH as top 1), then dips slightly but forms a higher low (HL) compared to the previous low. This lower point becomes the neckline – a temporary support level.

The price attempts to climb again but fails to create a new high, forming a second peak (often lower than the first; i.e., top 2). This failed attempt signals weakening buying pressure.

The price consolidates around the neckline before breaking down decisively below it. This breakthrough confirms the double top reversal.

Consolidation around the neckline is not essential, but it is a common, highly probable characteristic of a double top pattern.

Trading a double top

- A short trade entry can be considered after the price breaks decisively below the neckline.

- The stop-loss can be placed slightly above the neckline, or above the most recent high that's closer to the neckline.
- The target for the price decline is typically the distance between the neckline and the second peak (A to B), projected downwards from the breakdown point. This distance reflects the potential price movement based on the pattern's height.

Volumes play an important part in a double top. A neckline break with high volume suggests a stronger breakout. By using more analysis tools like candlestick patterns and volumes, you can get more insight into the pattern's probability of success.

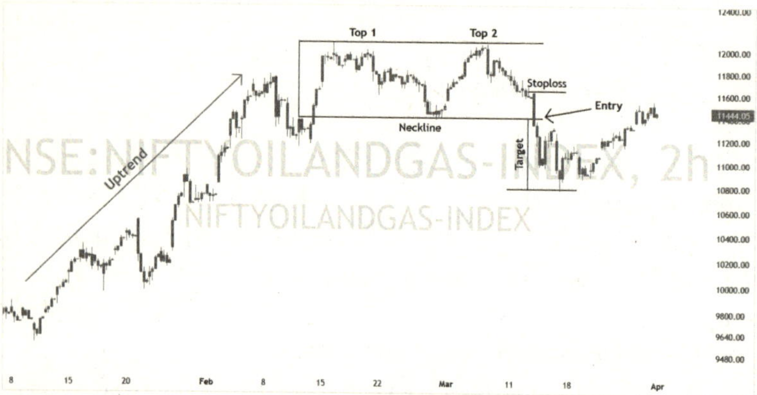

IMAGE 5.2: NIFTY Oil and Gas on a 2-hour chart with a double top pattern

Image 5.2 perfectly shows what a double top pattern looks like. Sometimes, it is difficult to identify patterns on candlestick charts, and it can be helpful to switch to a line chart to identify patterns.

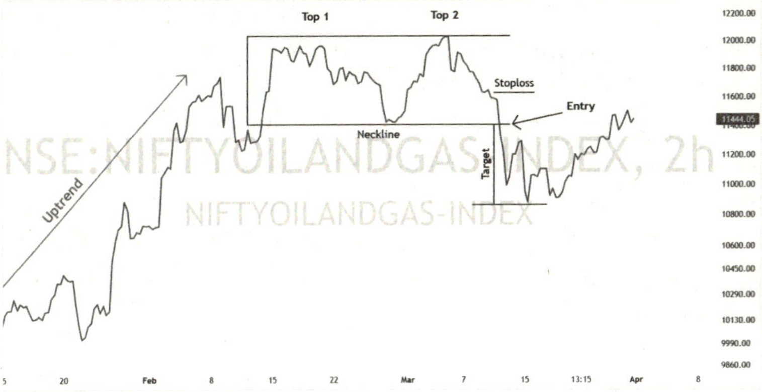

IMAGE 5.3: Nifty Oil and Gas on a 2-hour chart with a double top pattern (line chart)

Double Bottom Pattern

A double bottom is opposite of a double top. It is a bullish reversal pattern.

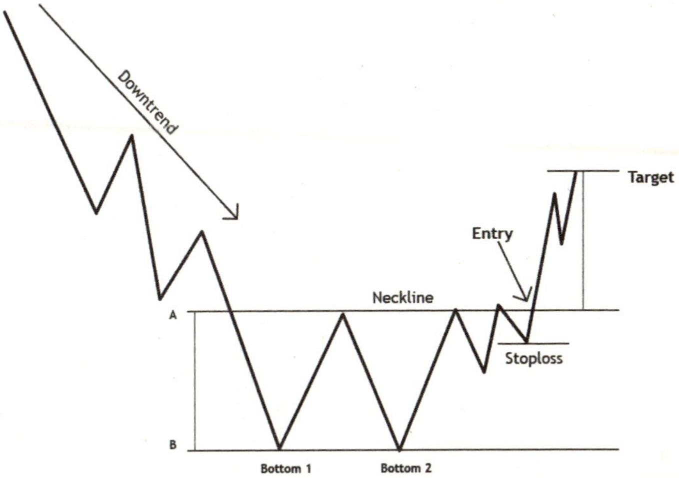

IMAGE 5.4: A double bottom pattern

A double bottom pattern looks like a capital W (Image 5.4). After a downtrend, the price reaches a low point (LL as bottom 1), then pulls back slightly but forms a lower high (LH) compared to the previous high. This lower point becomes the neckline – a temporary resistance level.

The price attempts to fall again but fails to create a new low, forming a second trough. This failed attempt signals weak selling pressure.

The price consolidates around the neckline before breaking up decisively above it. This breakthrough confirms the double bottom reversal.

Trading a double bottom

- A bullish trade entry can be considered after the price breaks decisively above the neckline.
- The stop-loss can be placed slightly below the neckline, or below the most recent low that's closer to the neckline.
- The target for the bullish trade is typically the distance between the neckline and the second trough (A to B), projected upward from the breakout point. This distance reflects the potential price movement based on the pattern's height.

IMAGE 5.5: BIRLACORP on a weekly line chart with a double bottom pattern

Usually, a reversal after a trend occurs when the price has gone through an accumulation or distribution phase (consolidation). In case of a double top or double bottom pattern, the reversal is rather swift, which gives less room for a lengthy consolidation, suggesting that the current price movement is either due to a weak trend or some news regarding the company that's affecting its stock price.

Triple Top and Triple Bottom Patterns

The triple top and triple bottom are extensions of the double top and bottom patterns. As the name suggests, the difference lies in the triple top or bottom formed by the stock price in an uptrend or downtrend respectively. A triple top or bottom also signify a lengthy consolidation after a trend.

See Image 5.6 for an example of a triple top pattern.

IMAGE 5.6: A triple top pattern on CREDITACCESS on a daily timeframe

Rounding Top Pattern

A rounding top is a bearish reversal pattern that occurs after a long uptrend. It resembles a dome-like shape, or an upside-down 'U', above a supporting neckline (as shown in Image 5.7).

After an extended uptrend, buyers lose momentum and struggle to push prices higher. This phase is often characterized by a lengthy consolidation period where the price fluctuates within the rounded area.

Sellers gradually gain control, eventually pushing the price decisively below the neckline, confirming the reversal.

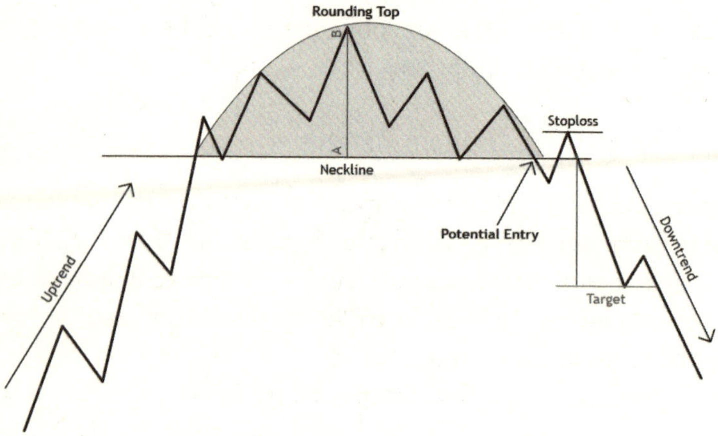

IMAGE 5.7: A rounding top pattern

Trading a rounding top

- A bearish entry can be taken once the price breaks the supporting neckline.
- A stop-loss can be placed slightly above the neckline or the most recent lower high near the neckline.
- The target for the price decline is typically the distance between the neckline and the highest peak (A to B), projected downwards from the breakdown point. This distance reflects the potential price movement based on the rounding top's height.

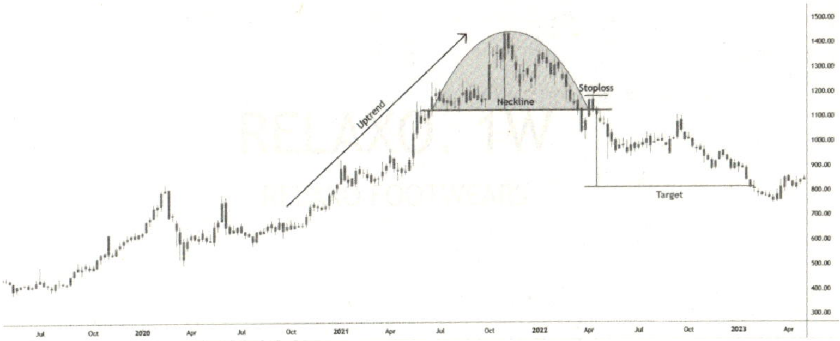

IMAGE 5.8: A weekly chart of RELAXO forming a rounding top pattern

Rounding Bottom Pattern

A rounding bottom is the opposite of a rounding top, and represents a bullish reversal pattern formed after a downtrend (as shown in Image 5.9). It resembles a wide 'U' shape.

After a sustained downtrend, sellers become exhausted, and buyers start accumulating. This phase is also characterized by a consolidation period where the price fluctuates within the rounded area.

Bulls eventually gain control, pushing the price decisively above the resistance neckline, confirming the reversal.

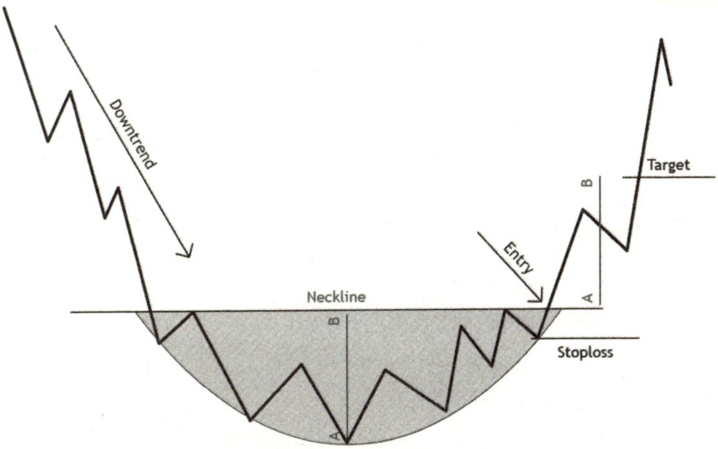

IMAGE 5.9: A rounding bottom pattern

Trading a rounding bottom

- Bullish trade entry can be considered after break of the resistance neckline.
- The stop-loss for the trade is slightly below the neckline, or below the higher low nearest to the neckline.
- The potential target is the distance between the resistance neckline and the lowest trough.

In Image 5.10, the weekly chart of BANKINDIA might be forming a rounding bottom pattern, indicating a potential trend reversal from the downtrend.

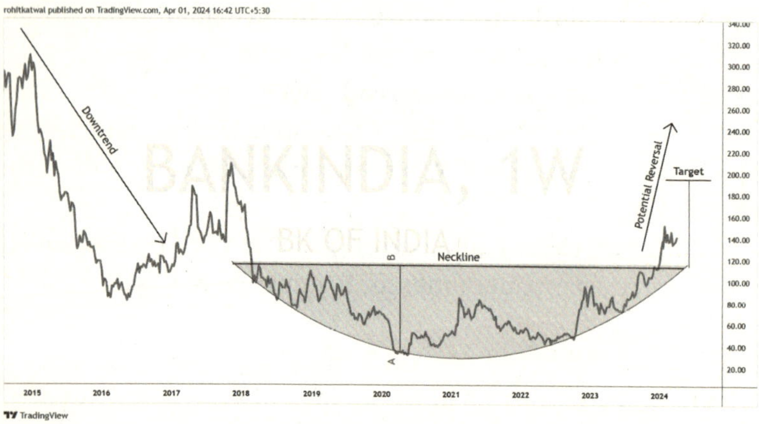

IMAGE 5.10: A weekly chart of BANKINDIA with a potential rounding bottom underway

Head and Shoulders Pattern

The head and shoulders pattern is a widely recognized and reliable bearish reversal pattern that appears after an uptrend. It's known for its relatively simple visual identification and can be a valuable tool for traders to spot potential trend reversals. The pattern emerges after a preceding uptrend, characterized by a series of higher highs and higher lows. The price reaches a peak, forming the left shoulder.

A neckline is established by connecting the swing lows (temporary price bottoms) before the head and shoulders formation. This line represents a support level where the price has previously bounced back up.

Crucially, the price rallies and surpasses the peak of the left shoulder, forming a higher central peak known as the head. This signifies a temporary resurgence of buying pressure, but ultimately fails to break new highs.

A right shoulder forms, typically lower than the head, as sellers start to gain control. The price may revisit the neckline for support before another downward move.

The key confirmation for the reversal is a decisive breakdown below the neckline. This signifies a shift in momentum from buyers to sellers.

The head and shoulders pattern differs from a triple top by having a central peak (head) that's usually higher than the other two, followed by a decline before the neckline breakdown.

Increased trading volume on the breakdown below the neckline can strengthen the bearish signal. While not essential, a more symmetrical pattern with well-defined shoulders tends to be more reliable.

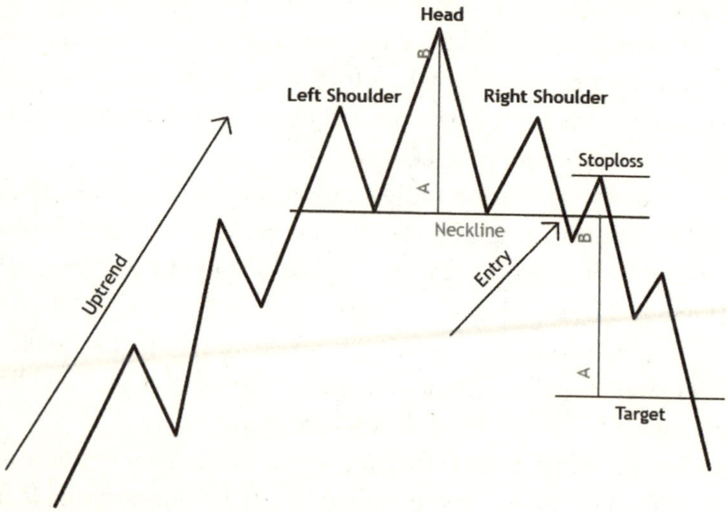

IMAGE 5.11: A head and shoulders pattern

Trading a head and shoulders

- A short trade entry can be considered after the price breaks decisively below the neckline.
- The stop-loss can be placed slightly above the neckline or above the highest point of the right shoulder.
- The target for the price decline is typically the distance between the neckline and the head, projected downwards from the breakdown point. This distance reflects the potential price movement based on the pattern's height.

A head and shoulders pattern can also form when the neckline is slanting and not horizontal.

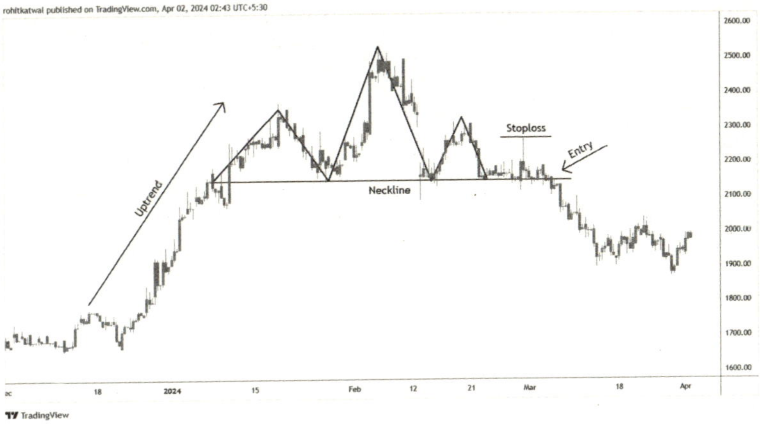

IMAGE 5.12: A head and shoulders pattern on a GLAXO 3-hour chart

Inverted Head and Shoulders Pattern

The inverted head and shoulders pattern is a widely recognized and bullish reversal pattern that appears after a downtrend. It shares some similarities with the head and shoulders pattern, but in reverse, and signifies a potential shift in momentum from sellers to buyers.

The pattern emerges after a preceding downtrend, characterized by a series of lower lows and lower highs. The price reaches a temporary low, forming the left shoulder.

A neckline is established by connecting the swing highs (temporary price peaks) before the inverted head and shoulders formation. This line represents a resistance level where the price has previously been rejected. The price dips lower and breaks below the left shoulder, forming a trough that acts as the head. This signifies a potential weakening of selling pressure.

A right shoulder forms, typically higher than the head, as buyers start to gain control. The price may revisit the neckline for resistance before another upward move.

The key confirmation for the reversal is a decisive breakout above the neckline. This signifies a shift in momentum from sellers to buyers.

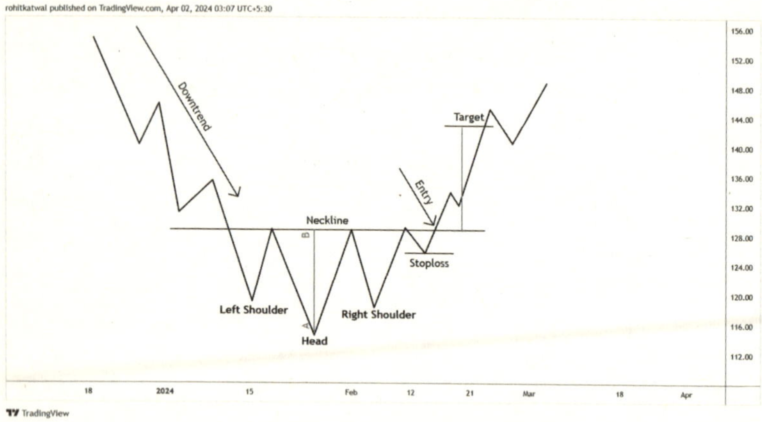

IMAGE 5.13: An inverted head and shoulders pattern

Observe the weekly chart of NAUKRI in Image 5.14 forming an inverted head and shoulders pattern. This is an example of inverted head and shoulders forming with a slanting line. Although the pattern with horizontal lines are considered more accurate, it does not mean that slanting necklines are invalid.

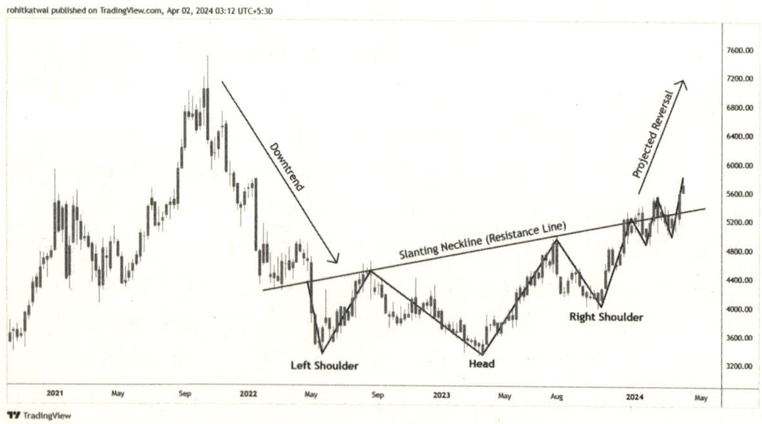

IMAGE 5.14: A weekly chart of NAUKRI with an inverted head and shoulders pattern (slanting neckline)

Here, we've covered some common trend reversal patterns: head and shoulders, inverted head and shoulders, and rounding tops and bottoms. It's interesting to note that these reversal patterns tend to coincide with specific phases of the market cycle. Bearish reversal patterns often appear during the distribution phase, which is the third stage, characterized by weakening buying pressure and potential price decline. Conversely, bullish reversal patterns tend to emerge during the accumulation phase, the first stage, where price consolidation might indicate buying pressure building up. While the specific shapes of these patterns (rounded, double tops, etc.) can vary, understanding this relationship between chart patterns and market cycles can be a valuable tool for traders. See Image 3.34 below for a better understanding.

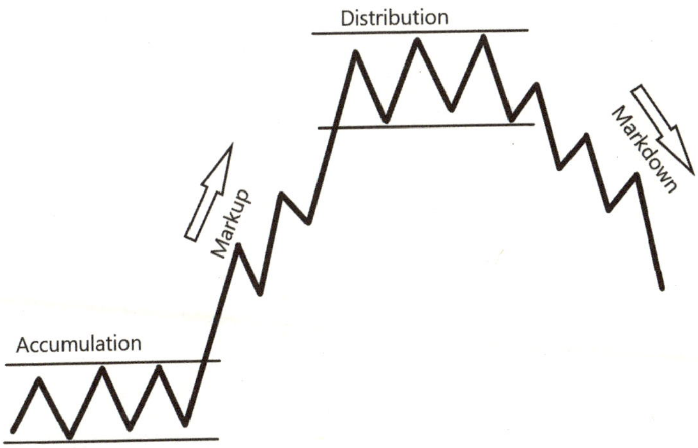

IMAGE 3.34: A market cycle showing the stages of the market

Trend Continuation Patterns

Trend continuation patterns are technical indicators used to identify potential continuations of the prevailing trend. Unlike reversal patterns, which suggest a shift in direction, continuation patterns signal that the current uptrend or downtrend is likely to hold. The 4-stage market cycle (accumulation, markup, distribution, markdown) is a guide, but sometimes markets surprise us.

Normally, Stage 3 (distribution) results in a price decline. But if a company's future looks bright (strong earnings, new products), investors keep buying, and Stage 3 secretly acts like Stage 1 (accumulation), the price might hold steady or even rise, defying expectations of a downturn and extending the uptrend for years!

That's how trend continuation patterns form. They might be disguised in a distribution, when it is instead in the accumulation phase. That is why we often say that only after a breakout can we say whether consolidation was accumulation or distribution.

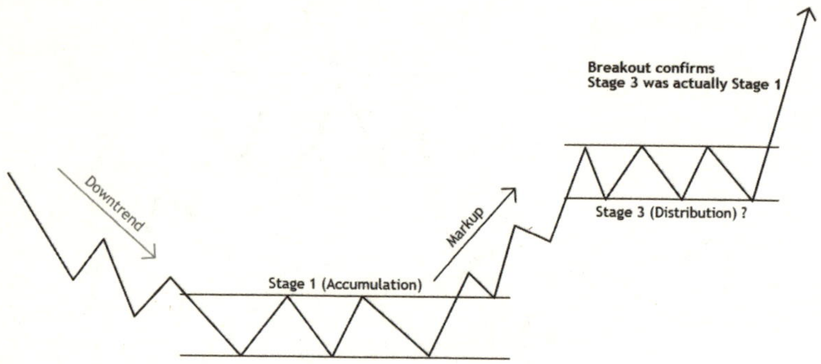

IMAGE 5.15: Stage 3 is sometimes Stage 1

Understanding this is important, because traders often make the mistake of confusing Stage 1 with Stage 3. Trend continuation patterns work when there is always an existing trend (bullish or bearish).

The most important trend continuation patterns are:

1. Bullish rectangle and bearish rectangle
2. Ascending triangle
3. Descending triangle
4. Cup and handle
5. Inverted cup and handle
6. Flag and pole

Bullish Rectangle and Bearish Rectangle Pattern

The rectangle is a common technical analysis pattern that suggest consolidation phase after a trend. It may also suggest a temporary pause in the price before it starts moving in the direction of the trend.

If the rectangle is formed in a bullish trend and breakout from rectangle is to the upside, it's a bullish rectangle. If the rectangle is formed in a bearish trend and the price breaks down, it's a bearish rectangle.

Long term consolidations can be termed as Phase 1 accumulation after an uptrend, or Phase 3 distribution after a downtrend. Since we are talking about trend continuation patterns, we are not going to talk about the trend reversal aspect of rectangles. Effectively, double top or bottom and triple top or bottom are also rectangles, but they represent trend reversals.

A rectangle is formed by two horizontal lines that connect price highs and lows. The price movement is confined within these parallel lines for a certain period. The rectangle pattern is confirmed if the price breaks above the resistance line or below the support line.

A rectangle pattern does not guarantee a direction. It just indicates that price is out of the consolidation phase, where bulls and bears were somewhat balanced.

The main limitations of a rectangle breakout is the false breakout that often occurs, which is why confirmation from other technical analysis tools is recommended for making better trading decisions.

Volumes play a crucial role in a rectangle pattern breakout. Volumes in a rectangle pattern are low, with occasional high volumes on certain candles, which indicates stock is getting accumulated or distributed. A breakout is often backed by strong volumes. A low-volume breakout tends to be less reliable.

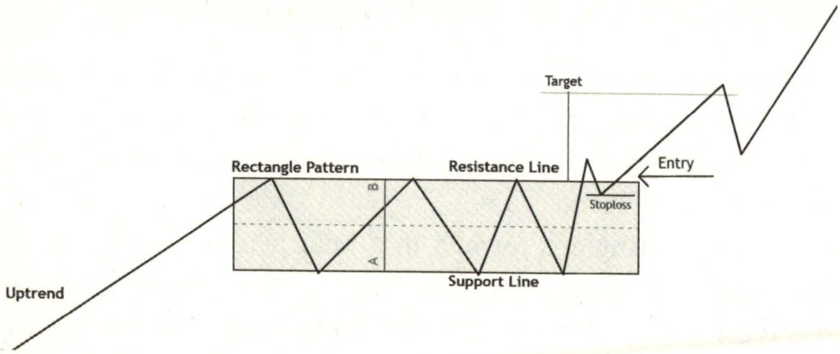

IMAGE 5.16: A bullish rectangle pattern

Trading a bullish rectangle

- **Identify the rectangle**: Look for a price movement confined within two roughly parallel horizontal resistance and support trendlines. The price should be bouncing between these lines for a while, indicating consolidation.
- **Wait for the breakout**: This is crucial. Don't enter the trade before a decisive breakout occurs. A breakout above the resistance level (upper trendline) suggests a potential continuation of an uptrend.
- **Volume confirmation (optional but important)**: While not essential, increased trading volume on the breakout can strengthen the signal. Higher volume on a breakout suggests more conviction behind the price movement.
- Place a buy order above the resistance level after a confirmed breakout. Place a stop-loss order below the nearest significant low. The distance between the resistance and support line is the target for the trade (Image 5.16).

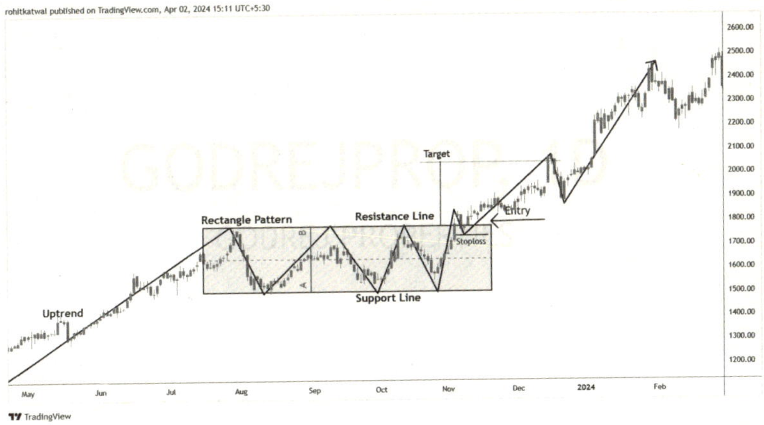

IMAGE 5.17: A daily chart of GODREJPROP with a rectangle pattern

A bearish rectangle pattern is the opposite of a bullish rectangle pattern. In a downtrend, the price starts consolidating between rectangle patterns. The break below the support line is the bearish entry. The stop-loss is slightly above the support line, or above the nearest lower high. The distance between the resistance and support lines is the target for the stock price.

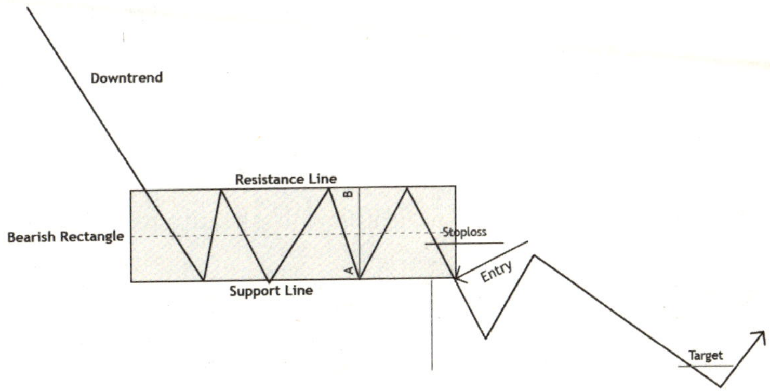

IMAGE 5.18: A bearish rectangle pattern

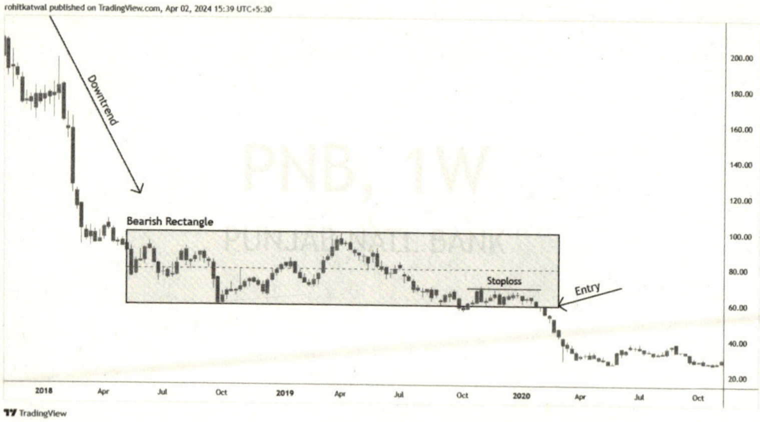

IMAGE 5.19: A weekly chart of PNB with a bearish rectangle

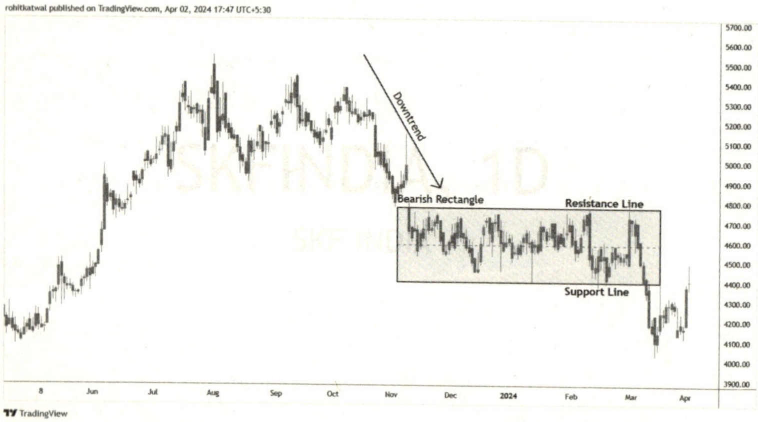

IMAGE 5.20: A daily chart of SKFINDIA with a bearish rectangle

Ascending Triangle

Now that we've explored rectangles, let's move on to triangle patterns. Interestingly, all these patterns can be thought of as a variation of rectangles.

Picture the price as a spring. The more you compress a spring, the stronger the force pushing back in the opposite direction. This principle of action and reaction can be applied to triangles, and is why all the triangle patterns work. The price squeezes, only to eventually break out in a direction.

In an ascending triangle, the price movement gets compressed within a specific area. A horizontal line connects the price highs, forming a ceiling. On the other hand, a rising trendline connects the price lows, creating a kind of floor that keeps rising.

This price squeeze, like compressing a spring, can be seen as a build-up of potential energy. The question is, in which direction will the price eventually break out?

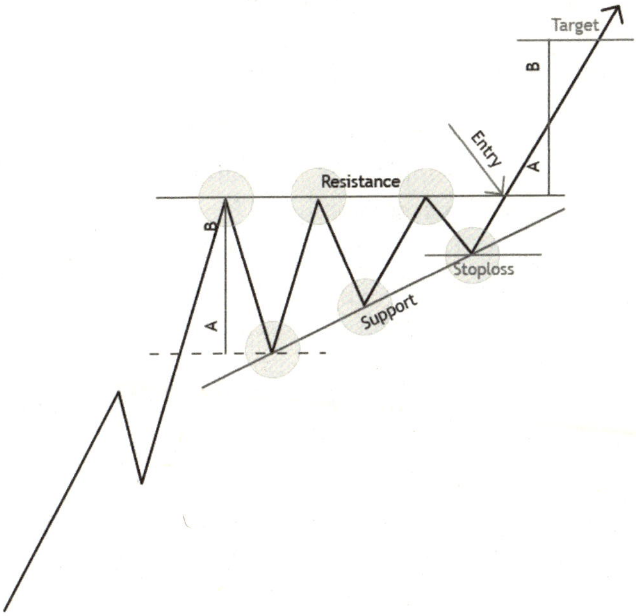

IMAGE 5.21: An ascending triangle pattern

An ascending triangle is a bullish continuation pattern, which signifies that buyers are getting very aggressive. After an uptrend, there is an attempt from sellers to push price lower, which is absorbed by the buyers. At the resistance, sellers again try to take control, which is absorbed by buyers more aggressively. This selling pressure at resistance could be created for multiple reasons, like investors booking profits or creating short positions, or even long-term investors who had been stuck at wrong prices in the past exiting their positions at breakeven prices. The important thing is that the selling pressure is absorbed by buyers creating a horizontal resistance line but a rising higher low, thus forming an ascending triangle.

Trading an ascending triangle

A confirmed breakout is crucial for the validity of an ascending triangle. Breakouts with higher trading volume are generally considered more reliable than those with lower volume. A higher volume signifies increased buying pressure and strengthens the bullish continuation signal.

- **Entry**: place a long trade (buy order) above the resistance line (upper trendline) after a confirmed breakout with strong volume. This suggests buyers are overcoming selling pressure, potentially leading to a continuation of the uptrend.
- **Stop-loss**: Set a stop-loss order to limit potential losses. A common approach is to place it below the nearest significant low. This could be the most recent low point along the rising trendline or slightly below the resistance line.
- **Target**: The target is the height of the triangle (the distance between the resistance line and the first higher low point, labelled A-B in Image 5.21).

In Image 5.22, observe how, after an uptrend, TCS starts forming an ascending triangle. While the resistance line is straight, higher lows are rising and the price is squeezing like a triangle, which shows buyers are getting more and more aggressive. Finally, the price breaks out with a high volume and achieves the target.

IMAGE 5.22: A weekly chart of TCS with an ascending triangle

Descending Triangle Pattern

Recall our exploration of the ascending triangle – a bullish pattern signalling potential price increases. The descending triangle serves as its counterpart, indicating a bearish continuation within a downtrend. Imagine the ascending triangle's spring, just flipped upside down.

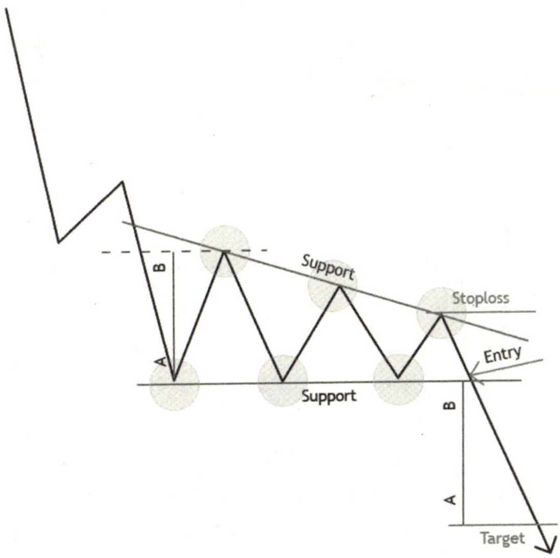

IMAGE 5.23: A descending triangle pattern

Descending triangles take shape during downtrends. Imagine price action confined within a specific area. A downward sloping trendline connects a series of price highs. As the downtrend progresses, these highs get progressively lower. A horizontal line connects a series of price lows. Unlike the ascending triangle, these lows don't necessarily create higher bottoms, but may fluctuate around a similar level.

This price compression forms a triangular shape, visually representing the increasing selling pressure pushing the price downwards. Each time the price tests the support level (horizontal line), it's like a compressed spring attempting to bounce back up. However, unlike the ascending triangle where buyers win those battles, here, sellers overpower buyers, forcing the price lower.

Trading a descending triangle

The key to the descending triangle lies in a confirmed breakout. This happens when the price decisively falls below the horizontal support line (lower trendline) with a surge in trading volume. Strong selling pressure overwhelming buyers is the underlying force behind this downside breakout, potentially leading to a continuation of the downtrend.

- **Entry**: After a confirmed downside breakout with strong volume, a short trade (sell order) can be initiated below the support line. This aims to capitalize on the potential continuation of the downtrend.
- **Stop-loss**: A common approach is to place it above the nearest significant high. This could be the most recent high point along the downtrending line, or slightly above the support line.
- **Target**: The target is the height of the triangle (the distance between the support line and the first lower high point, labelled A-B in Image 5.23).

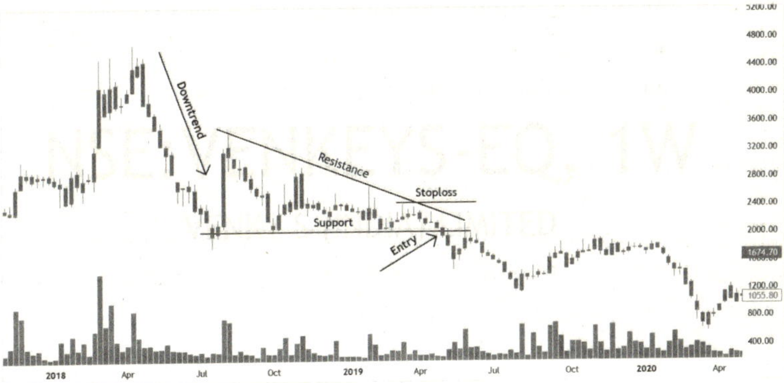

IMAGE 5.24: A weekly chart of VENKEYS with a descending triangle

The weekly chart of VENKEYS in Image 5.24 is a perfect example of a descending triangle pattern.

Cup and Handle Pattern

A cup and handle is a bullish trend continuation pattern. It gets its name due to its resemblance to a cup and a handle. After an uptrend, the price creates a resistance level (neckline) due to selling pressure. The price then enters a consolidation phase (cup) where a 'U'-shaped pattern forms. This consolidation reflects a tug-of-war between bulls (buyers) and bears (sellers).

Seller psychology during consolidation

During this phase, several factors can motivate sellers to participate:

- **Profit-taking**: Early buyers who entered during the uptrend might take profits, especially as the price nears the resistance level.
- **Stop-loss orders**: Some traders might have placed stop-loss orders below certain price points. If the price dips during consolidation, these stop-loss orders might trigger, forcing some buyers to exit their positions (weak hands being shaken out).

- **Bearish outlook**: Some traders might fundamentally believe the stock's outlook is bearish, leading them to sell regardless of the pattern formation.

Testing the neckline and handle formation

The price eventually tests the resistance (neckline) again. This could be due to renewed buying pressure, or a final attempt by sellers to push the price down. If buyers overpower the sellers, the price may rise, forming the handle (a brief downward movement) before a potential breakout.

Breakout

The pattern is complete once the price decisively breaks above the neckline with strong volume. This breakout suggests a shift in market sentiment, with bulls (buyers) gaining control. The surge in volume signifies increased buying pressure, potentially leading to a continuation of the uptrend.

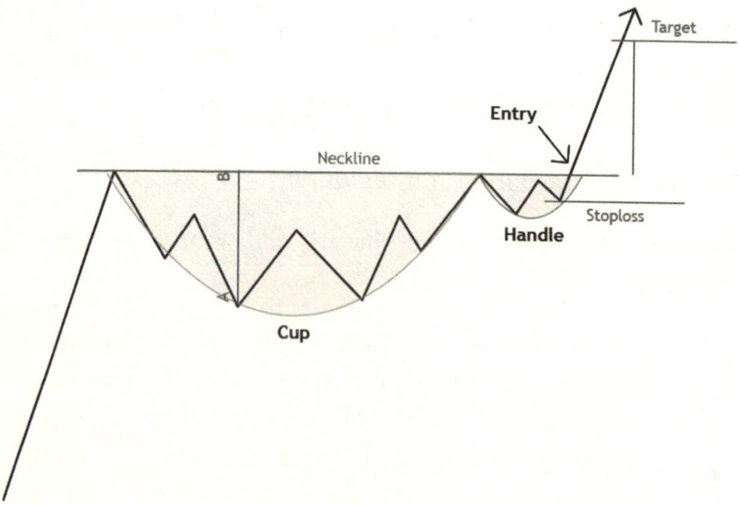

IMAGE 5.25: A cup and handle pattern

Trading a cup and handle

- **Breakout**: The most crucial aspect is a confirmed breakout. This occurs when the price decisively moves above the neckline (Image 5.25) with a significant increase in trading volume. This surge in volume signifies strong buying pressure potentially overpowering sellers, hinting at a continuation of the uptrend.
- **Entry**: Once a confirmed breakout with strong volume is established, a long trade (buy order) can be initiated above the neckline.
- **Stop-loss**: The stop-loss is placed below the handle's low point or slightly below the cup's bottom. This limits potential losses if the price movement doesn't follow expectations.
- **Target**: The profit target is based on the height of the cup. Measure the vertical distance between the cup's bottom and the rim (line A-B in Image 5.25). This distance, projected upward from the neckline, is the target.

Be aware that false breakouts can occur, where the price pierces the neckline but fails to sustain the move higher. Look for confirmation with strong volume to avoid entering these trades.

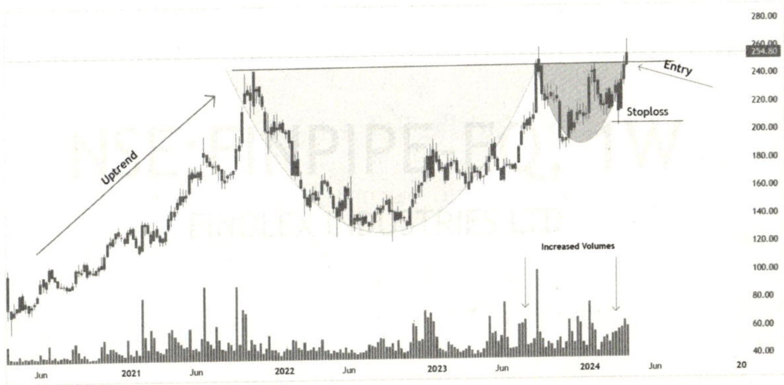

IMAGE 5.26: A weekly chart of FINPIPE with a cup and handle pattern

Another example of cup and handle can be observed in the weekly chart of TATACONSUM in Image 5.27. Observe how the price made a high after an uptrend, started trading sideways forming a rounded bottom, tested the resistance, made a handle, and broke out.

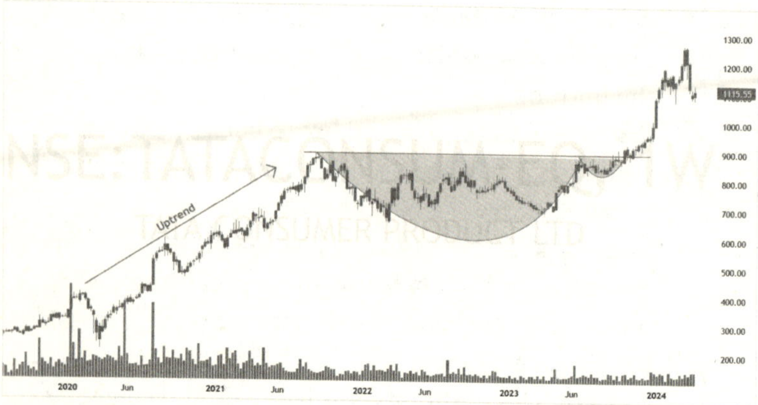

IMAGE 5.27: A weekly chart of TATACONSUM with a cup and handle pattern

Before we close the discussion on the cup and handle pattern, one must understand that this pattern can have variations, like deeper handles or double handles. As long as the basic structure of the cup and handle is maintained (U-shaped cup, neckline, handle, breakout), one must not confuse these variations with the core market psychology the pattern signifies (consolidation, buying and selling pressure, potential breakout).

Inverted Cup and Handle Pattern

An inverted cup and handle pattern is the bearish counterpart to the bullish cup and handle we discussed earlier. This pattern signifies a potential reversal from an uptrend to a downtrend. It looks like an inverted 'U', which signifies consolidation.

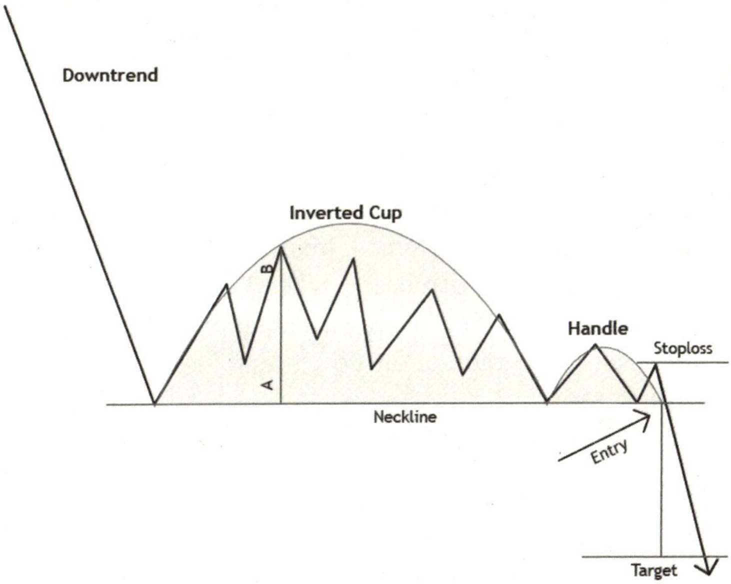

IMAGE 5.28: An inverted cup and handle pattern

Psychology during consolidation

Similar to the cup and handle, this pattern reflects a battle between bulls and bears during consolidation:

- **Profit-taking**: Bulls who entered during the previous uptrend might try to close their positions at breakeven, hoping to get out without a loss.
- **Bearish sentiment**: Some traders might fundamentally believe the overall market outlook is bearish, leading them to short the stock or sell existing positions regardless of the pattern formation.

Testing the neckline and handle formation

The price eventually tests the support level (neckline) again. This could be due to renewed selling pressure or a final attempt by bulls to push the price higher.

If sellers overpower the bulls, the price may fall, forming the handle (a brief upward movement) before a potential breakdown.

Breakdown

The pattern is complete once the price decisively breaks below the neckline with strong volume. This breakdown suggests a shift in market sentiment, with bears (sellers) gaining control. The surge in volume signifies increased selling pressure, potentially leading to a continuation of the downtrend.

Trading an inverted cup and handle

- **Breakdown confirmation**: The most crucial aspect is a confirmed breakdown. This occurs when the price decisively moves below the neckline (support line) with a significant increase in trading volume. This surge in volume signifies strong selling pressure potentially overpowering bulls, hinting at a continuation of the downtrend.
- **Entry**: Once a confirmed breakdown with strong volume is established, a short trade (sell order) can be initiated below the neckline.
- **Stop-loss**: The stop-loss is placed above the handle's high point or slightly above the cup's top. This limits potential losses if the price movement doesn't follow expectations.
- **Target**: The profit target is based on the height of the cup. Measure the vertical distance between the cup's bottom and the rim (line A-B in Image 5.28). This distance projected downward from neckline is the target.

Like the cup and handle, one has to be aware about the false breakdowns that could happen with this pattern.

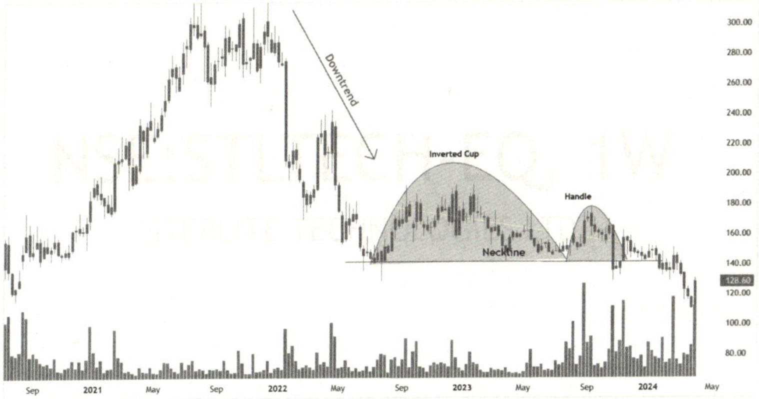

IMAGE 5.29: A weekly chart of STLTECH with an inverted cup and handle pattern

Observe Image 5.29, which shows a weekly chart of STLTECH with an inverted cup and handle pattern.

Neutral Chart Patterns

Neutral chart patterns don't inherently signal a trend reversal or continuation. Instead, they indicate periods of price consolidation, where buyers and sellers are somewhat balanced, making the future price direction unclear. These patterns can serve as precursors to either breakouts (the price moving decisively above resistance in an uptrend or below support in a downtrend) or breakdowns (the price failing to hold support).

The context of the chart plays an important role in how a neutral pattern unfolds. What seems like a bullish continuation might still be a sideways movement with more data on the chart.

The following are some of the important neutral chart patterns:

1. Rising channel
2. Falling channel
3. Rising wedge
4. Falling wedge
5. Symmetrical triangle

Rising Channel

A rising channel is also called an ascending channel. A rising channel is a technical chart pattern commonly found within an uptrend. It's formed by two upward sloping trendlines, one connecting the higher lows (support line) and the other connecting the higher highs (resistance line). The price tends to bounce between these lines as the uptrend progresses. If the price breaks the resistance line, it indicates a trend continuation. If price breaks the support line, it can be a trend reversal. However, be cautious of false breakouts above resistance or below support before entering positions.

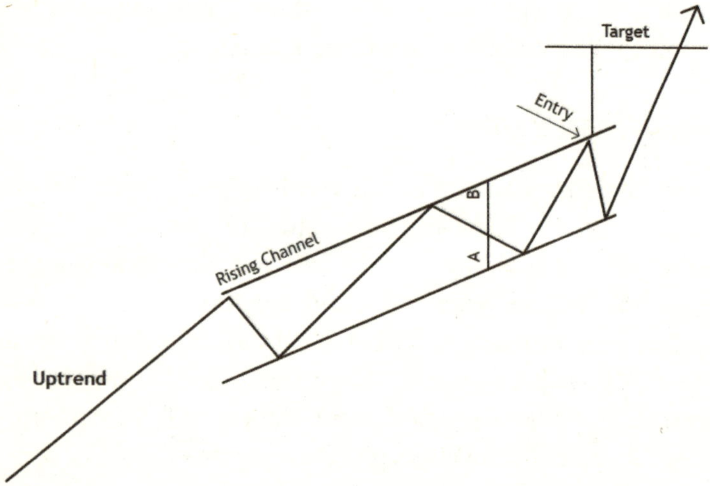

IMAGE 5.30: A rising channel trend continuation pattern

In Image 5.30, we can see how a rising channel trend continuation forms. Also observe the daily chart of ZOMATO in Image 5.31 showing a rising channel trend continuation pattern.

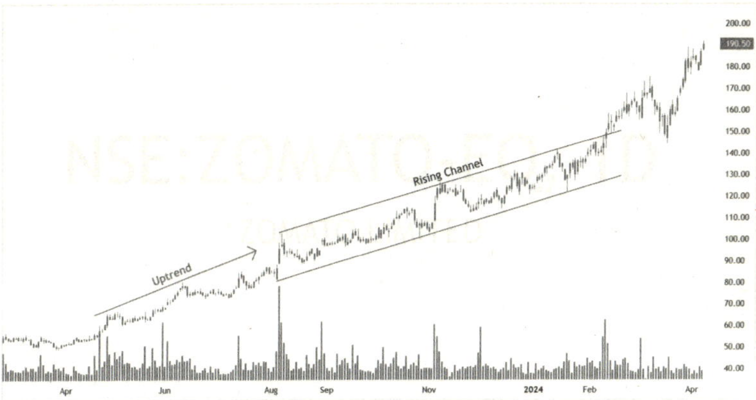

IMAGE 5.31: A daily chart of ZOMATO forming a parallel channel

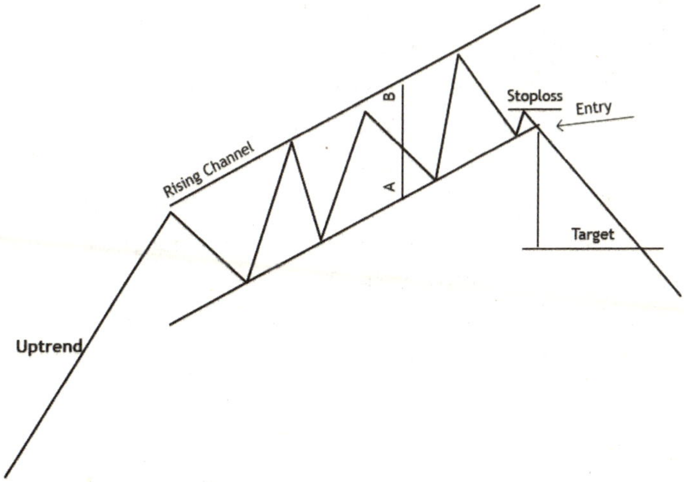

IMAGE 5.32: A rising channel trend reversal pattern

Image 5.32 is an illustration of a rising channel trend reversal. Observe how, in the SUNTV daily chart shown in Image 5.33, the price forms a parallel channel and finally breaks the lower rising trendline to start a downtrend.

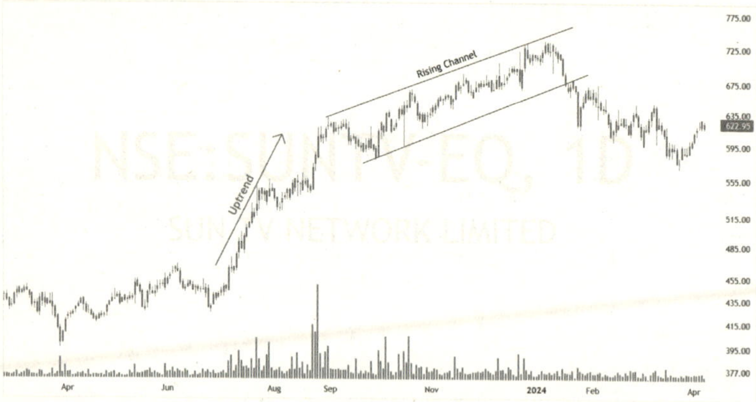

IMAGE 5.33: A daily chart of SUNTV forming a rising channel trend reversal

I have observed, over time, that rising channel trend continuation breakouts are fast and swift. They can hit the profit target rapidly. But at the same time, we cannot rule out false breakouts – lengthy consolidation period of no activity which can make it difficult to trade. You also cannot rule out the possibility that the parallel channel will not increase its width. Look at the MCDOWELL-N daily chart in Image 5.34 – I have been waiting for a bullish breakout in the stock for the last 3 months, and I'm still waiting.

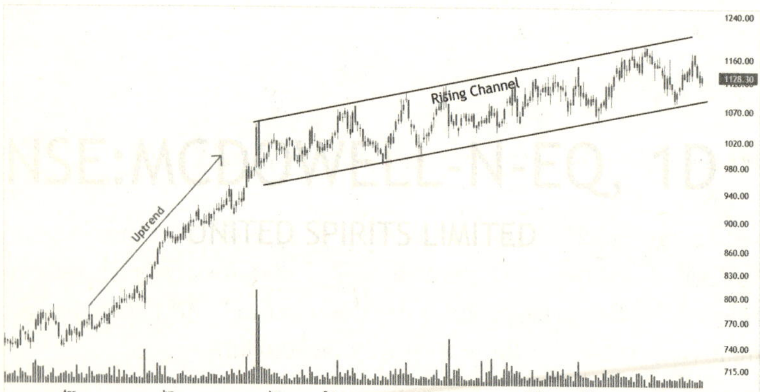

IMAGE 5.34: A daily chart of MCDOWELL-N forming a rising channel

Trading a rising channel

Regarding breakouts:

- **Long positions (buy)**: A breakout above the resistance line, ideally with strong volume, is a bullish signal suggesting trend continuation. Traders might initiate long positions after a confirmed breakout.
- **Short positions (sell):** Conversely, a breakdown below the support line, particularly with strong volume, suggests a potential trend reversal. Traders might exit existing long positions or initiate short positions after a confirmed breakdown.
- **False breakouts**: Caution is advised regarding false breakouts, where the price pierces a trendline but fails to sustain the move. Look for confirmation with strong volume to avoid entering trades based on false signals.
- **Stop-loss**: A stop-loss can be placed for long positions at the nearest higher low to the resistance line. A stop-loss for short positions can be placed at the nearest lower high to the support line. Some experts advise to put the stop-loss at the opposite trendline, which is the wrong approach, in my opinion, as it distorts the risk/reward balance of the trade.
- **Target**: The profit target is based on the height of the channel (the vertical distance between the upper and lower trendlines).

Additional considerations: volumes during a rising channel are low, comparatively, and usually increase once there is a genuine breakout. Lower volumes are a further sign of an ongoing consolidation. Hence a breakout with volume is a sign of a reliable breakout.

The steeper the slope of the channel, the more aggressive the uptrend, which can also indicate higher potential volatility. Manage your position size accordingly.

Falling Channel

A falling channel is also called a descending channel, and is the opposite of a rising channel. A falling channel is a technical chart pattern commonly found within a downtrend. It's formed by two downward-sloping trendlines, one connecting the lower highs (resistance) and the other connecting the lower lows (support). The price tends to bounce between these lines as the downtrend progresses. If the price breaks the support line, it indicates a trend continuation. If price breaks the resistance line, it can be a trend reversal.

The psychology of the market participants remain the same for a falling channel as for a rising channel. There exists a balance between buyers and sellers, which can be observed from lower trading volumes. A breakout from the channel with volume confirms either the trend continuation or the trend reversal aspect of the pattern.

Rising and falling channel patterns are neutral patterns, but it is always preferred to take a trade in the direction of the trend.

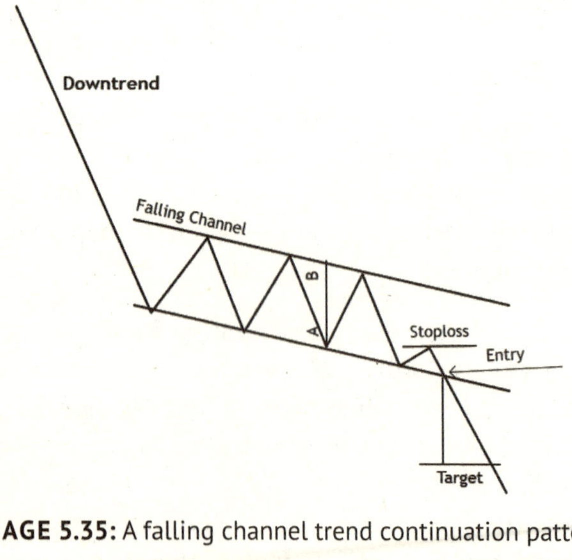

IMAGE 5.35: A falling channel trend continuation pattern

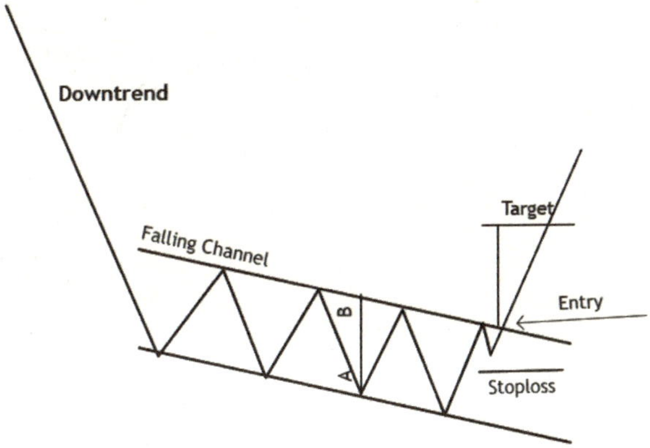

IMAGE 5.36: A falling channel trend reversal pattern

Rising Wedge

A rising wedge is bearish reversal pattern. If the pattern forms during an uptrend, it signifies a bearish reversal. If the pattern forms during a downtrend, it forms a bearish trend continuation.

A rising wedge is formed by two upward sloping trendlines that converge as the price moves higher. Imagine a funnel pointing upwards, with the price getting squeezed between narrow trendlines. The upper trendline acts as the resistance. The lower trendline acts as the support. If the price breaks to the upper side, it is considered a trend continuation; otherwise, it is a trend reversal.

Like other chart patterns, higher volumes during a breakdown suggest a more reliable trade signal.

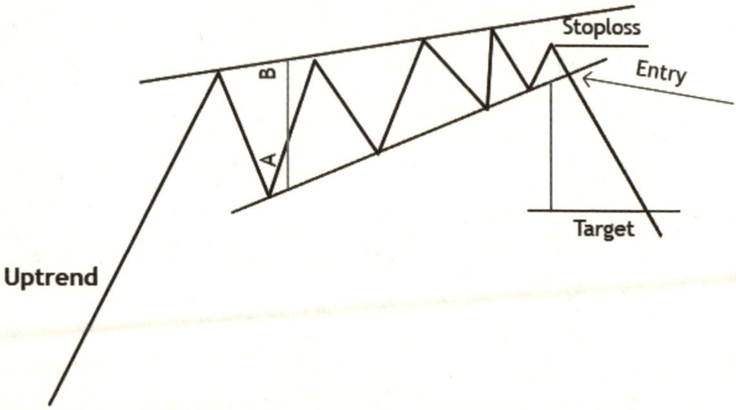

IMAGE 5.37: A rising wedge in an uptrend

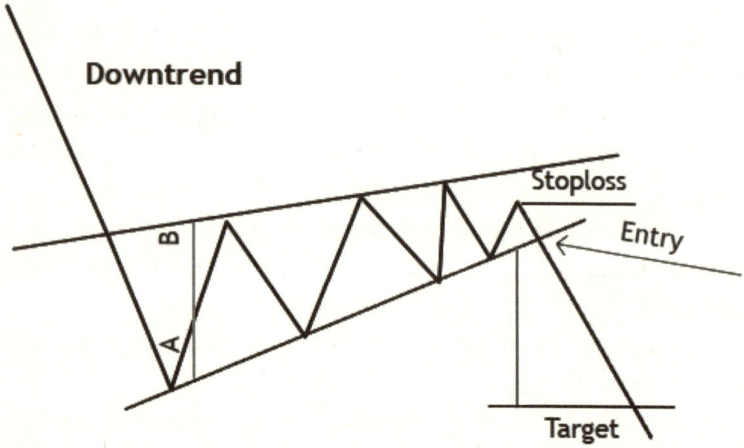

IMAGE 5.38: A rising wedge in a downtrend

Understanding the psychology of market participants is important in rising wedge patterns. When the price breaks the previous higher high, it should result in prices going up, but instead sellers push the price down. This cycle of creating higher highs and higher lows continues with the price barely moving up. It only results in price contraction and the formation of a rising wedge. Failure to take the price higher after every breakout of a higher high signifies weakness. A confirmed breakout above the resistance line (with strong volume) suggests a possible continuation of the uptrend or a potential trend reversal, while a confirmed breakdown of the support (with strong volume) suggests sellers taking control.

Trading a rising wedge

The rising wedge, while a neutral pattern, can offer selling opportunities based on confirmed breakdowns.

- **Entry**: Look for a confirmed breakdown below the lower trendline of the rising wedge, ideally accompanied by strong volume. This suggests a potential resumption of a downtrend (if already a downtrend) or a trend reversal (if in an uptrend). Strong volume during the breakdown reinforces the bearish signal.
- **Stop-loss**: Place a stop-loss order slightly above the nearest lower high to the support line. This limits potential losses if the breakdown turns out to be a false breakout.
- **Profit target**: The distance between the first higher low and higher high of the rising wedge is the profit target of the trade.

A rising wedge is generally looked up in an uptrend for trend reversal.

Falling Wedge

A falling wedge is a bullish reversal pattern. In a downtrend, it signifies a trend reversal. In an uptrend, it signifies a trend continuation.

It is formed by two downward-sloping trendlines that converge as the price moves lower within a downtrend. It suggests a potential weakening of the downtrend and a possible trend reversal towards an uptrend. As sellers become less aggressive and buyers start accumulating, the price decline slows down, forming the wedge pattern.

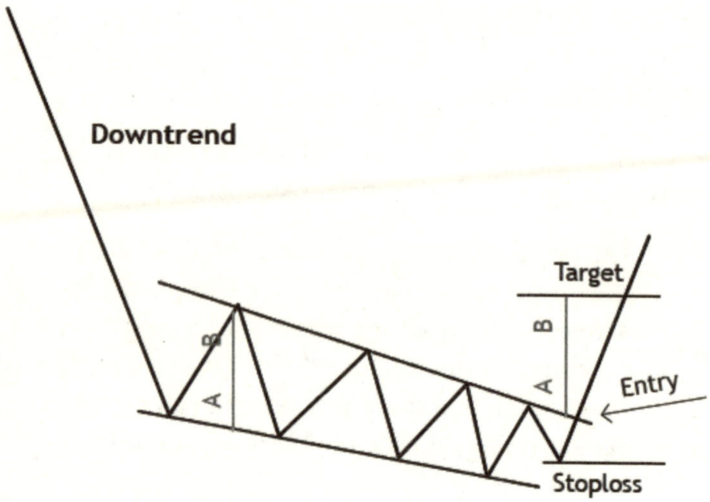

IMAGE 5.39: A falling wedge in a downtrend

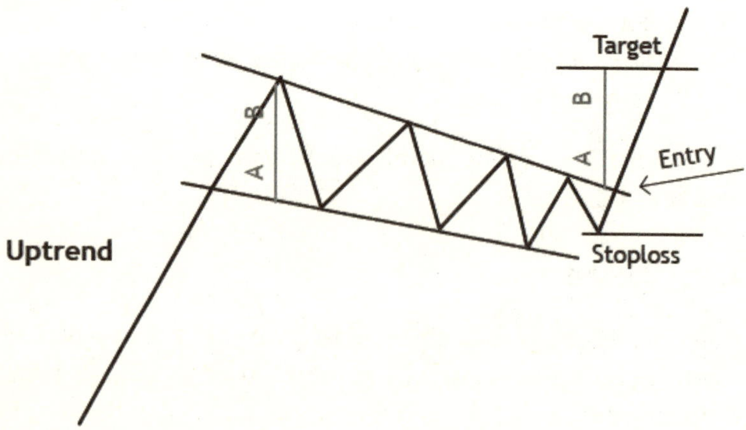

IMAGE 5.40: A falling wedge in an uptrend

Market psychology in a falling wedge is converse to that of a rising wedge. In a falling wedge, sellers are trying to take control of the market by pushing prices below the lower high. Sellers even succeed in creating a LL-LH structure, but they are unable to push the price down, dramatically showing the inherent strength of the buyers. The pattern is confirmed once the price breaks the resistance line to the upside.

Trading a falling wedge

The falling wedge, while a neutral pattern, can offer buying opportunities based on confirmed breakouts.

- **Entry**: Look for a confirmed breakout above the upper trendline of the falling wedge, ideally accompanied by strong volume. This suggests a potential trend reversal (if a downtrend) or a trend continuational (if in an uptrend). Strong volume during the breakout reinforces the bearish signal.
- **Stop-loss**: Place a stop-loss order slightly below the nearest higher low to the resistance line. This limits potential losses if the breakout turns out to be a false breakout.
- **Profit target**: The distance between the first lower high and lower low of the falling wedge is the profit target of the trade.

A falling wedge is generally looked up in a downtrend for trend reversal.

Symmetrical Triangle Pattern

The symmetrical triangle is a neutral chart pattern that can appear within an established uptrend, downtrend, or even a choppy, trendless market. It doesn't inherently signal a trend reversal or continuation, but it suggests a period of consolidation where buyers and sellers are somewhat balanced.

The symmetrical triangle is formed by two converging trendlines, one sloping upward and the other sloping downward. As the price fluctuates, the highs get progressively lower (upper trendline) and the lows get progressively higher (lower trendline), creating a triangular shape.

The trendlines converge as the price action gets squeezed within the triangle, indicating a potential breakout in either direction (up or down).

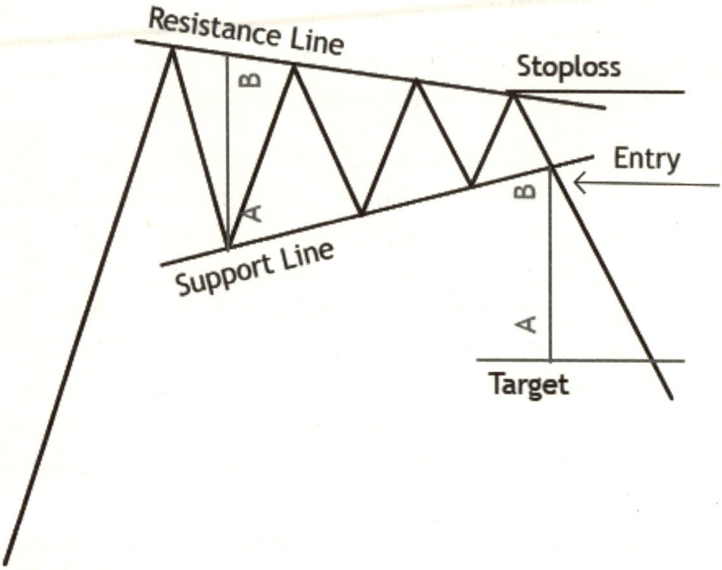

IMAGE 5.41: A symmetrical triangle pattern

A confirmed breakout above the upper trendline or below the lower trendline, ideally with strong volume, can signal a potential trend direction. Breakout above the resistance (established uptrend) suggests a continuation of the uptrend. Breakout below the support (established downtrend) suggests a continuation of the downtrend. Breakout in either direction (no established trend) is less clear and requires further confirmation. Be aware of false breakouts, where the price pierces a trendline but fails to sustain the move. Confirmation with strong volume is crucial for reliable signals.

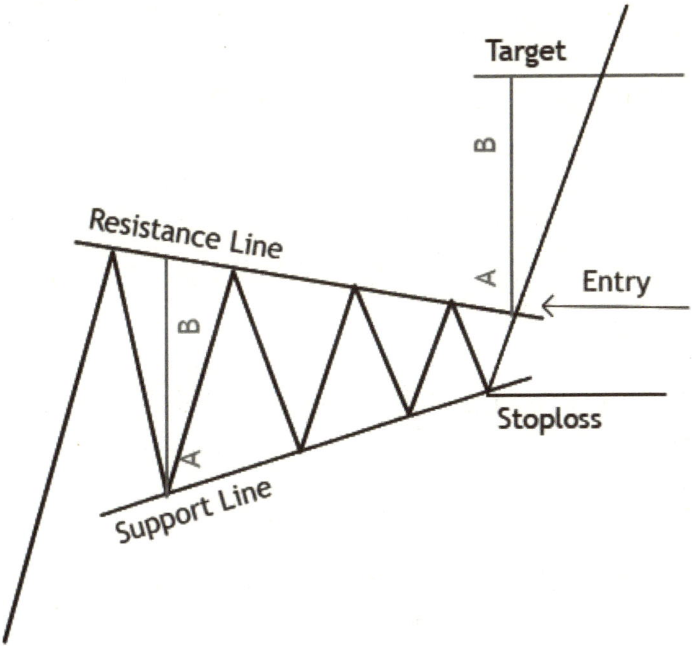

IMAGE 5.42: A symmetrical triangle pattern

Trading a symmetrical triangle

- **Entry**: Look for a confirmed breakout above the upper trendline or lower trendline ideally with high volumes.
- **Stop-loss**: Place a stop-loss slightly above the resistance line if the price breaks down, or slightly below the support if the price breaks up.
- **Profit target**: The distance between first lower high and lower low of the symmetrical triangle is the profit target of the trade.

During a symmetrical triangle, there's a balancing act between buyers and sellers. As the price approaches the upper trendline, buyers might become more active, pushing the price higher. Conversely, as the price nears the lower trendline, sellers might step in, pushing the price down. The converging trendlines reflect this ongoing struggle.

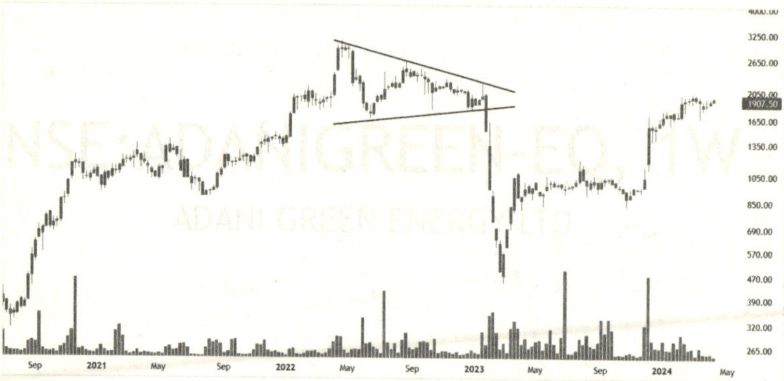

IMAGE 5.43: A weekly chart of ADANIGREEN forming a symmetrical triangle

Rohit's Trend Explosion Pattern (RTEP)

Among all the chart patterns I have discussed with you till now, the RTEP is my favorite pattern. It is a very powerful, advanced bullish pattern that occurs in an uptrend.

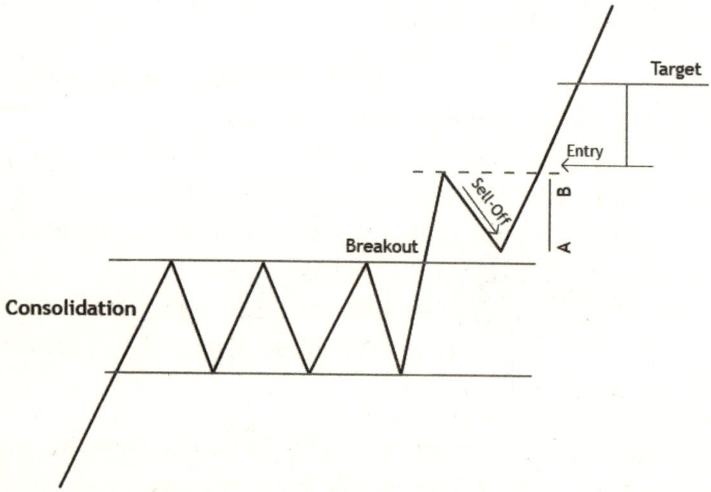

IMAGE 5.44: An RTEP pattern

After a breakout from consolidation, the price starts an uptrend. There are traders who might try to sell in an uptrend because of wrong analysis, profit-booking, hitting stop-losses, etc. that causes the occasional HH-HL structure. But this might not always be the case. If spotting an uptrend were this easy, then everyone would ride the trend. That is why, during an uptrend, there are multiple attempts by institutional investors to shake out weak buyers and collect more stock. After a breakout from consolidation (Image 5.44), during an uptrend, there is often a sharp sell-off in the stock price. This pullback might induce weak buyers to exit their positions. In some markets, this could also entice short sellers to enter expecting a downtrend.

This is where institutional buyers might step in and start accumulating the stock, pushing the price higher. Once the price decisively breaks above the previous high, it can lead to a significant and rapid upward move for several reasons:

1. Aggressive buying negates selling pressure, confirming the uptrend's continuation.
2. Fear of missing out (FOMO) by other investors can lead to further buying pressure.
3. In markets where short selling is prevalent, aggressive buying after a pullback can trigger a short squeeze. Short sellers who entered during the pullback are forced to buy back the stock to cover their positions as the price rises, further accelerating the upward move.

Volumes play an important role in trading decision. Buying after a sharp sell-off is with high volumes gives more validation to the RTEP pattern.

Short selling regulations differ across markets. In the Indian stock market, aggressive short selling practices like naked shorting (selling borrowed stock without owning it) are restricted. However, intraday short selling is allowed. This means traders can sell stocks they believe will decline in price during the same trading day, but they must repurchase them by the day's end. If an intraday short position is carried forward inadvertently, it can attract penalties from the exchange. Therefore, in the RTEP pattern context, if the price decisively breaks above the resistance after a pullback, it can force intraday short sellers to cover their positions quickly, adding to the buying pressure and upward move.

In contrast, many global markets allow positional short selling, where investors can borrow and sell stocks they believe will go down, holding the short position for an extended period. If the price falls, they can later buy back the stock at a lower price to return to the lender and pocket the profit. However, short selling can be risky. If the price starts to rise unexpectedly, short sellers may be forced to buy back the stock at a higher price to close their positions, leading to potential losses. This situation, where short sellers are forced to buy due to a rising price, is known as a short squeeze, and can further accelerate the upward price movement.

Trading the RTEP

- **Entry**: Look for a decisive breakout above the previous swing high following a period of consolidation in the uptrend. The pullback after the breakout might take the form of a sharp sell-off or a retracement to a key support level. Regardless of the specific price action, a clear break above the previous high (resistance line) is the ideal entry point for the RTEP pattern.
- **Stop-loss**: Place the stop-loss below the nearest higher low to the resistance line (previous high) used for entry. This ensures you exit the trade if the buying pressure weakens, and the price falls back below the breakout level.

- **Target**: The target is the distance between the previous high (resistance line) and the low point reached during the pullback (sell-off dip). This provides a healthy risk/reward ratio.

Case Study 1

Observe the chart in Image 5.45 of NATIONALUM on a 3-hour timeframe. The price is in an uptrend and faces a sharp sell-off near 116 levels, forming a shooting star pattern. Buyers start pushing the price higher at 102 and the resistance line is broken with heavy volumes, followed by rapid momentum, which achieves the target in next 3-4 days. A stop-loss for such a trade can be slightly below the consolidation near the resistance line.

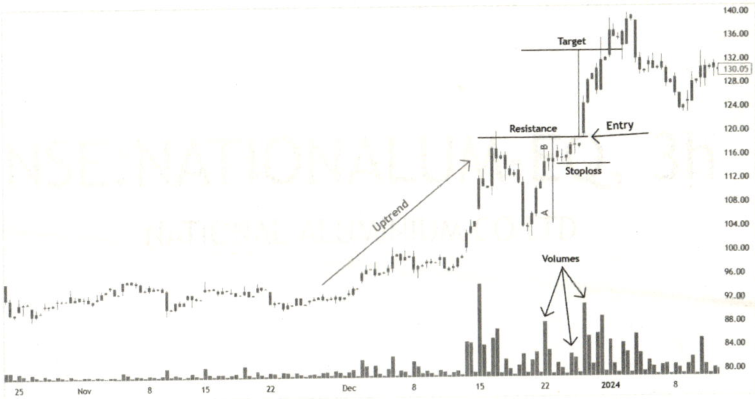

IMAGE 5.45: A chart of NATIONALUM on a 3-hour timeframe with an RTEP pattern

Case Study 2

Observe the chart in Image 5.46 of PNB on a 3-hour timeframe. The price forms an uptrend, followed by consolidation, followed by a sharp sell-off. The price immediately recovers and breaks the resistance line with heavy volumes. The target for the trade is achieved in 2-3 days without the trade ever getting into a loss.

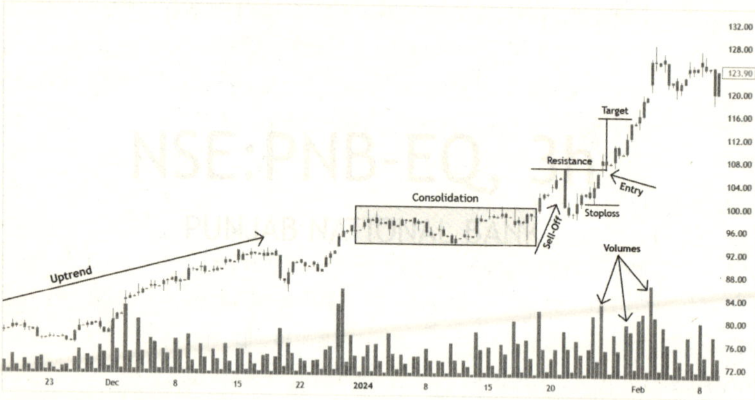

IMAGE 5.46: PNB on a 3-hour chart with an RTEP pattern

In later chapters, we will learn the trailing stop-loss method with which we can target bigger profits on trades with smaller stop-losses while continuously locking in profit.

Case Study 3

In Image 5.47, DLF was forming an uptrend on daily charts. There was a sudden sell-off. Buyers jumped in and broke the resistance line, and the price achieved the target in 3-4 days.

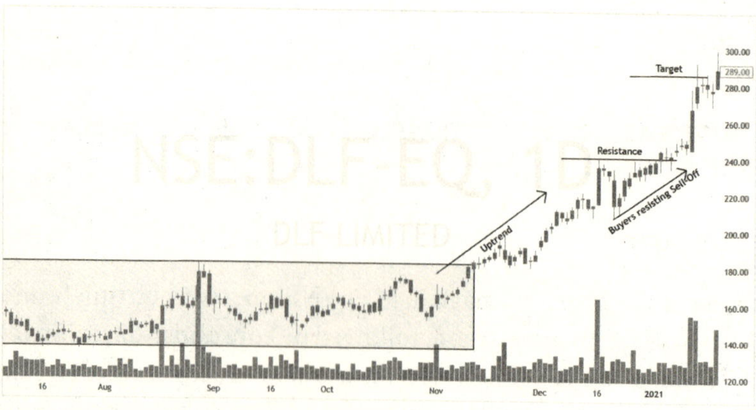

IMAGE 5.47: A daily chart of DLF with an RTEP pattern

Case Study 4

In Image 5.48, on a daily chart, IDFCFIRSTB broke out of consolidation and started to trend, and there was a sudden sell-off. Buyers started buying, and once the price broke the resistance line, the stock price jumped more than 20% in 20 days.

Traders must remember that this pattern gives an illusion of a reversal. Sell-off does not result in a downtrend; i.e., a Lower Highs, Lower Lows structure. If an LH-LL structure has been formed, then trading the pattern should be avoided.

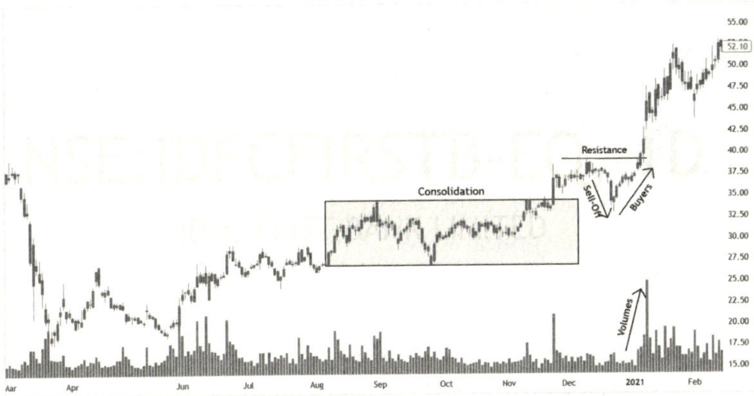

IMAGE 5.48: A daily chart of IDFCFIRSTB with an RTEP pattern

Short Selling Explained (Tesla Case Study)

Tesla, led by the charismatic Elon Musk, had a passionate fanbase and a reputation for innovation.

However, many traditional investors doubted Tesla's long-term viability and profitability. This led to a high short interest, meaning a significant amount of borrowed stock was being held by investors betting on the price to go down.

The squeeze: In 2020 and 2021, Tesla's stock price experienced a meteoric rise, defying analyst expectations. This upward surge forced short sellers to buy back borrowed shares to cover their positions (as the price rose, their potential losses grew).

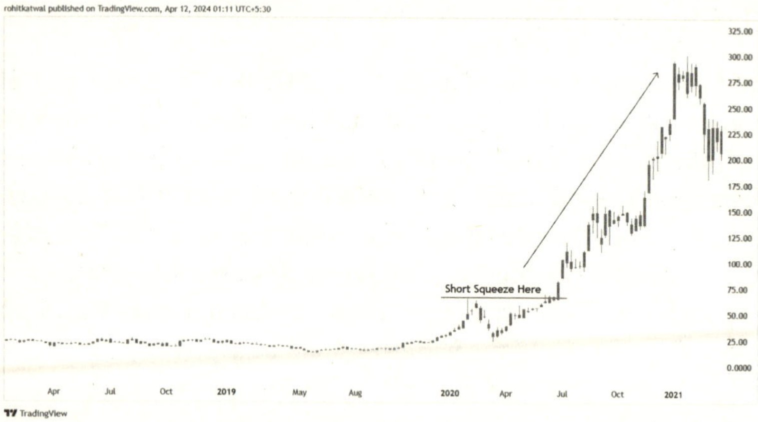

IMAGE 5.49: A weekly chart of TSLA indicating a short squeeze

This buying pressure further fuelled the stock price, creating a snowball effect known as a short squeeze.

Impact: Short sellers who did not exit their positions in time suffered substantial losses. The event garnered significant media attention and highlighted the potential risks and rewards associated with short selling.

If you remember our volume analysis, short covering is actually a short squeeze. While short squeezes can be dramatic, the Rohit's Trend Explosion Pattern focuses on identifying potential buying pressure that can lead to trend continuation, regardless of whether a short squeeze occurs.

CHAPTER 6

Gap Analysis

Unveiling the stories of price imbalance

When the price opens considerably higher or lower than the previous day's close, it is called a gap. On a chart, it looks like a big empty space between two candles.

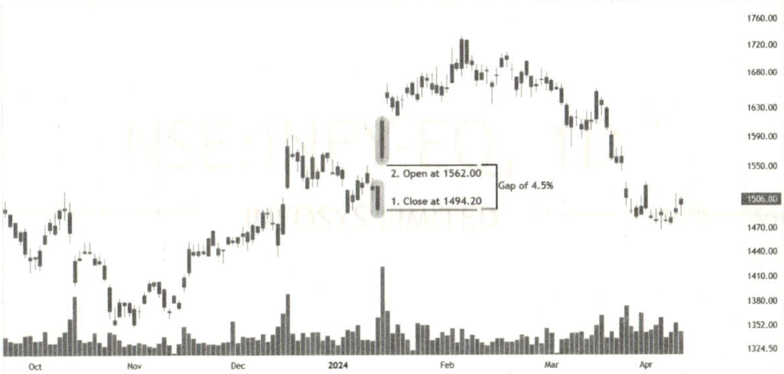

IMAGE 6.1: A daily chart of INFY with a gap

In the chart in Image 6.1, look at the highlighted candles. Observe how the price closed at 1494 with a bearish candle and opened at 1562 the next day. The price gapped up by 4.5%. This scenario could have been good or bad for a trader, depending on the trade executed when the price was closing at 1494.

Bearish trade

- The trader would be looking at a 4.5% loss immediately at the next day's opening.
- The stop-loss below 1562 would not have been executed because the price never traded at that level, which further meant that the trader is starting at a loss beyond his risk appetite.
- If the trader waits for the price to come down to exit at a breakeven or at a lesser loss, by the end of day, his loss would have increased to 8%.

Bullish trade

- The trader would be looking at an immediate profit of 4.5% at the next day's opening.
- By the end of day, the trader would be making a profit of 8%.

From the above observations, we can understand that gaps are good when they favor our trading direction, but can be devastating if they go against our trading direction. The above observation is only relevant when we have an open position and a gap happens, which is out of our control. The important question is how to trade the stock once the gap has happened, and you don't have an open position. How do you analyze the stock price and psychology of market participants to take a trade? That is where gap analysis comes in.

Advanced traders use hedging techniques to reduce the risk of gaps or unknowns, which are beyond the scope of this book.

A gap on a stock chart signifies a price opening significantly higher or lower than the previous day's close. This can be caused by certain events or news related to the company or the broader market. Analyzing where these gaps occur on the chart can help us understand market psychology and potentially inform trading decisions.

There are 4 types of gaps:

1. Common gaps
2. Breakaway gaps
3. Runaway (or continuous) gaps
4. Exhaustion gaps

Common Gaps

Common gaps are uneventful gaps that often occur during accumulation or distribution zones. These zones form during a trend as the price consolidates after a strong move. Large investors and institutions may be actively accumulating or distributing shares in this zone, creating uncertainty about the stock's next direction.

Common gaps reflect this indecision, with the price opening significantly higher or lower than the previous day's close due to a lack of overnight trading activity. These gaps are typically accompanied by low trading volume, further indicating a period of low conviction among market participants.

While some common gaps may eventually 'fill' as the price retraces to trade at the level skipped during the gap, this is not guaranteed. The filling process depends on various factors, and some common gaps may persist for a long time or never fill completely.

Common gaps can be triggered by various events, including news specific to the company, such as dividend announcements or stock splits, unexpected economic data releases that impact the broader market, or changes in investor sentiment due to external factors.

Image 6.2 is an example showing common gaps on the weekly chart of HDFCBANK for the past four years, where the stock has been consolidating between 1400 and 1700. Observe the number of gaps that occurred during this period.

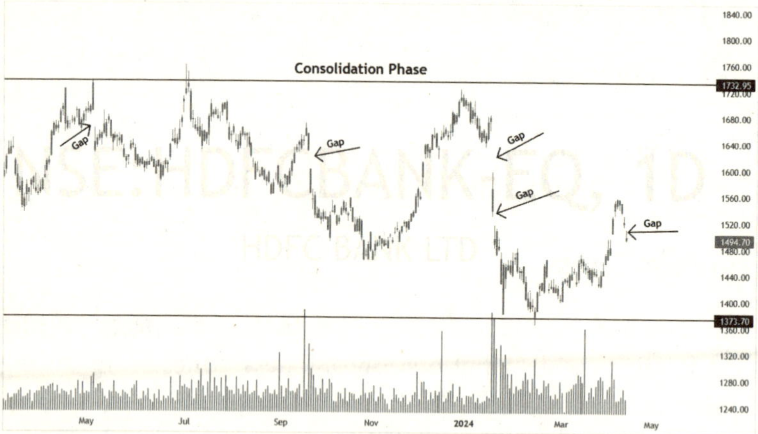

IMAGE 6.2: A daily chart of HDFCBANK with common gaps

As discussed earlier, common gaps tend to get filled eventually due to the sideways nature of the market in consolidation zones. However, there's no guarantee that all gaps will fill. In the HDFCBANK chart, the gaps likely formed due to events like quarterly results or stock weightage updates in various indices.

It's crucial for traders to understand the different types of gaps and develop trading strategies accordingly. Gaps can lead to significant losses if not approached cautiously.

IMAGE 6.3: A daily chart of DRREDDY with a gap-down

As you can observe, these gaps are not normal and are varying within the range of 5-10%. Look at another example of LAURUSLABS in Image 6.4 on a daily timeframe. The price closed at 400 and opened at 360 the next day with a gap-down of 10% while the price is in a sideways parallel channel. And later, the gap got filled after 7 trading days.

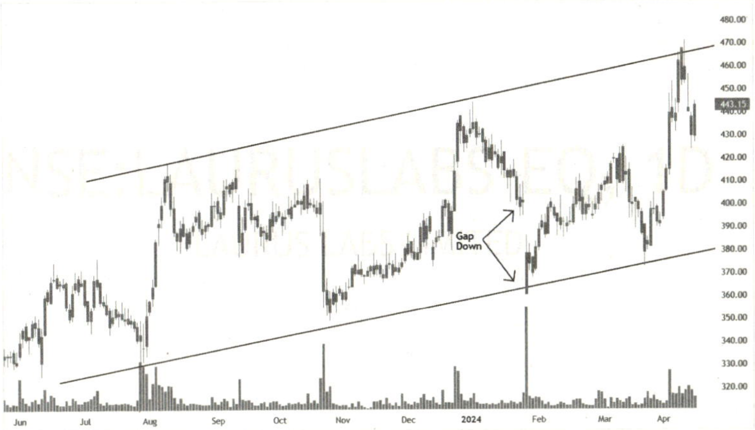

IMAGE 6.4: A daily chart of LAURUSLABS in a parallel channel with a common gap.

Common gaps are also the reason why almost all market veterans always swear by the most famous market quote of all times:

The trend is your friend until the end, when it bends.

Trends are where most of the money is made in the stock market. Sideways markets (consolidation or accumulation or distribution) are where most of the money is lost in the stock market, and one of the major reasons for them is common gaps.

Let us revisit our example of HDFCBANK once again. From 2021 till 2024, the stock is in a consolidation zone. One of the trading strategies often (wrongly) used by traders is to identify a sideways channel, mark the support and resistance, and:

1. Buy when price rejects the support with a stop-loss slightly below the support line and profit target at the resistance; or conversely
2. Sell when price rejects the resistance with a stop-loss slightly above the resistance and profit target at the support.

This strategy has a very good risk/reward ratio – probably 1:3 or more.

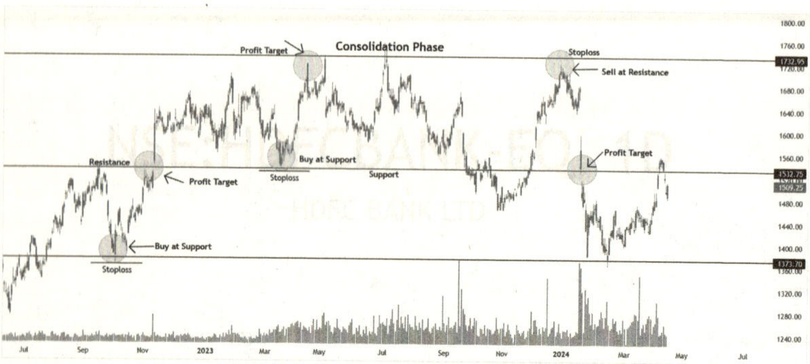

IMAGE 6.5: HDFCBANK in a sideways channel with gaps

On paper this strategy looks good, but the problems are:

1. We can never know what the real rejection of the support or resistance is, candle-wise.
2. The sideways channel could be a rectangle, triangle, erratic, or even a parallel channel that can change at any time.

Therefore, by the time we enter the trade, we are not exactly at the support or resistance level, but in the center of the accumulation or distribution zone, which is most susceptible to common gaps. Observe HDFCBANK again in Image 6.6. The gaps are highlighted.

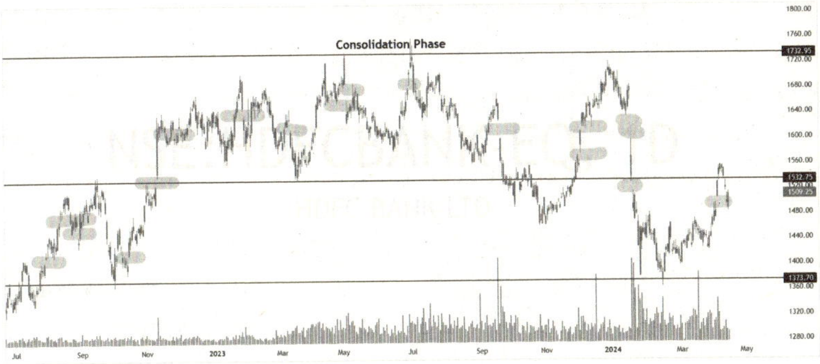

IMAGE 6.6: HDFCBANK on a daily timeframe, highlighting gaps

Most common gaps occur in the middle of a sideways zone. When we take a trade at the support or resistance, our initial risk/reward ratio is 1:3, which is good even if we have a 50% winning probability. But when we take a trade into middle of a sideways zone, our winning probability might again be 50%, but our risk/reward ratio has worsened from 1:3, likely to 1:1. A single random gap against our position might deteriorate the risk/reward ratio further. Secondly, in a sideways zone, the common gaps are random, which might make it difficult to exit from the trade at the intended stop-loss point.

Breakaway Gaps

Breakaway gaps are exciting moments when the price explodes out of a trading range with a surge in volume. This heavy buying or selling suggests one side (buyers or sellers) has taken control, potentially signalling a new trend.

Breakaway gaps signify that market participants have accumulated or distributed the stocks. A breakout signifies that it was accumulation and that the stock price is ready for an uptrend. A breakdown signifies that it was distribution and that stock price is ready for a downtrend.

In consolidation, the price has been revolving within a range for a long time. The fact that market participants are ready to trade the stock outside that range signifies that they have decided the direction, and either buyers or sellers have taken control of the market, so don't expect that this gap will be filled soon and trade in the direction of the trend.

Breakaway gaps are also susceptible to failure. Depending on the strength of the candle, a trader can decide to:

1. Enter once the candle has formed with strength; or
2. Wait for the stock price to trade above or below the breakaway candle to confirm a trend continuation.

Look at the chart of DELTACORP in Image 6.7 and the daily chart of INFY in Image 6.8 of INFY. News of government-imposed taxes induced a sell-off in the stock price. The price took support at the previous turnaround point. The price struggled and bounced at this support line for some time and finally broke down with a breakaway gap.

IMAGE 6.7: A daily chart of DELTACORP with a breakaway gap

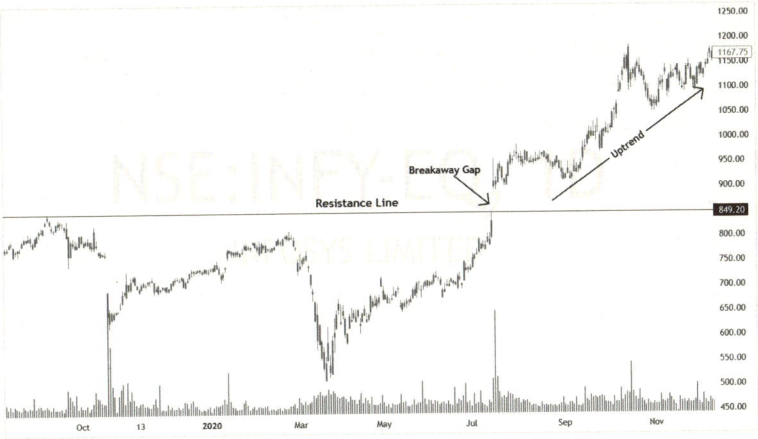

IMAGE 6.8: A daily chart of INFY with a breakaway gap

Runaway Gaps

Runaway gaps represent a significant price movement within a trending market, accompanied by a surge in trading volume. They often occur after a breakout from a trading range, where the price continues its directional move (upward or downward) without the anticipated pullback. This unexpected continuation can leave some traders scrambling to enter positions, leading to a surge in buying or selling activity, reflected in the gap.

Understanding the psychology behind runaway gaps:

Uptrend (runaway gap-up): Following a breakout, some traders might initially hesitate to enter, anticipating a pullback for a better entry point. However, if the price continues to rise steadily with lower volume, a sense of urgency can develop. Fear of missing out (FOMO) can then trigger a surge in buying activity from those who missed the initial move, pushing the price higher and creating a runaway gap-up.

Downtrend (runaway gap-down): In a downtrend, some investors might hold onto a stock, waiting for a price rebound or hoping for a trend reversal. However, if the price continues to decline steadily, fear can take hold. Investors who were waiting to sell may panic and exit their positions in a hurry, leading to a surge in selling volume and a runaway gap-down.

Observe the charts of OFSS and CUMMINSIND in Images 6.9 and 6.10 respectively, both showing runaway gaps.

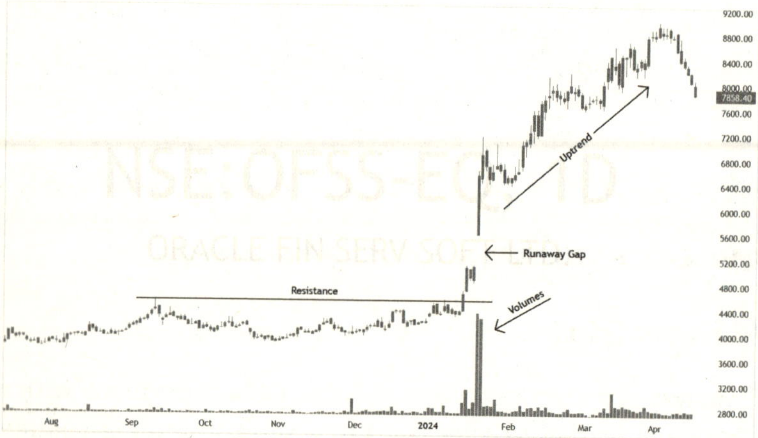

IMAGE 6.9: A chart of OFSS on a daily timeframe with a runaway gap

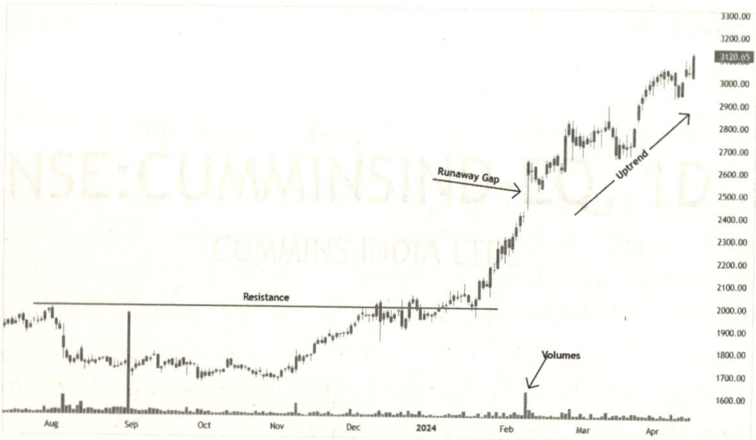

IMAGE 6.10: A chart of CUMMINSIND on daily timeframe with a runaway gap

Exhaustion Gaps

Exhaustion gaps signal a possible weakening of the current trend. They appear as significant price movements with a gap and typically occur near the end of an extended uptrend or downtrend.

Uptrend: In an uptrend, an exhaustion gap appears as a sudden and sharp downward price movement with a gap, often accompanied by increased trading volume. This suggests that the buying pressure that was driving the uptrend may be starting to wane. Exhaustion gaps can occur when buyers become exhausted from continually pushing the price higher and there aren't enough new buyers to sustain the momentum.

Downtrend: In a downtrend, an exhaustion gap appears as a sudden and sharp upward price movement with a gap, again accompanied by increased volume. This suggests that the selling pressure that was driving the downtrend may be losing steam. Exhaustion gaps can form when sellers become exhausted from continually pushing the price lower and there aren't enough new sellers to maintain the downtrend.

Like breakaway gaps, in exhaustion gaps, it is better to take bearish or a bullish trade in the next candle when the price starts going below or above the previous day close's respectively.

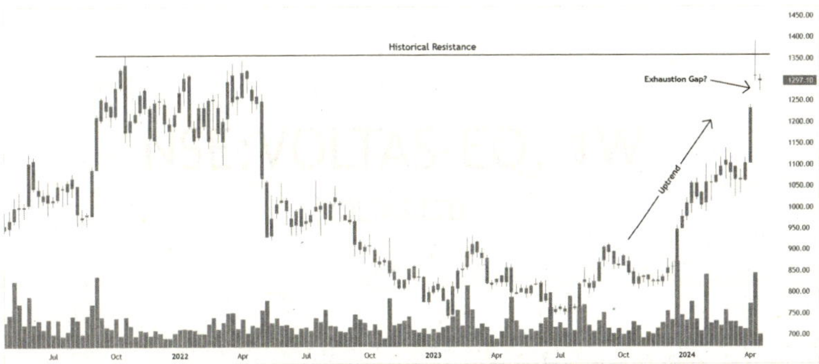

IMAGE 6.11: A chart of VOLTAS with a probable exhaustion gap

An exhaustion gap can reflect a shift in market psychology, where one side (buyers or sellers) is losing control, and the other side starts to gain an upper hand. In Image 6.11, observe how VOLTAS formed a bearish candle with high volume near the historical resistance. Trading of the price below the close of the candle might signify an immediate trend exhaustion.

But look at the chart of IRFC in Image 6.12. After an uptrend, IRFC formed an exhaustion candle with low volumes. The follow-up candle broke the exhaustion candle low with high volumes. This suggested a trend reversal. Remember our analysis in Table 3.3, where we said a rising market and decreasing volume is a sign of a weak market. Followed by a sell signal with heavy volumes, it signals that a probable top is in place.

Therefore, it's always advisable to understand the context of the price with respect to volume before making a trading decision.

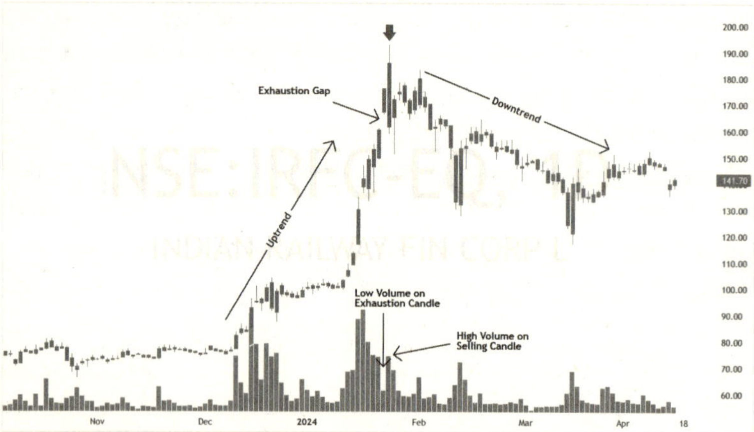

IMAGE 6.12: A chart of IRFC with an exhaustion gap

Now that we have understood candlesticks, chart patterns and different type of gaps, let's move on to the next important part of technical analysis; i.e., technical indicators.

CHAPTER 7

Technical Indicators

Technical analysis doesn't work all the time.
But then again, neither does fundamental analysis.

Technical indicators are tools designed to simplify price action trading. Technical analysis can be complex. One has to analyze price structure, candlestick and chart patterns, volume analysis, etc., which can be exhaustive for a new trader. It takes years of practice for a trader to master the art of price action trading; after all, technical analysis is the study of human behavior around certain price levels.

Think back to how you learned to ride a bike. Initially, your father held you steady. As you gained confidence, you gradually needed less support, eventually riding independently. It's the same case with technical indicators; they can help you understand the market structure initially, and with practice, you'll rely on them less and become a more adept trader, interpreting price action with greater skill.

Technical indicators are also called lagging indicators because the mathematical values used to create indicators are derived from the price itself. Therefore, price action analysis is the leading indicator, whereas technical indicators are first-order derivatives of the price and so are called lagging indicators.

In Table 7.1:

- I have taken the closing price of VEDL on a daily basis from 2 March 2024 to 18 April 2024.
- From 15 March 2024, I have taken the average of closing prices for the last 10 days using the AVERAGE formula in Excel and have applied this formula to every subsequent day that VEDL has traded.
- I have taken the difference between the price and the average price in the next column. A red cell (negative value) indicates that price of VEDL is below the 10-day moving average (MA), and a green cell (positive value) indicates the price is above the 10-day moving average. The intensity of the color is based on how negative or positive the difference is.

We can observe from Table 7.1 that before 20 March, the prices of VEDL were trading below its 10-day moving average. Which further means that in the last 10 days, sellers were in control of the market, as they were willing to sell even below the average trading price in 10 days.

Which further means that something is wrong with the stock price. If eggs are selling for Rs. 60/dozen, a shopkeeper isn't going to suddenly start selling eggs at Rs. 50/dozen unless there's something wrong with the eggs or if there is an absence of demand. The same principle applies to stocks, too.

On 21 March 2024, the price of VEDL suddenly jumped and started trading above its 10-day moving average, which means buyers were now willing to buy the stock above its average price. Post this, the price of VEDL continuously kept closing above its 10-day moving average by a huge difference, which signified that traders were willing to buy the stock at an above-average price. Within a matter of one and a half months, the stock rose from 280 to 388; i.e., a gain of 38%.

Symbol	Date	Close Price	10 Days MA	Price Diff from MA
VEDL	02-Mar-24	273.05		
VEDL	04-Mar-24	276.35		
VEDL	05-Mar-24	285.7		
VEDL	06-Mar-24	282.45		
VEDL	07-Mar-24	282.85		
VEDL	11-Mar-24	275.35		
VEDL	12-Mar-24	270.3		
VEDL	13-Mar-24	251.9		
VEDL	14-Mar-24	260.15		
VEDL	15-Mar-24	265.1	272.32	-7.22
VEDL	18-Mar-24	271.05	272.12	-1.07
VEDL	19-Mar-24	266.65	271.15	-4.5
VEDL	20-Mar-24	267.65	269.345	-1.695
VEDL	21-Mar-24	273.4	268.44	4.96
VEDL	22-Mar-24	271.1	267.265	3.835
VEDL	26-Mar-24	268.55	266.585	1.965
VEDL	27-Mar-24	271.6	266.715	4.885
VEDL	28-Mar-24	271.65	268.69	2.96
VEDL	01-Apr-24	287.5	271.425	16.075
VEDL	02-Apr-24	301.3	275.045	26.255
VEDL	02-Apr-24	301.3	278.07	23.23
VEDL	03-Apr-24	298.8	281.285	17.515
VEDL	03-Apr-24	298.8	284.4	14.4
VEDL	04-Apr-24	309.95	288.055	21.895
VEDL	05-Apr-24	318.95	292.84	26.11
VEDL	08-Apr-24	323.3	298.315	24.985
VEDL	09-Apr-24	338	304.955	33.045
VEDL	10-Apr-24	361.8	313.97	47.83
VEDL	12-Apr-24	372.95	322.515	50.435
VEDL	15-Apr-24	370.55	329.44	41.11
VEDL	16-Apr-24	378.2	337.13	41.07
VEDL	18-Apr-24	388.5	346.1	42.4

TABLE 7.1: A simple example of a 10-day moving average calculated on the closing price of VEDL

IMAGE 7.1: A chart of VEDL on a daily timeframe with a 10-day moving average

This is just an example of how a simple/day moving average indicator can be used to understand whether the price is trading below or above its average price. We can use this information to negotiate a better price for the stock. And secondly, we didn't need to study the HH-HL structure or identify a rectangle pattern or conduct volume analysis to ascertain that the price was in an uptrend, or that the trend was changing. Mere information through an indicator that the price was above or below the average was enough to identify the change in market behavior. Thirdly, and most importantly, the information was derived from the price itself, and hence it is called a lagging indicator.

I am not advocating that technical indicators are better than price action analysis, but merely making you understand that they are tools that can make your task of analyzing the markets easier. As we go on to understand technical indicators, we will not focus on the mathematical calculations used for deriving the value of these indicators. We will focus on how you can best use these indicators to identify trends and probable trading opportunities. All the technical indicators that we will discuss are available freely on most broker platforms.

There are four types of technical indicators:

1. Trend-following
2. Momentum
3. Volume
4. Volatility

Trend-Following Indicators

Trend-following indicators help identify the overall trend direction of the security. The following are the most important trend identification indicators that we are going to study.

1. Simple moving average
2. Exponential moving average
3. Williams Alligator

Simple Moving Averages

Simple moving averages (SMAs) are a simple and effective trend-following indicator. They smooth out price fluctuations by calculating the average price over a specific period (*n* days). In our VEDL example (Table 7.1 and Image 7.1), the *n* was 10 days. As the stock price moves up, the SMA also rises. Conversely, when the price goes down, the SMA follows suit, but with a slight delay. This is because moving averages are based on historical data and inherently lag behind current price movements.

We can double-click the indicator and input the range of candles to be used for calculations.

In an uptrend, the price typically trades above the moving average. In a downtrend, the price is usually below the moving average. When the trend starts to change, say from an uptrend to sideways or a downtrend, the prices can immediately react to supply and demand fluctuations, crossing the moving average or starting to trade below it. The moving average itself might not change as quickly because it considers the average price over a set number of days. This is why moving averages are sometimes used to smooth out other, more erratic indicators.

Parameter n

The parameter *n* determines the sensitivity of the moving average. A lower *n* (fewer days) will result in a moving average that reacts more quickly to price changes. Conversely, a higher *n* (more days) will create a smoother trend line, but may be slower to reflect recent price movements.

When the price is frequently criss-crossing the moving average to the upper or lower side, it means there is no trend and we are in a sideways market (Image 7.2).

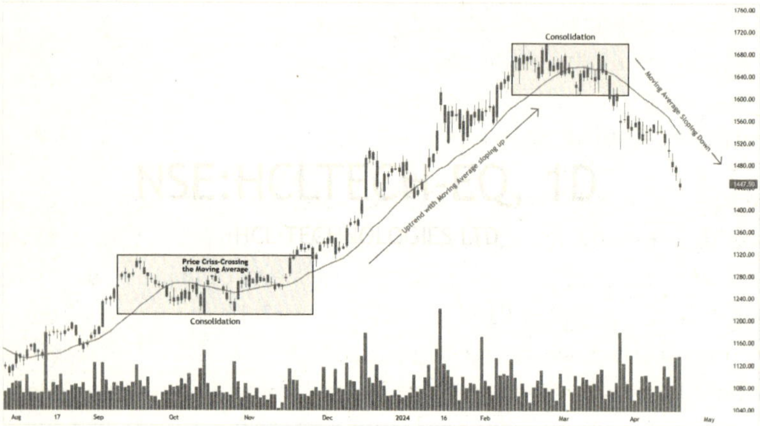

IMAGE 7.2: HCLTECH with MA(20)

Angle or slope of the moving average

The angle or slope of the moving average play an important role in determining the strength of the trend. If the slope is steeper, the trend is strong; otherwise, it is weak. If we observe HCLTECH in Image 7.2, you will notice that MA(20) is at an approximate angle of ~45 degrees. Compare this to VEDL in Image 7.3 with MA(20) and you can observe that the angle is upwards of 71 degrees. A greater degree of moving average slope to the upside or downside signifies a strong trend.

IMAGE 7.3: A daily chart of VEDL with MA(20)

Another observation you can make from the VEDL chart is the difference between the price and the moving average. This distance can provide some insight into market psychology. In the VEDL example, the price is trading 17% above the moving average, which suggests strong bullishness from market participants who are willing to buy the stock at a premium. This could be a sign of a potential long-term uptrend. However, a large price difference can also indicate an overbought condition, where the price may be inflated and due for a pullback as the market normalizes. This is the time when all the news and media outlets start talking about the stock, and retail traders in the fear of missing out end up buying a stock at an inflated price. The possibilities are endless. But one moving average can give us a detailed glimpse into market psychology.

It's important to remember that not all stocks exhibit the same price movements. Some stocks might trend upwards in a strong, impulsive manner, while others might move in a more gradual, stair-step pattern with pullbacks.

For example, compare the charts of HCLTECH (Image 7.2) and VEDL (Image 7.3) with their respective 20-day moving averages. HCLTECH's uptrend appears less impulsive, with price fluctuations and pullbacks along the way. In contrast, VEDL's uptrend shows a steeper rise with limited pullbacks so far.

This highlights that interpreting technical indicators like moving averages should consider the individual stock's behavior and overall market conditions.

The Fibonacci Sequence

Using the Fibonacci sequence with moving averages (n days)

While moving averages with a fixed number of days (like 20, 50, 100) are common, some traders explore using Fibonacci numbers for the *n* parameter. The Fibonacci sequence is a mathematical series where each number is the sum of the two preceding numbers (1, 1, 2, 3, 5, 8, etc.). This is where the concept of 8-, 13-, 21-, 34- or 55-day moving averages comes from. As to why it works? It's because when enough people start using a method, it starts reflecting on the charts as human behavior.

Previously, we discussed *n* as the parameter for moving averages, representing the number of days used to calculate the average price. For better accuracy, it's important to clarify that *n* actually refers to the number of candlesticks used in the calculation.

- In technical analysis, indicators like moving averages are typically applied to charts with specific timeframes (e.g., daily, hourly).
- Regardless of the timeframe you're analyzing (daily, hourly, etc.), the *n* parameter in a moving average refers to the number of candlesticks considered within that timeframe.

For example, a 20-day moving average on a daily chart would consider the average closing price of the past 20 days. Similarly, a 20-day moving average on an hourly chart would consider the average closing price of the past 20 hours.

With custom programming, some traders can calculate moving averages based on one timeframe (e.g., daily) and plot them on a different timeframe chart (e.g., hourly). However, this is an advanced concept beyond the scope of this book.

Choosing the right moving average

There's no one-size-fits-all for moving averages. The ideal choice depends on your trading style:

- **Short-term traders (20-50 days)**: Focus on short-term trends and frequent signals. The 20-day MA is popular due to its proximity to the average number of trading days per month (around 20). The 50-day MA offers a slightly broader timeframe.
- **Long-term traders (100-200 days)**: Identify long-term trends and major support/resistance levels. The 100-day and 200-day MAs are widely used to gauge these aspects.

Crossover, pullback, and trailing stop-loss

Traders use one or more moving averages of different length to identify trends. Crossover means when a lower-length moving average crosses over to a higher-length moving average. A lower-length moving average is also called a fast-moving average, and a higher-length moving average is called a slow-moving average. Moving average crossovers can signal potential trend reversals. A shorter-term moving average crossing above a longer-term moving average (a golden cross) might suggest a shift to an uptrend, while the opposite (a death cross) might indicate a downtrend. Popular crossover combinations include 20/50, 50/200, and even 50/100/200.

Pullbacks, however, are temporary price retracements within a trend. Moving averages can help identify potential pullback zones. For example, in an uptrend, if the price dips back towards the moving average but doesn't break below it, this could be a buying opportunity for some traders. The effectiveness of using a specific moving average for pullbacks can vary depending on the stock's volatility. Less volatile stocks might find support at a lower moving average (e.g., 20-day) compared to more volatile stocks that might find support at a higher moving average (e.g., 50-day).

Moving averages can also be a helpful tool for trailing stop-losses. Trailing stop-loss orders can be used to lock in profits and limit potential losses. The stop-loss price can be set at the moving average and then gradually trailed upwards (in an uptrend) or downwards (in a downtrend) as the price moves favorably.

Moving averages offer a simple yet powerful tool for technical analysis. However, it's important to remember that they are not a guaranteed path to profits. Analysis using moving averages requires practice and experience to interpret signals effectively. Even with practice, moving averages are prone to whipsaws (false signals) and wrong trades. Therefore, it's crucial to use them in conjunction with other technical indicators and proper risk management techniques.

As emphasized throughout this book, never rely on a single technical indicator to make trading decisions. Always consider confirmation from other indicators to increase the probability of a successful trade. Certain technical indicators can complement each other and provide stronger signals when used together. For example, stochastic oscillators and Bollinger Bands, or stochastic oscillators and MACD, can be effective combinations for some traders. Remember, technical analysis provides insights into potential price movements, but there's no absolute certainty in the markets. The only thing that will work with absolute certainty in the market is proper risk management by using appropriate position sizing and stop-loss orders.

Let us look at Image 7.4, showing a chart of BSOFT on daily timeframe with moving averages of 20 and 50 applied.

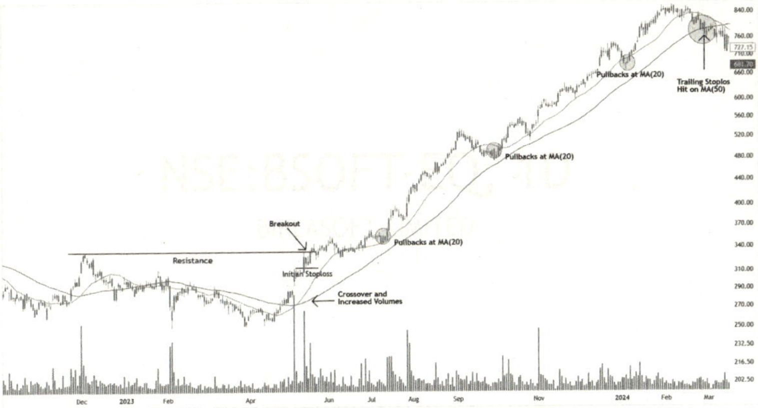

IMAGE 7.4: A daily chart of BSOFT with MA(20) and MA(50)

- Observe how the price breaks the resistance at 335. The initial stop-loss is placed just below the breakout point at the recent HL (higher low).
- The price consolidates at the breakout level near MA(20) (orange line) and starts moving up.
- The price retraces back to MA(20) and bounces back.
- The blue line is MA(50), which indicates a slow-moving average, is the trailing stop-loss. As long as the price does not touch MA(50), we ride the uptrend.
- The price gives 3 pullbacks to MA(20) and finally hits the trailing stop-loss at 770.
- BSOFT gave a clean 100% move in 1 year.

Look at another example: Image 7.5, showing CDSL on a daily chart with 20, 50 and 100 moving averages.

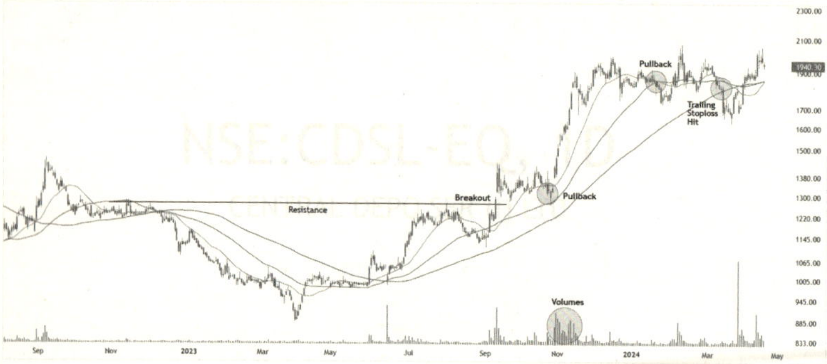

IMAGE 7.5: A daily chart of CDSL with MA(20), MA(50) and MA(100)

- Observe how the price gave a breakout above the resistance line at 1266.
- The movement of CDSL is volatile, compared to BSOFT. If we plot the stop-loss at MA(50), it will immediately stop us out from the stock without any benefit.
- MA(100) gives the stock enough room to be volatile and yet continue moving up in its uptrend without hitting the stop-loss.
- The price gives a pullback at 1830 but fails to continue the uptrend.
- After a few days, the trailing stop-loss is hit at MA(100) at 1845. Although the stock was volatile, in 8 months, it gave a clean return of 50%.

These examples highlight two crucial aspects of trading with moving averages:

- **Understanding stock movement:** Analyzing historical price movements can help identify a stock's typical behavior (volatile vs. less volatile).
- **Risk management:** Stop-loss placement and position sizing should be adjusted based on volatility to avoid emotional trading decisions influenced by price fluctuations.

Exponential Moving Average (EMA)

The exponential moving average (EMA) is a variation of the moving average that places more weight on recent prices, making it react faster to price changes than a traditional moving average.

This is achieved through a weighting factor (alpha) applied in the EMA calculation. Common alpha values include 0.2 for a fast EMA, 0.5 for a moderate EMA, and 0.8 for a slow EMA.

Compared to the simple moving average (SMA), the EMA's higher weight on recent data makes it more responsive to recent price movements but also more susceptible to noise (false signals).

Traders often use EMAs to identify trends and confirm signals from SMAs. They might employ multiple EMAs with different weights to capture both short-term and long-term trends.

The rest of the concepts – angles, pullbacks, trailing stop-losses, crossovers, etc. – are the same as those for the simple moving average.

Williams Alligator

Bill Williams developed the Williams Alligator as a tool to identify trends in the market. Markets and individual stocks spend most of their time (70-85%) in sideways consolidation, with strong trends emerging only 15-30% of the time. Williams believed that traders capitalize during these trending periods, and that is why he created the Williams Alligator.

Unlike a single moving average, the Alligator uses three moving averages with Fibonacci numbers (13, 8, 5) as periods, and depict an alligator's features. See Image 7.6:

- **The jaw (blue line)**: The slowest and strongest, representing the long-term trend (typical period: 13).
- **The teeth (red line)**: The intermediate layer, reflecting the mid-term trend (typical period: 8).

- **The lips (green line)**: The fastest and most agile, representing the short-term trend (typical period: 5).

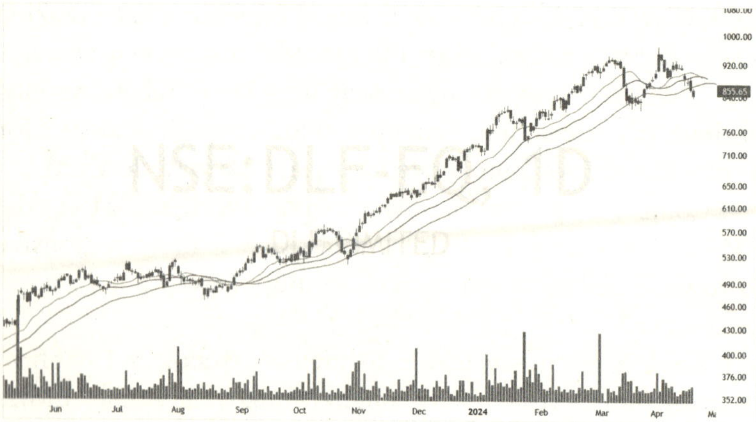

IMAGE 7.6: A daily chart of DLF with a Williams Alligator

How the Williams Alligator is different from moving averages

- The jaw, teeth and lip lines of the Alligator indicator are smoothed. Imagine a price line that is erratic. Smoothening takes the average price of a certain period to plot a smoother line. Smoothening is applied to the Williams Alligator to give better trend identification.
- There is an offset parameter in the Williams Alligator due to which the jaw, teeth and lips are plotted further, to the current day, to give early entry or exit if the price starts trending or reversing.

How to use the Williams Alligator

- **Sleeping Alligator (flat lines)**: When the jaw, teeth, and lips criss-cross, the Alligator is considered 'sleeping', indicating a sideways market.
- **Hunting Alligator (fanned lines)**: When these lines begin moving up or down, fanning out as they do, the Alligator is 'hunting', suggesting a trending market.

We generally avoid trading when the Alligator is sleeping and look for entry opportunities when it's hunting. Combined with other technical analysis tools, the Williams Alligator can be a valuable trend-following indicator to capture strong moves.

Image 7.7 shows a chart of COALINDIA on a daily timeframe with various aspects of the Williams Alligator clearly illustrated.

Observe the elements of the Williams Alligator:

- The price was sideways when the Alligator lines were criss-crossing. This means the Alligator is sleeping or sated.
- The price broke out and the jaw, teeth, and lip started to fan out, signalling a trending move. It signifies the Alligator is waking up for hunting.
- Look at the jaw, teeth, and lip plotted 8, 5 and 3 candles further to the last available trading day, due to the offset parameter.

IMAGE 7.7: A daily chart of COALINDIA with a Williams Alligator

The Williams Alligator offers a distinct advantage over traditional moving averages for trend identification. By using multiple lines with different smoothing periods, it provides a more comprehensive view of short-term, mid-term, and long-term trends simultaneously.

Momentum Indicators

Momentum indicators help identify the underlying momentum of the stocks. These are the important momentum indicators:

1. Relative strength index (RSI)
2. Moving average convergence/divergence (MACD)
3. ADX

The indicators that we used till now were the overlay indicators that are put on the price directly. Momentum indicators are standalone indicators, but are still derived from the price itself.

Relative Strength Index (RSI)

The RSI was created by J. Welles Wilder to identify the momentum in the price. The first thing you need to understand about the RSI is that it is an oscillating indicator; i.e., the value of RSI (typically 14 periods) oscillates between 0-100.

When the price moves up, the RSI moves up, and when the price moves down, the RSI moves down (Image 7.8).

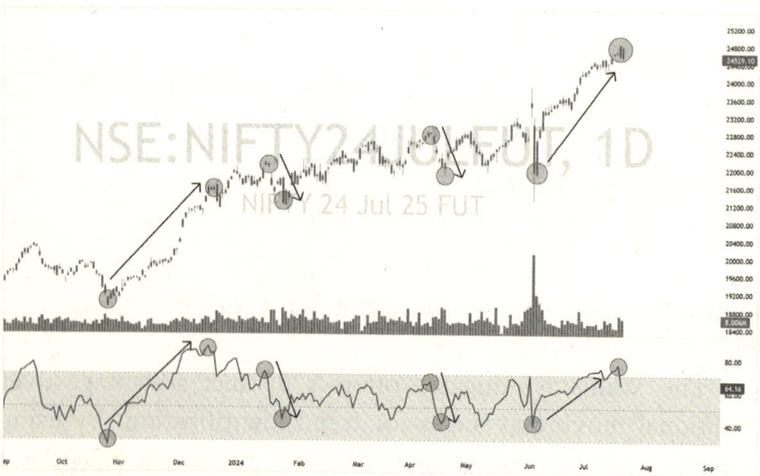

IMAGE 7.8: RSI plotted on a daily chart

See how the RSI is moving in tandem with the price – rising and falling with the price. But can trading with the RSI be that simple? Just buy when the RSI is moving up, and sell when it's moving down? No. If trading were that easy, everyone would do it. Every tool has its nuances which you must understand.

Overbought and oversold zones

The RSI oscillates between 0 and 100. When the RSI is above 80, it is considered overbought, and when the RSI is below 20, it is considered oversold. Many new traders make the mistake of considering these as sell and buy zones. But the problem is that on any timeframe, specifically in a trending market, stocks can stay in overbought or oversold zones for extended periods of time, giving you whipsaws on your trade. The price can stay in an overbought zone and keep on rising. The price can also stay in an oversold zone and keep on falling. But why does this happen? It's because although stocks or markets are sideways most of the time, if they start trending in one direction, that trend can last for a long duration (Image 7.9).

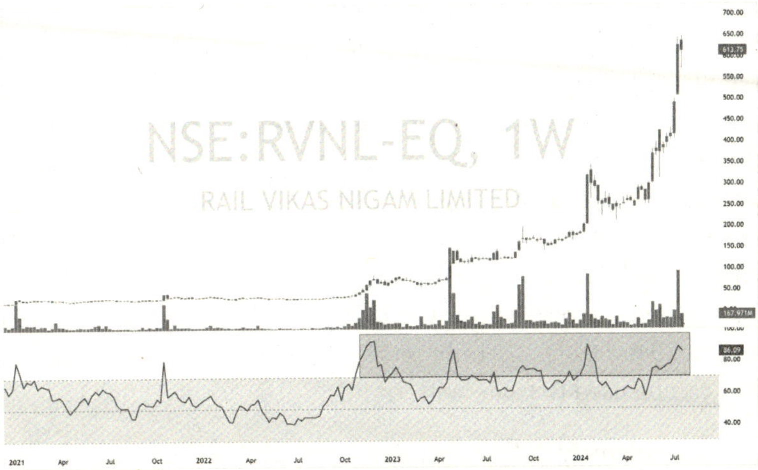

IMAGE 7.9: A weekly chart of RVNL in an overbought zone

In Image 7.9, we can see that in an established uptrend, even when the RSI is above the overbought zone, the price is making a Higher Highs, Higher Lows pattern formation. You can also see that in an established uptrend, the RSI does not fall below the oversold zone. It either stays in the overbought zone or keeps bouncing back into it. The inverse is true in a downtrend.

RSI can be used to trade in two ways:

1. Trend continuation
2. Trend reversals

Trend continuation

The RSI can remain in the oversold zone (above 70) and overbought zone (below 30) for an extended duration. If the price is forming a Higher Highs, Higher Lows (HH-HL) pattern and continues to be in an overbought zone, then any retracements of the price followed by the RSI rising up can be used to trade with the trend. But the question remains, how much of a retracement of the price is sufficient to look for buying opportunities with the RSI in a strong uptrend? Well, there is no definitive answer to that. But we can take help of other indicators here to make things easy, like moving averages, for example. We already established that there is no one-size-fits-all approach when it comes to the parameters of a moving average. Nonetheless, there are some widely used parameters by traders for moving averages. I personally prefer a mix of 14/22/39 moving averages in regular trading. But in long-term trend trading, I might prefer 20/50/100/200 moving averages.

When a stock is in a strong uptrend, moving averages of length 20 or 50 act as strong retracement points. Here is how the RSI can be used to trade with trends:

1. Identify a clear uptrend.
2. Buy when the RSI starts moving upward along with the price, bouncing off a moving average of 20.

3. Larger moving averages, like 50 or a price break below higher low, can be used as a stop-loss.

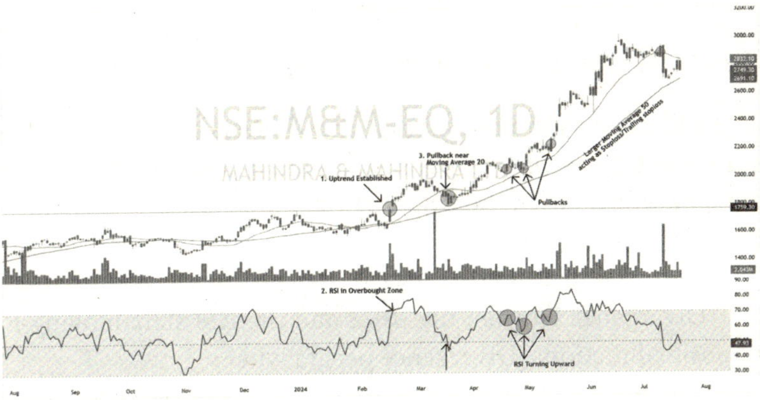

IMAGE 7.10: M&M on a daily chart

Let's take the example of the M&M daily chart in Image 7.10.

1. The price broke out of an all-time high establishing an uptrend.
2. The RSI started trading above 70.
3. The price pulled back to the moving average (20) and bounced back, taking support. The RSI also moved up with that price bounce.
4. Throughout the uptrend, the price retraced towards moving average 4 times, with the trailing stop-loss at closing below moving average (50).

Image 7.10 shows just one way how one can use the RSI for trend trading. It is different from the conventional method of using RSI, where it is suggested that one should buy once the price is oversold and sell when the price is overbought.

I have seen traders who use the RSI according to their unique trading style. Some prefer to buy in an overbought zone once the trend is established. Some prefer to use two RSIs of different length and use a faster RSI crossover above the slower RSI as a buy signal. I have also seen traders applying EMA on the RSI to determine the point at which the RSI crosses above/below its EMA to buy or sell. Technical indicators are just tools, and it all comes down to how the traders use them.

Trend reversals (concept of divergence)

The RSI can also be used to trade trend reversals, but it is not as simple as buying when the RSI starts moving above an oversold zone or selling when the RSI starts falling below an overbought zone. We have to understand the concept of divergence to trade trend reversals efficiently.

Divergence is when the price and the RSI start moving in opposite directions. Divergence occurs when:

1. The price is making higher highs and the RSI is making lower highs. This is called a bearish divergence.
2. The price is making lower lows and the RSI is making higher lows. This is called bullish divergence.

One thing must be kept in mind. We match highs with highs and lows with lows. We cannot match higher highs with higher lows, or lower lows with lower highs, and call it a divergence.

Observe how, in Image 7.11 and 7.12, bearish divergence and bullish divergence occur on MUTHOOTFIN and TATACONSUM respectively. Also note how highs on the price are matched with highs in the RSI, and conversely, how lows on the price are matched with lows in the RSI.

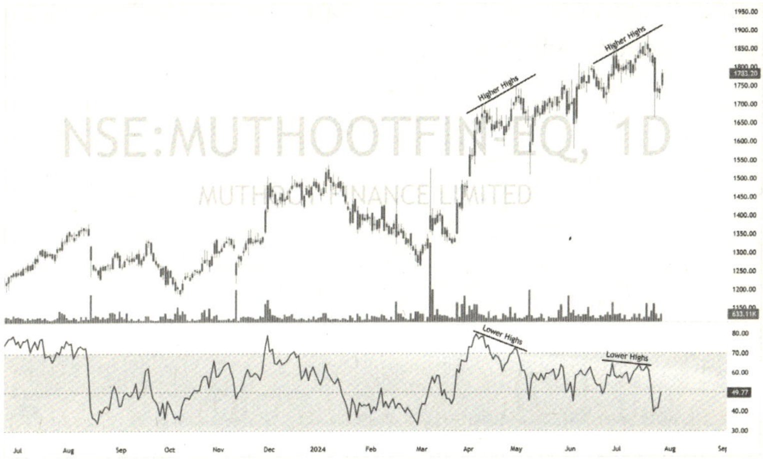

IMAGE 7.11: Bearish divergence on MUTHOOTFIN

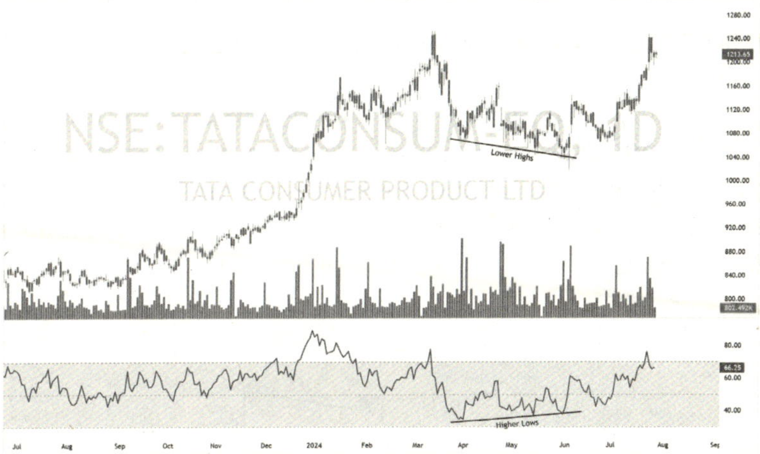

IMAGE 7.12: Bullish divergence on TATACONSUM

But how exactly do you take a trade after identifying a divergence? You need to use other technical methods to identify the exact entry price. I prefer a break of the support line combined with bearish divergence, or a break of the resistance line combined with bullish divergence, to initiate a trade.

For a stop-loss, one can use methods discussed earlier in the book based on their own winning probability and position sizing. From here on, I will not share stop-loss techniques for each and every indicator or strategy.

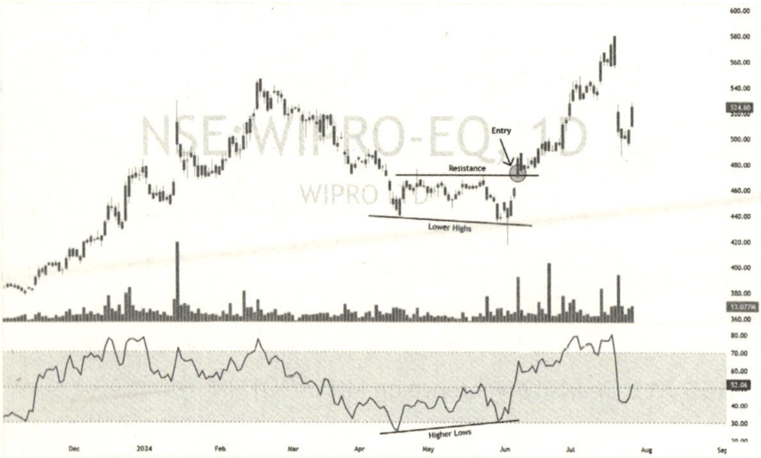

IMAGE 7.13: A daily chart of WIPRO with bullish divergence

In Image 7.13, look at the bullish divergence forming on WIPRO on daily charts with the price forming lower highs and the RSI forming higher lows, followed by a breakout above the resistance line. The resistance line break is the entry point for a bullish trade.

IMAGE 7.14: A daily chart of HINDCOPPER with bearish divergence

In Image 7.14, we can see bearish divergence on daily charts of HINDCOPPER, where the price is forming higher highs and the RSI is forming lower highs. The break of the support line is the entry point for a bearish trade.

Divergence can also sometimes be tight. What this means is that the price divergence can occur in such a small time interval on candlestick charts that it might be difficult to spot such a divergence with the naked eye. In such a scenario, one can use line charts to identify a tight divergence. For instance, look at Image 7.15, which shows PHOENIXLTD on daily charts. At first glance, it might be difficult to spot any divergence on the charts. But if we switch to the line chart, as in Image 7.16, we can easily spot a tight divergence forming. A break of the trend line or support line is the entry point for a short trade.

IMAGE 7.15: A daily chart of PHOENIXLTD

IMAGE 7.16: A daily chart of PHOENIXLTD with tight bearish divergence

But why exactly does divergence work?

The RSI calculates the relative strength of the price over the last *n* periods (usually 14). If the price is getting stronger with each candle, the RSI will usually move higher. But after a trend, momentum starts to wane, with every subsequent candle having less strength than the previous candle. The price may keep on going higher, but the RSI starts to reflect this weakness, and hence the divergence forms. For this reason, even though the RSI is lagging indicator, RSI divergence is considered a leading indication of price movement.

Before we move on to our next indicator, there is a quote of Bruce Lee that comes to mind:

I fear not the man who has practiced 10,000 kicks once,
but I fear the man who has practiced one kick 10,000 times.

No indicator is perfect, and every indicator has its nuances. It is only after considerable study and practice that you can understand the true behavior of an indicator with respect to a stock.

Moving Average Convergence/Divergence (MACD)

MACD is a momentum indicator. It has three components: the MACD line, the signal line, and the histogram. The default settings of MACD are generally 26, 12, and 9. To understand how the signal is generated for any indicator, as a trader, we must know how it is calculated.

There are four components of MACD:

1. MACD line – 12 EMA - 24 EMA
2. Signal line – 9 EMA of MACD Line
3. Histogram – MACD Line - Signal Line
4. 0 line – Equilibrium point

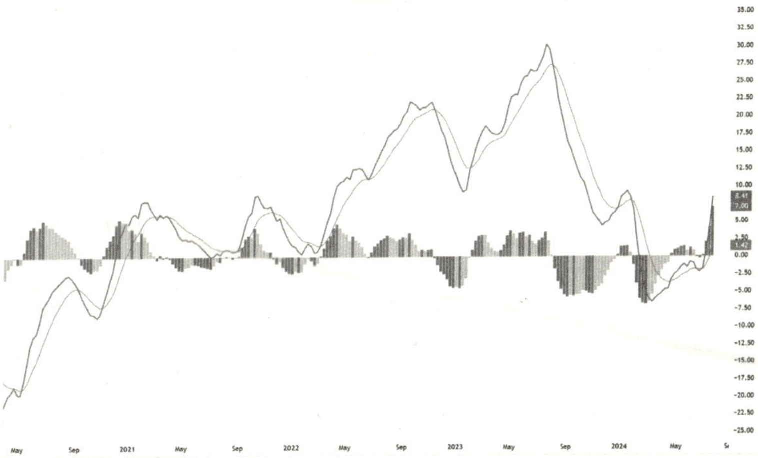

IMAGE 7.17: MACD

In Image 7.17, the blue line is the MACD line, the orange line is the signal line, and then there is the histogram.

A general interpretation of MACD is: when the MACD line crosses above the signal line, it's a bullish signal. When the MACD line crosses below the signal line, it's a bearish signal. MACD is a manifestation of moving averages. When the price starts rising for a certain period of time, moving averages start to rise, and this constant rise or fall in EMA is what drives the

MACD line higher or lower. MACD in itself tells us that 12 EMA has been moving above or below 26 EMA. If the MACD line is tilted to the upside, that means 12 EMA has been above 26 EMA. If the MACD line is tilted to the downside, that means 12 EMA has been below 26 EMA.

The signal line is the 9-period EMA of the MACD line. When the MACD crosses above the signal line, it is a signal that the first fast-moving average crossed above the slow-moving average, and now those moving averages have been above its own 9 EMA, and this acts as a buy trigger when the MACD crosses above the signal line, and a sell trigger when the MACD line crosses below the signal line.

The histogram plots the difference between the MACD line and signal line. When the MACD is moving farther from 9 MACD, it signals a trend. A green histogram represents an uptrend and a red histogram represents a downtrend. The height of the histogram signals the strength of the trend.

The 0 line is actually the equilibrium point. It is the point where the value of 12 EMA and 26 EMA are almost same, which further means that at this point of time, the 12 and 26 EMA are actually criss-crossing and there is no decisive trend. Therefore, as the MACD and signal line approach the 0 line, it becomes necessary to use additional technical analysis methods to gauge further direction.

The general interpretation of the MACD signal in the public domain is wrong. I have seen analysts turning bullish as soon as below the 0 line, the MACD line crosses above the 0 line. Conversely, I have also seen traders and analysts turning bearish when above 0 line MACD crosses below the signal line. They could not be wronger.

Look at Image 7.18.

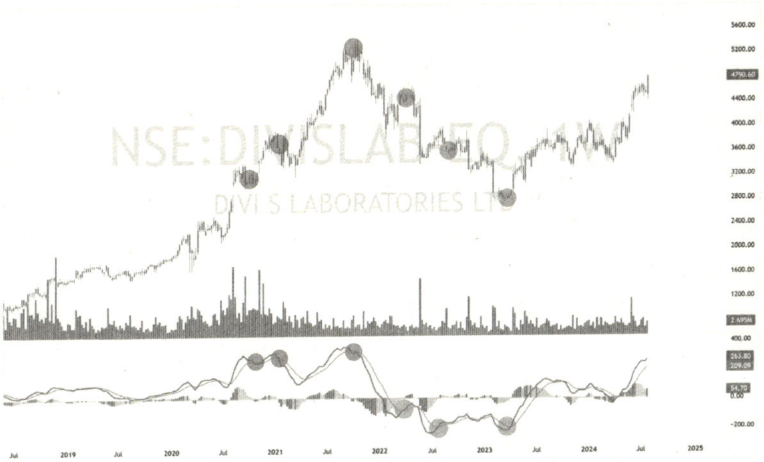

IMAGE 7.18: A daily chart of DIVISLAB with MACD

The red circles are where MACD crossed below the signal line and supposed to be bearish. The green circles are where MACD crossed above the signal line and supposed to be bullish. But the first two signals were fake before the third signal turned right. So, the question that needs to be asked is this: is MACD crossover above or below the signal line enough for it to be a buy or sell signal? The answer is no.

When MACD crossover above the signal line below 0 line happens, it just signifies that an existing downtrend might be coming to an end, or it can be a pullback in an existing trend. Remember the market cycle? After a trend, there is accumulation or distribution followed by a trend again. Mere crossover of MACD above the signal line is just indication of a slowdown in the trend. It might as well continue moving in the direction of the existing trend.

In Image 7.18, even after the MACD crossing above or below the signal line, the price continued to move in its existing direction. This is where the 0 line comes in play. The real momentum on the buy side comes when the MACD line starts trading above the 0 line. Conversely, real momentum on the sell side comes when the MACD line starts trading the below 0 line.

Understanding the 0 Line

Once the MACD has reached the 0-point, the price enters into a consolidation zone. At this point, the value of 12 EMA and 26 EMA are almost equal, and the price is in an accumulation or distribution zone. For any trade to be successful, the price must decisively move outside this consolidation along with the MACD.

When the MACD starts trading above the 0 line, it must be breaking out of a consolidation zone through the resistance to the upper side. When the MACD starts trading below the 0 line, it must be breaking out of a consolidation zone through the support to the lower side.

How to trade with MACD

1. Let the MACD cross above the 0 line for a buy trade, or cross below the 0 line for a sell trade. It will automatically be above or below the signal line in the respective cases.
2. Initiate a buy trade if the price is breaking out of consolidation through the resistance. Initiate a sell trade if the price is breaking out of consolidation through the support.

Let us understand this with an example in Image 7.19.

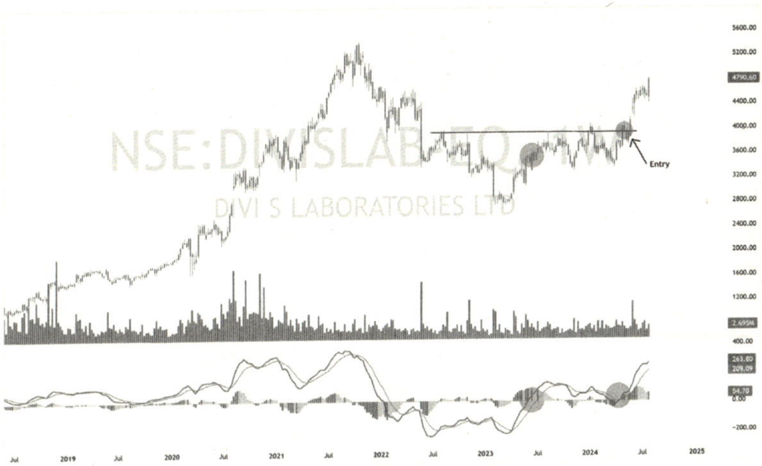

IMAGE 7.19: A daily chart of DIVISLAB with MACD

1. The MACD crossed above the 0 line, but the price is still below the resistance line. Just because the price is above the 0 line does not mean we have to buy. The price has to break above the resistance line along with the MACD trading above 0.
2. The price breaks above the resistance line with the MACD crossing above the signal line and trading above 0. This is a valid buy trade. Observe how fast the price started moving in momentum after that.

Let us observe a sell-side example in Image 7.20.

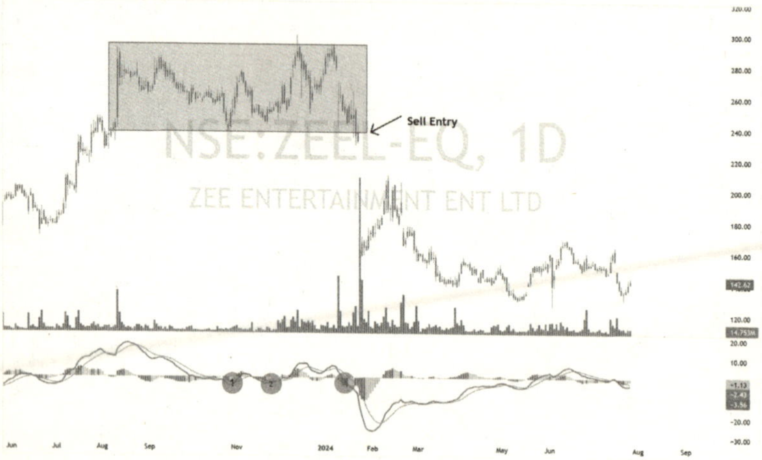

IMAGE 7.20: A daily chart of ZEEL with MACD

1. The first time the MACD crosses below the 0 line, there is no consolidation or established support line.
2. The second time the MACD crosses below the 0 line, the price fails to break the support line.
3. The third time when the MACD crosses below the 0 line, we have an established rectangle channel, and the price breaks the support line and is a valid short entry.

As you can observe from the two examples above, real momentum picks up when the MACD actually starts trading above or below the 0 line, and mere crossover of the signal line is not enough to take a trade. At the 0 line is consolidation. For a trend to establish, the MACD must trade above or below the zero line in confirmation with the price breaking above or below the consolidation zone. The MACD crossing above or below the signal line is just a pullback in an existing trend.

Like every other indicator, MACD is not perfect, and is susceptible to whipsaws and false breakouts. Even when everything is right, the trade can be wrong. As a trader, it is our duty to ensure proper risk management and study before initiating a trade.

Average Directional Index (ADX)

ADX in itself is a complete trading system. ADX has three components.

1. ADX Line measures strength of the trend
2. +DI Line measures strength of upward price movement
3. -DI Line measures strength of downward price movement

The thick blue line in Image 7.21 is an ADX line. The red line is -DI, or MDI. The green line is +DI, or PDI. When the PDI is greater than the MDI, the trend is upward. When the MDI is greater than the PDI, the trend is downward. When the ADX is greater than 25, underlying is trending.

If ADX > 25 and PDI > MDI, the stock is in an uptrend.

If ADX > 25 and MDI > PDI, the stock is in a downtrend.

ADX < 25 signifies a sideways bias.

This is the general interpretation of ADX. But ADX is more than this, and is a complete system in itself.

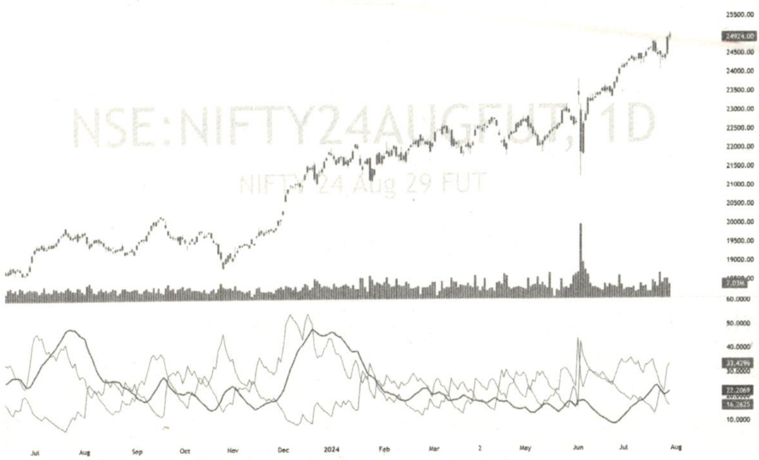

IMAGE 7.21: A daily chart of NIFTY with ADX

Let's explore the various components of ADX.

PDI and MDI

PDI and MDI identify the current direction bias of the market. If the PDI is above the MDI, the stock is trading with a bullish bias. If the MDI is above the PDI, the stock is trading with a bearish bias. Bias means that there is a probable bullish or bearish move underway. It could very well be sideways and not a definitive trend. But as long as conditions meet, we always infer:

- PDI > MDI = Bullish bias
- MDI > PDI = Bearish bias

Let us look at Image 7.22. It shows a chart of GOLD with MDI and PDI plotted. For ease of understanding, ADX is hidden for now.

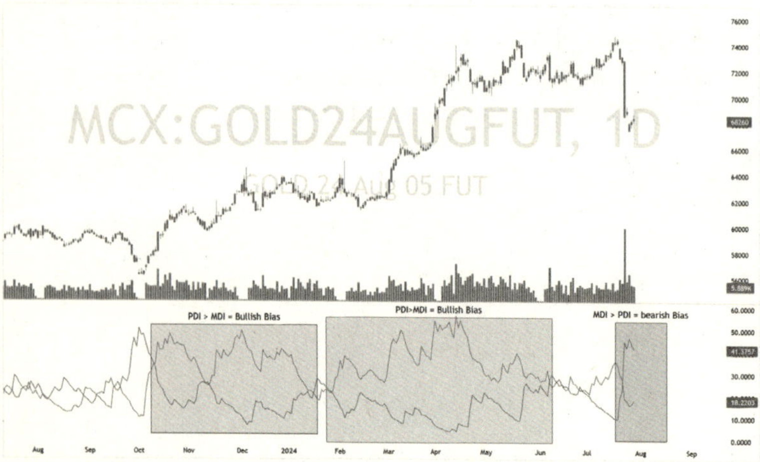

IMAGE 7.22: A daily chart of GOLD with PDI and MDI

1. In the first rectangle, the PDI crossed over the MDI, indicating the bullish bias has started. We are only going to look for bullish trades.
2. In the second rectangle, the PDI, after briefly falling below the MDI, again crossed above the

MDI, indicating bullish bias. GOLD did trade with bullishness, but this is just an indication for us to take bullish trades.

3. In the third rectangle, the PDI fell below the MDI, and we can infer that a bearish bias has started.

In all the above cases, we only get a probable idea of bullish or bearish bias. It's an inbuilt indicator inside ADX that helps decide if the ADX is trending, and then in which direction the market is trending. Or, if the market is about to start trending, which direction it might pick up. We will get to that analysis later on.

Let us look at another example for better understanding.

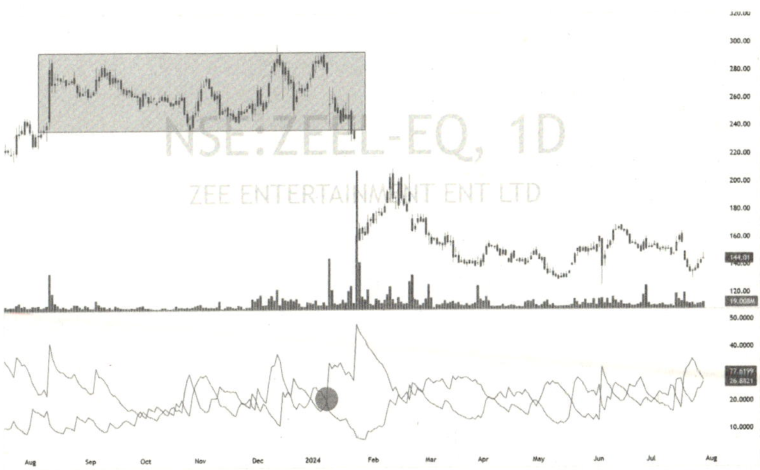

IMAGE 7.23: A daily chart of ZEEL with PDI and MDI

Look at the circle in Image 7.23 when the PDI went above the MDI, indicating a bearish bias. It was followed by a rectangle pattern breakout of ZEEL. PDI (plus or +DI) and MDI (minus or -DI) thus identify the direction in which we should trade.

As far as direction of the trend is concerned or the bullish or bearish bias is concerned, crossover of PDI or MDI is not a holy grail. Unlike other indicators, it has whipsaws.

Kiss and touch of the MDI and PDI

Let us look at the daily chart of ZEEL once again in Image 7.24.

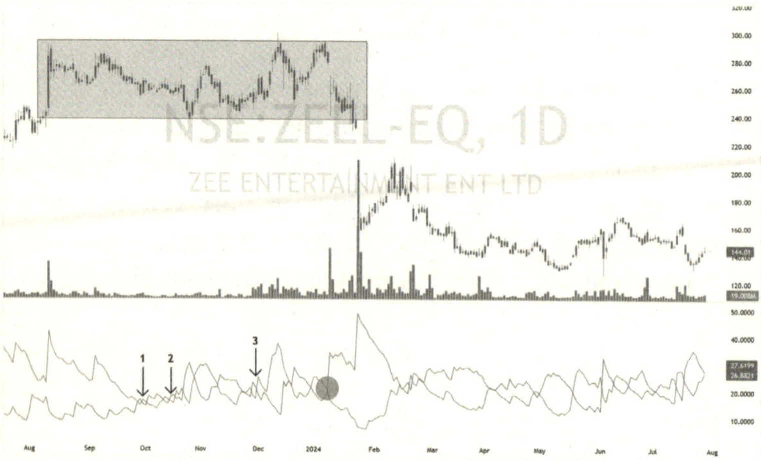

IMAGE 7.24: A daily chart of ZEEL with PDI and MDI

At points 1, 2, and 3, the MDI and PDI tried to cross over above each other briefly. This crossover is called a kiss and touch of the PDI and the MDI. Such crossovers can lead to unravelling of a bigger trend, or it can be a whipsaw. That is why when we take a direction signal from PDI or MDI crossover, it is always advised to take confirmation from another technical analysis tool that the direction is indeed correct to increase the winning probability of the trade. In Image 7.23, at the point where the MDI crossed over the PDI, it established a bearish bias. The trigger for the trade was a breakout of a rectangle pattern at the neckline. If you once again look at Image 7.24, you will notice that at points 1, 2, and 3 (a kiss and touch of the MDI and the PDI), the price was still inside the rectangle formation and there was no secondary confirmation from the price action that a trade has to be initiated.

ADX line

Now that we know about the direction, let's look at the ADX line. It is a belief among the trading community that ADX values above 20 or 25 indicate a trending ADX. This observation is partially true, but as every stock has a different pattern of moving up or down, the universally attributed number of 20 or 25 is wrong. We should rather focus on clear movement of the PDI or MDI for direction and a clear uptrend on the ADX line suggesting strength of the trend. Such clear movement of ADX might come above 20 or 25 or 30, depending on the stock.

In Image 7.25, look at highlighted portion of ADX on a BPCL chart. ADX has been sideways between 14-33. It's only once the ADX crossed above this rectangle that the stock price started to trend upward. The PDI had already crossed above the MDI, suggesting a bullish bias on BPCL. For ADX to start a new trend, the move on the ADX should come from the lower levels; i.e., it should be a fresh trend on the ADX line.

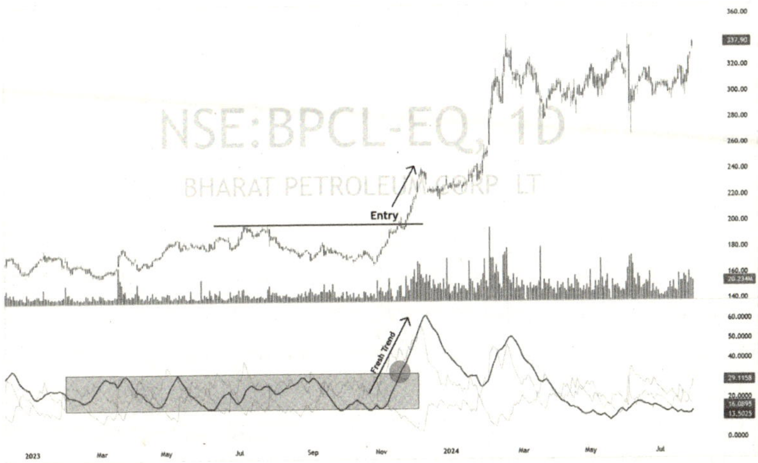

IMAGE 7.25: A daily chart of BPCL with ADX

Once trend strength has been established on the ADX, it can also be used to trade pullbacks. Such pullbacks on the ADX in an established trend are strong pullbacks. Whenever the ADX in an established trend creates a U-formation, it's generally indicative of a strong pullback in an existing trend.

Look at Image 7.26. The ADX on BPCL established a trend. The ADX touched 62 levels and started falling down and gave a U-turn pullback. The price bounced back more aggressively and made a new high. Such trends exist unless the ADX line falls below the 20-25 line and stay sideways for an extended period of time, or change visibly on the charts.

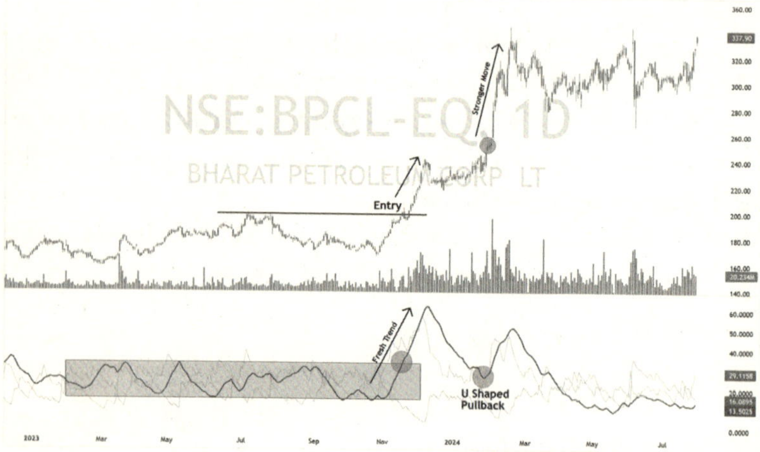

IMAGE 7.26: A daily chart of BPCL with ADX pullback

Look at one more example in Image 7.27. TATAMOTORS is sideways on 3-hourly charts. Barring budget day, there were 6 occasions when the PDI crossed above the MDI, giving a bullish signal. But every time, the signal was coming in the middle of sideways channel, and had to be ignored. Finally, the PDI crossed above the MDI with the price breaking out decisively from a rectangle channel, giving a clear buy. The ADX line is also trending to the upside, suggesting strength in the trend. I hope this clears how to avoid whipsaws in a PDI and MDI crossover. Use of price action is only one way to avoid whipsaws. I have seen traders using secondary indicators like 'stochastics' to avoid taking a whipsaw trade. Ultimately, it is on the traders to find the optimal method that works for them.

We never trade in the middle of a sideways channel, as discussed in our interpretation of price action.

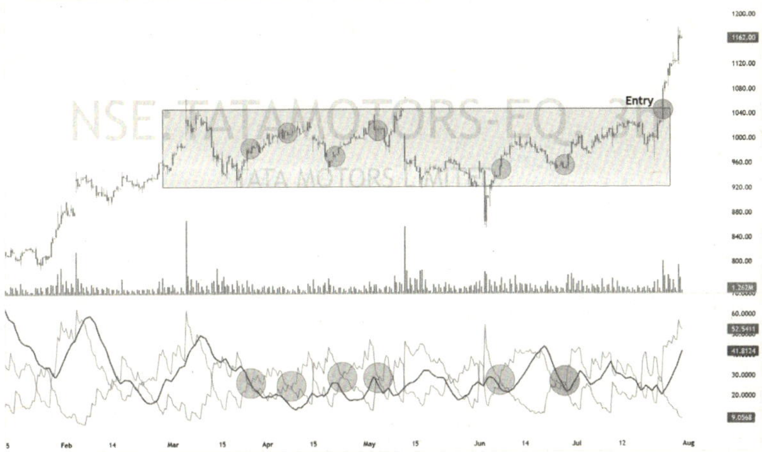

IMAGE 7.27: A 3-hour chart of TATAMOTORS with ADX

Ultimate bullish pattern

The ADX line forms a specific pattern which I consider extremely bullish or bearish based on PDI and MDI. When ADX is forming lower highs in such a way that a resistance trend line can be formed by joining the lower highs, a break of such a trendline by an ADX line can result in a strong bullish or bearish signal based on crossover of PDI above MDI, or vice versa.

Let us understand this through the example in Image 7.28.

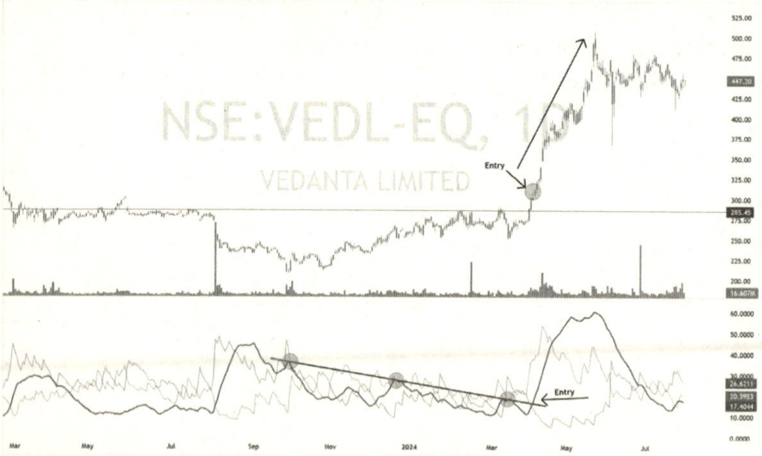

IMAGE 7.28: A daily chart of VEDL with ADX

1. Observe how the price is sideways and the ADX has been forming lower highs.
2. We can connect a clear trendline connecting the lower highs.
3. The PDI crosses above the MDI.
4. The price breaks above the resistance line decisively.

VEDL went up by 43% in ~45 days.

The same pattern can be observed on the EXIDEIND daily charts in Image 7.29. The ADX line is forming lower highs. The ADX breaks the trendline. The price breaks the all time high with volumes. The stock price jumped 46% in 2 months.

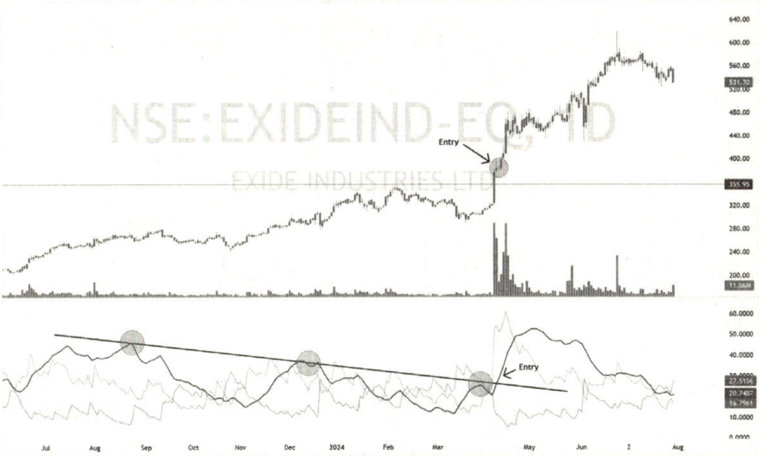

IMAGE 7.29: A daily chart of EXIDEIND with ADX

As mentioned earlier in the chapter, ADX is just not an indicator, but a trading system in itself. The more you use it, the more refined your trading approach will get with time.

Volume

Volume is arguably the most authentic indicator in trading. In Chapter 3, we delved into the correlation between price and volume to understand when a stock or market (used interchangeably) is weak or strong. Let's recap Table 3.3:

1. **When price is rising, and volume is rising**: This signals a strong or bullish market.
2. **When price is rising but volume is falling:** This indicates a weak market. While it's not a bearish market or a bearish trigger, it lacks the strength for an upward move.
3. **When price is falling, and volume is rising:** This suggests a weak or bearish market.
4. **When price is falling, and volume is falling:** This signals a strong market because the lack of selling volume indicates capitulation. While not necessarily a buy trigger, it hints at potential selling exhaustion.

Price	Volume	Market Outlook
Rising	Up	Strong Market
Rising	Down	Weak Market
Falling	Up	Weak Market
Falling	Down	Strong Market

TABLE 3.3: Price and volume interpretation

It's crucial to note that volume, like any technical indicator, should never be viewed in isolation. Interpretation must be in conjunction with other indicators or price action analysis—or both. While more confirmation can lead to better clarity, excessive confirmation might result in decision paralysis. Therefore, it's more effective to identify the pattern first and then seek confirmation from the volume.

Volume Analysis: Daily Chart of LICI

Let's analyze the daily chart of LICI (Image 7.30) to understand the first concept of volume analysis.

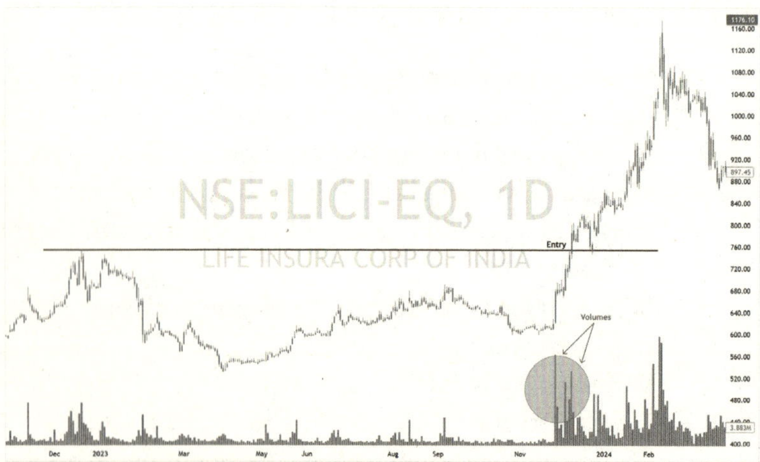

IMAGE 7.30: A daily chart of LICI

1. **Sideways trading with negligible volumes (Dec '22 to Dec '23)**: Throughout this period, LICI's price remained relatively flat, indicating a lack of strong buying or selling interest. The low volumes suggest that both retail and institutional traders were not significantly involved.
2. **Price surge with heavy volumes (Dec '23)**: In December 2023, LICI's price began to rise sharply, accompanied by a significant increase in trading volume. This surge indicates strong buying interest, likely driven by institutional investors. The price breaking the 52-week high of 754 is a crucial technical milestone, as it signifies market strength and attracts further attention from traders and analysts.
3. **Resistance turned support:** After breaking the 52-week high, the price encountered resistance at 754. Once surpassed, this resistance level transformed into support. The price retested this support level, successfully held, and resumed its upward trajectory, confirming the strength of the new support level.
4. **Significant price increase (770 to 1160)**: Following the successful retest of the support, LICI's price continued to climb, reaching a high of 1160 from 770 in just 45 days, marking a 50% increase. This rapid rise, supported by high volumes, indicates strong bullish sentiment and sustained buying interest.

Key takeaways:

1. **Volume as a confirmation tool**: The increase in volume during the price surge confirms the strength of the move. High volumes during price increases are indicative of strong buying interest, often from institutional investors.
2. **52-week high significance**: Breaking the 52-week high is a significant technical event that often

attracts attention from traders and analysts, leading to increased trading activity.

3. **Support and resistance dynamics**: The transformation of a resistance level into support is a bullish signal, especially when accompanied by high volumes. The successful retest of this new support level further confirms the strength of the bullish trend.
4. **Rapid price movement**: A substantial price increase over a short period, supported by high volumes, highlights strong market momentum and investor confidence.

Volume Analysis: Daily Chart of JIOFIN and UNITDSPR

Now that we've understood the first concept of volume analysis through the example of LICI, let's delve into the second concept by analyzing the daily chart of JIOFIN (Image 7.31) and the weekly chart of UNITEDSPR (Image 7.32).

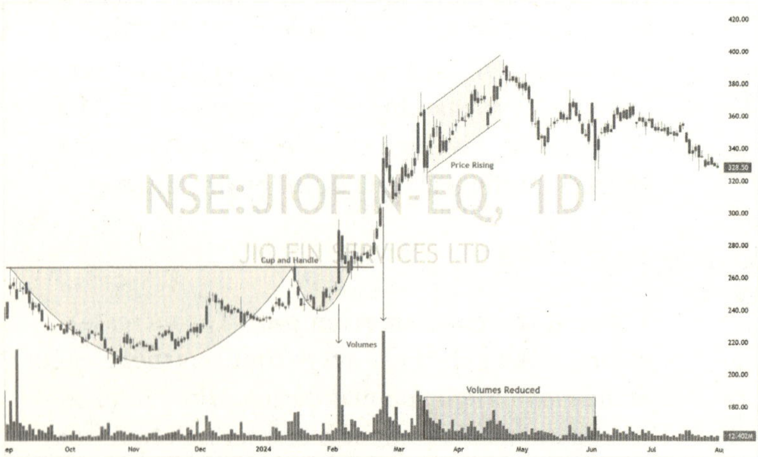

IMAGE 7.31: A daily chart of JIOFIN

1. **Cup and handle breakout (Feb '24)**: In February 2024, JIOFIN formed a textbook cup and handle pattern, a bullish continuation pattern. The breakout from this pattern was supported by high trading volumes, indicating strong buying interest and confirming the validity of the breakout.
2. **Rising prices with high volumes (end of Feb '24)**: Following the breakout, JIOFIN's price continued to rise until the end of February 2024, accompanied by high trading volumes. This sustained volume during the price increase signifies robust bullish sentiment and further buying pressure.
3. **Selling pressure (mid Mar '24)**: In mid-March 2024, JIOFIN faced selling pressure, leading to a temporary price decline. The volumes during this period were significant, highlighting the presence of strong selling interest.
4. **Rising prices with diminishing volumes (post Mar '24 to Apr '24)**: After the initial selling pressure, JIOFIN's price resumed its upward trajectory for the next 45 days, but with diminishing trading volumes. By the last week of April 2024, the price started to consolidate, gradually declining as the market lost momentum.

Key takeaways:

1. Breakouts accompanied by high trading volumes increase the probability of trade success. The high volume during the cup and handle breakout in JIOFIN is a classic example of this principle.
2. A continued upward price movement without high volumes can indicate a weak market. This does not necessarily signal a bearish trend but suggests a lack of conviction in the market's bullish or bearish direction.

This example of JIOFIN highlights a weak market when prices are moving up without considerable volume. However, it is not a sell trigger. Price action analysis involves understanding human behavior. If low volumes suggest that market participants haven't decided to buy, and the price pattern is still under formation, it may also mean that market participants haven't decided to sell yet. Let's look at the daily chart of UNITDSPR (Image 7.32).

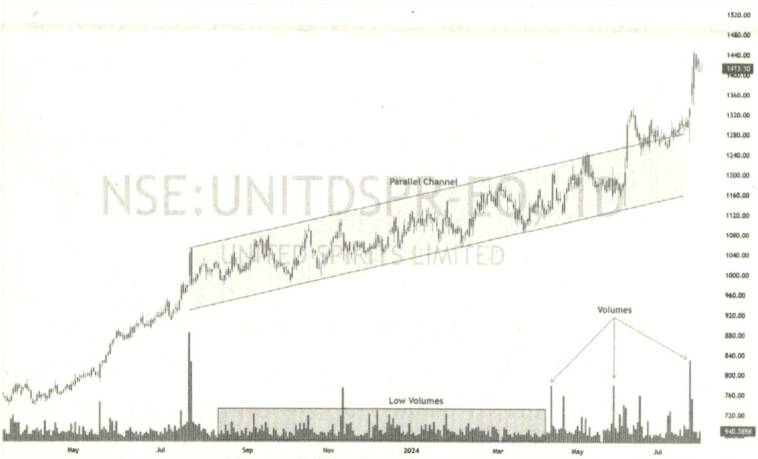

IMAGE 7.32: A daily chart of UNITDSPR

1. From Sep '23 to Apr '24, UNITDSPR formed a parallel channel with low volumes.
2. From May '24 to Jun '24, volumes started to rise along with sudden breakout attempts.
3. On 7 Jun '24, the price finally broke the channel, and a bull run started.

Key takeaways:

Rising price and low volume indicate a weak market, but it is not necessarily a sell signal. It signifies that market participants haven't decided on the trend direction. Any further direction may depend on various factors like price pattern, quarterly results, government policy, etc., which might be the reason for market participants being in a wait-and-watch mode.

Volume Analysis: Daily Chart of DELTACORP

When prices are falling and volumes are increasing, it signifies a weak market or a bearish market. Let us look at the daily chart of DELTACORP (Image 7.33) to understand how a change in government policy triggered a bearish market for the stock. As soon as the adverse news came into the public domain, the price started falling with increased volumes. Even when the broader markets were bullish in the years 2023-2024, DELTACORP never recovered from the massive selling that it witnessed after the government's adverse decision.

IMAGE 7.33: A daily chart of DELTACORP

Volume Analysis: Daily Chart of SUNTV

When the price falls without significant volume, it signifies a strong market. Why a strong market? Because at lower prices, market participants are not willing to sell. To push prices further down, there needs to be an increased supply. At this point, we often see a big sell candle with reduced volumes, which signifies that we have reached a point of selling capitulation. This is where bears try one last time to push prices further down, but more market participants do not join in their effort, preventing further decline.

The opposite of this is bullish capitulation, which might happen at the top with a big bullish candle and low volumes, potentially hinting at a reversal.

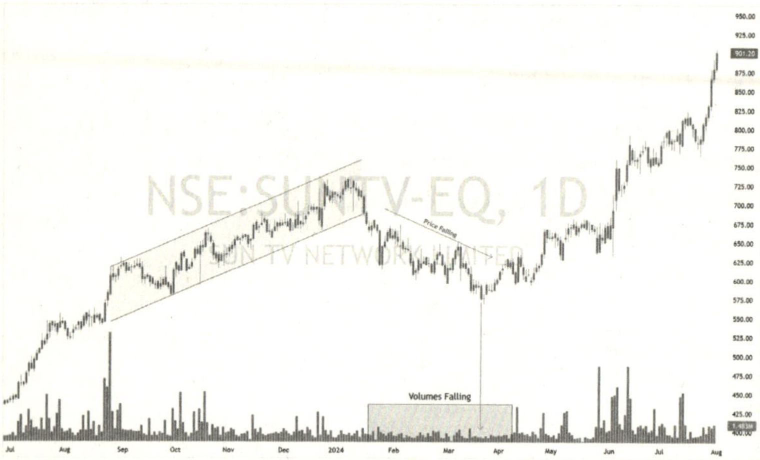

IMAGE 7.34: A daily chart of SUNTV

1. **Parallel channel formation**: SUNTV forms a parallel channel where the price is rising with falling volumes, signifying weakness. Eventually, the price breaks down from the parallel channel.
2. **Downtrend initiation**: SUNTV starts a downtrend. Observe how the price is falling with low volumes, which signifies the absence of sellers.
3. **Selling capitulation**: Sellers make one final attempt to push the price lower, but the volumes are missing, signifying selling capitulation.
4. **New uptrend**: Buyers take control in the next few trading sessions, and SUNTV starts a new uptrend with the price rising backed by increased volumes.

Key takeaways:

1. **Rising price with falling volume**: Indicates weakness, as the upward move lacks conviction.
2. **Falling price with low volume**: Suggests a strong market because there is an absence of significant selling pressure.
3. **Selling capitulation**: When a final sell-off attempt lacks volume, it signifies that sellers are exhausted, potentially marking the end of the downtrend.
4. **Volume-backed uptrend**: A new uptrend confirmed by rising prices and increased volumes indicates strong buying interest and a potential reversal of the previous downtrend.

Volume is one of the key indicators in technical analysis. Market participants often try to hide their trading activities to maintain a first-mover advantage, but one thing they cannot hide is their trading volume. This is why volume plays a crucial role in all price action and technical analysis. Whether it's trend-following, momentum trading, or identifying trend reversal signals, volume is a vital component. Mastering the interpretation of volume will come with practice and experience.

Volatility Indicators

Volatility simply refers to how wildly the prices are fluctuating in a given time period.

The obvious question that comes to mind is: how would volatility help me in trading? Prices are bound to fluctuate. How does it matter to know how much they are fluctuating?

Measuring volatility means getting an idea of:

1. How fast the stock fluctuates.
2. For what duration it fluctuates.
3. How far up or down it swings during that fluctuation.

Volatility therefore helps us understand the potential target or stop-loss for a trade. Volatility helps us identify probable mean reversal or trend continuation patterns. By taking consideration of volatility, we can create efficient trading strategies.

One of the most common used volatility-based indicators is Bollinger Bands.

Bollinger Bands

Bollinger Bands use the concept of standard deviation.

Standard deviation

Imagine a population where the average height is 5 feet 9 inches, with a standard deviation of 3 inches.

What this means is that in a sample of 100 people, their heights will range from 5 feet 6 inches to 6 feet. The average height of 100 people will be 5 feet 9 inches, with the maximum height being 6 feet and the minimum height being 5 feet 6 inches.

It has been observed that, over a larger set of data:

1. 68% of data falls within 1 standard deviation of the average. Therefore, 68/100 people will most probably have a height between 5 feet 8 inches and 5 feet 10 inches.
2. 95% of data falls within 2 standard deviations of the average. Therefore, 95/100 people will most probably have a height between 5 feet 7 inches and 5 feet 11 inches.
3. 99.7% of data falls within 3 standard deviations of the average. Therefore, ~99/100 people will most probably have a height between 5 feet 6 inches and 6 feet.

The remaining 0.03% can fall beyond 3 standard deviations of the average; that means heights shorter than 5 feet 6 inches or greater than 6 feet are improbable, but still possible.

Therefore, the first statement (i.e., the average height is 5 feet 9 inches with a standard deviation of 3 inches) means that in a sample of 100 people, 99/100 will have their height fall within the given range. 1 person may have a height shorter than 5 feet 6 inches or greater than 6 feet.

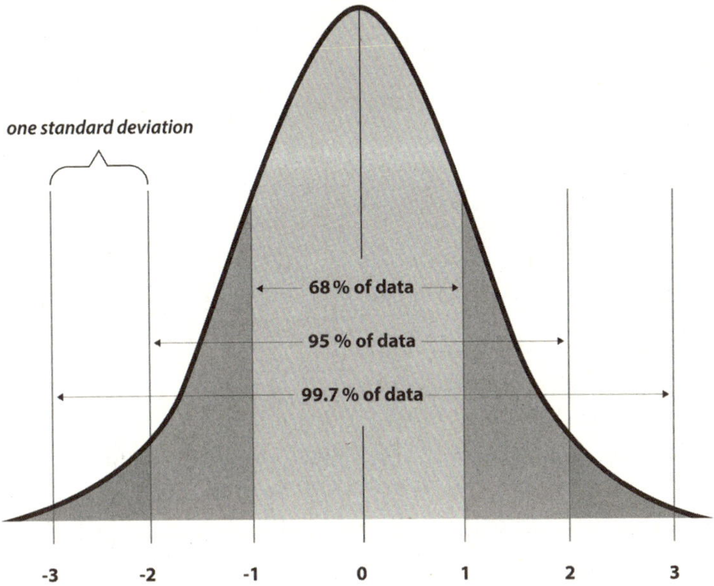

IMAGE 7.35: A standard deviation bell curve

Further simplifying, this means that in a given sample of data, 68% of data will most commonly lie within -1 to +1 standard deviation. 95% will lie in -2 to +2 standard deviations. And -3 to +3 standard deviations will encapsulate 99.7% of the data.

In the stock market, we can apply this principle to price for a particular period of time for (e.g., 14 days) and calculate the standard deviation to understand how much the price is deviating from the mean, or average, price. If the deviation is great (i.e., it is beyond 2 standard deviations), we can say that the stock is volatile. If the stock price is deviating by 3 standard deviations, it means the stock is highly volatile. If the deviation is more than 3, it could be an outlier event. This data point –

how many standard deviations from the mean the price is – can, mixed with price action, tell us whether the stock will revert to the mean, or will continue moving up or down in its current direction.

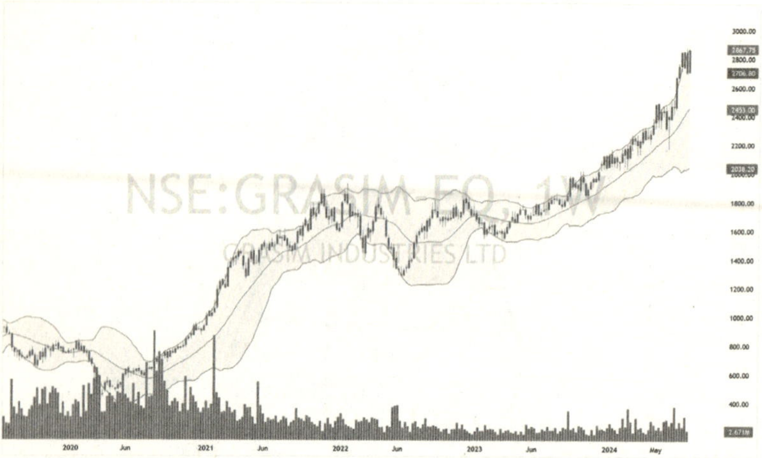

IMAGE 7.36: A daily chart of GRASIM with Bollinger Bands

Image 7.36 shows what Bollinger Bands looks like. Bollinger Bands requires two key parameters:

1. **Period length**: This determines the number of data points used to calculate the moving average (middle band) and standard deviation. A common value used is 20. The reason is because there are ~20 trading days in a month, but traders can explore other values. If we increase the length, we get a smoother Bollinger Band. If we decrease the period length, the Bollinger Band will be erratic.
2. **Standard deviation multiplier**: This value determines the distance between the middle band and the upper/lower bands. The most common setting is 2, but traders can experiment with different multipliers (e.g., 1.5, 2.5). The standard deviation number determines how far away from the middle

line the upper and lower bands are plotted. If the standard deviation multiplier is 2, then prices within the Bollinger Band signify that 95% of the price is within the 2 standard deviation range.

Traders have different way of interpreting Bollinger Bands. In price action trading, we understood that price moves in a zig-zag way – consolidation followed by a trend, and vice versa. A similar concept can be visualized using Bollinger Bands. During the consolidation period, Bollinger Bands squeeze, and start to expand once the price breaks to the upper or lower side. This breakout is when the price starts trading beyond its standard deviation. But we have to understand Bollinger Bands in more detail quantitatively to understand how to effectively use them.

Interpreting the value of the standard deviation

Standard deviation 2: SD2 encapsulates 95% of the price movement. It signifies that the price movement is within the normal range and traders are behaving normally within an expected range. Therefore, SD2 leads to the formation of a price squeeze or a normal distribution of the price. Till the time the price is within a Bollinger Band with standard deviation 2, there is an absence of a trend. Even if there is any kind of trend, there is a lack of strength or momentum. If the price closes outside the Bollinger Band, it might signify a breakout. For such a breakout to be successful, we might need further confirmation, like a follow-up move in the next trading session.

When the price trades outside the SD2 range, it signifies that someone is willing to pay a higher price for a stock or is willing to sell at a lower price than the prevailing market price. This can be further correlated with volumes to understand whether the breakout move is genuine or not.

Let us understand this using Image 7.37, which shows GRASIM on weekly charts.

1. The price of GRASIM was consolidating from Nov '21 to Aug '23, witnessing a resistance at 1860.
2. On 11 Sep '23, GRASIM closed above Bollinger Band SD2, coinciding with a breakout above the all-time high. The breakout was backed by heavy volumes and started a bull rally which is still in play.

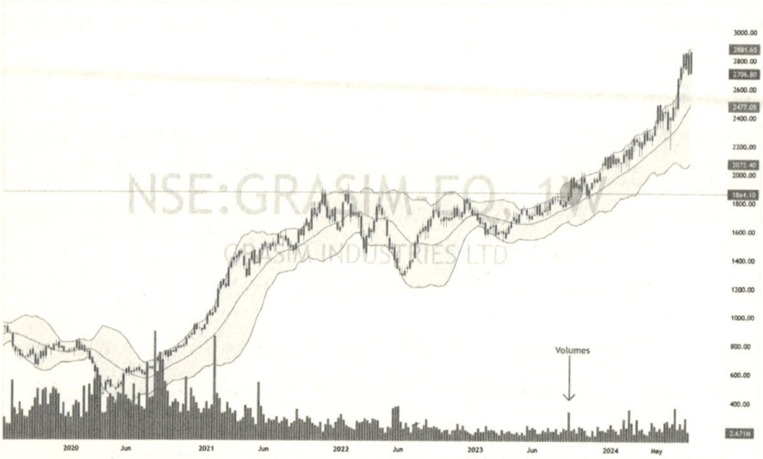

IMAGE 7.37: A weekly chart of GRASIM with Bollinger Bands (20, 2)

Notice how the Bollinger Band started to expand after the breakout.

Standard deviation 3: SD3 encapsulates 99.7% of the price movement. It signifies a clear anomaly: a 1/100 event has occurred. The height is either shorter than 5 feet 6 inches, or taller than 6 feet. Someone is willing to buy the stock at an inflated price or is willing to sell stock at a depressed price. It can signify either a strong trend or a trend reversal.

See EXIDEIND (Image 7.38).

1. On 8 Apr '24, the price closed at an all-time high and outside Bollinger Bands SD3.

2. The next day, buyers showed a continuous interest in pushing the price even higher, with increased volumes signifying a trend continuation. From 354, the price touched a high of 604 in two and a half months.

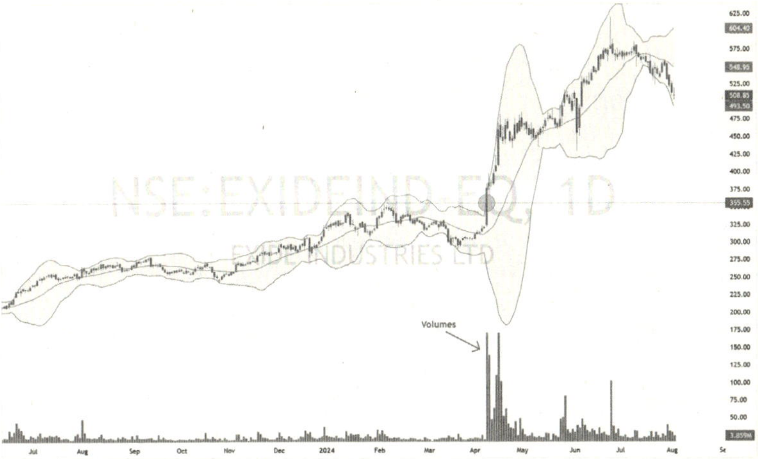

IMAGE 7.38: EXIDEIND on a weekly chart with Bollinger Bands (20, 3)

See INFY (Image 7.39).

1. On 4 Jun '24, the price fell to a low of 1365 trying to go below Bollinger Band SD3.
2. Buyers stepped in immediately and pushed the price higher. From the next day, the price started to increase, backed by high volumes.
3. The price bounced from long-term support, forming a double bottom pattern.

IMAGE 7.39: INFY on a daily chart with Bollinger Bands (20,3)

In both cases, buyers and sellers behaved differently. In EXIDEIND, buyers recognized it as a buying opportunity as a part of a trend continuation move. In INFY, buyers recognized it as a buying opportunity as a part of a trend reversal move.

These are just a few examples of how Bollinger Bands can be used in different ways. Bollinger Bands can also be used for identifying probable support and resistance points. Bollinger Bands can be used for trend identification as well as to identify trend reversal trades. Bollinger Bands can also be used to take mean reversal trades. To increase the accuracy of Bollinger Bands, they can also be used with indicators like RSI or stochastics. Once you understand how human psychology works around price and understand the concept of standard deviation, you can use Bollinger Bands in varied ways. The applications are limitless.

These are just few of the indicators that a trader must understand. If you want to explore more, I suggest you read about Supertrend, VWAP, anchored VWAP, the Zig Zag indicator, the Donchian Channel, Ichimoku Indicators, etc. for further insight into different indicators.

With this, we come the end of our discussion on technical indicators. In further chapters, we will discuss trading strategies in more detail, and we will see advanced applications of these indicators, or mixing up more than one indicator or price pattern for making trading decisions. Closing note: indicators are derived from price, and their success is based on sound risk management and position sizing.

In markets, sometimes everything works,
and sometimes nothing works.

CHAPTER 8

Breakout Trading

The market is always telling you something.
You just have to learn to listen.

The market is a reflection of human behavior. Human behavior, for the most part, is subtle. In trading, this subtle human nature becomes volatile due to the human emotions called greed and fear. The greed of missing out on profit and the fear of losing money are significant drivers. Breakout trading represents such human behavior. Prices often consolidate within a specific range, creating a state of equilibrium. But then, suddenly, the human emotions around the stock price start to change, possibly due to earnings reports, government regulations, or changed investor sentiment. Such shifts in sentiment can dramatically impact stock prices, leading to rapid price movements. This is where breakout trading comes into play: benefitting from the stock price movement when the price is volatile to capture a rapid move quickly.

In trading, there are essentially two patterns that repeat in different ways: the rectangle pattern and the triangle pattern (Image 8.1). Breakout trading is identifying such patterns and trading them for low risk and high reward. Compared to trend trading or momentum trading, the duration of trades in breakout trading is short.

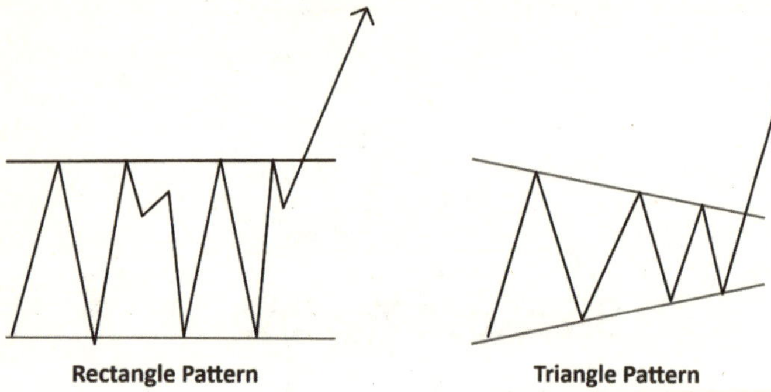

IMAGE 8.1: A rectangle pattern and triangle pattern

Imagine a spring compressed tightly. It's under immense pressure, coiled and ready to spring forward. Once released, the spring extends rapidly, releasing its stored energy.

Similarly, in breakout trading, a stock price consolidates within a range (the compressed spring). As the price remains confined within this range, pressure builds up. When the price finally breaks out of this range, it's like releasing the compressed spring. The price moves rapidly in the direction of the breakout.

Essentials of Breakout Trading

1. Support and resistance: to identify breakout levels
2. Pattern identification around such supports and resistances
3. Breakout volume
4. Stop-loss
5. Target

All these concepts have been discussed in previous chapters. Let's delve into some case studies.

Case Study 1 – BPCL

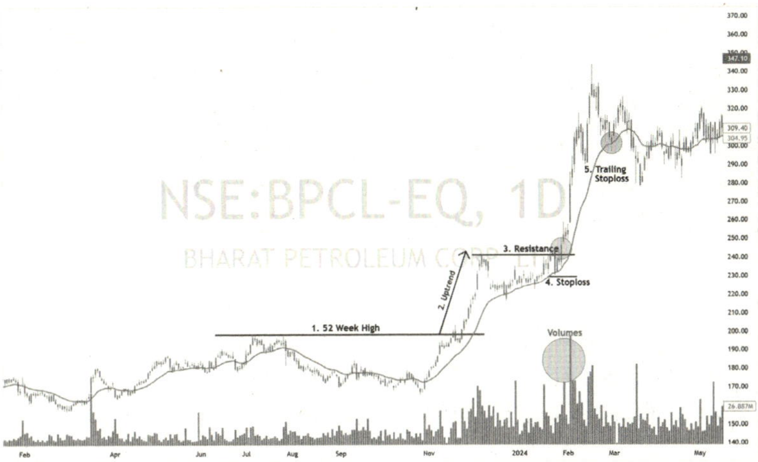

IMAGE 8.2: A daily chart of BPCL

1. BPCL broke a 52-week high, indicating an uptrend (Image 8.2).
2. An uptrend is established with an upmove followed by a sideways consolidation. Breakouts work best in the direction of an established uptrend.
3. The recent high acts as a resistance line. On 23 Jan '24, the price tried to break the resistance line, but volumes were low. Sellers try to take control of the price by pushing the price lower. Buyers take control of the price by rejecting selling pressure, and within three days, there's a breakout of the price above the resistance line with high volumes. This breakout with volume is an entry for fresh buy positions at 247.
4. The recent low near the resistance is the stop-loss for the trade at 229. Risk on the trade is 18 points.
5. For the trailing stop-loss, we use an exponential moving average of 20 periods. The price hits the stop-loss at 302 in 25 days.

- Risk = 18 points
- Profit = 55 points

Why did we choose a 20-period EMA for *trailing* stop-loss? Breakout trading is fast. The idea is to stay with the trade until the price is moving up. A smaller period results in a faster but more erratic moving average, whereas a larger period results in a slow but smooth moving average. Therefore, a smaller-period EMA results in a steeper curve of the plotted average. As long as the price after the breakout doesn't touch the EMA(20), we can consider it a strong breakout because market participants are willing to buy the stock above an average price of 20 days. Once the price touches the EMA(20), we close the trade and book profit as the price attains normalcy.

Case Study 2 – CHAMBALFERT

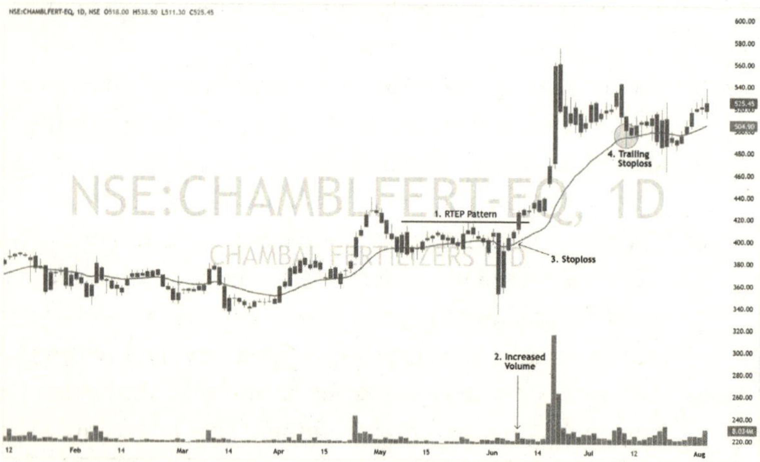

IMAGE 8.3: A daily chart of CHAMBALFERT

1. The price is trading in an uptrend and consolidating. The price witnessed a massive sell-off on 4 Jun '24 (Image 8.3).

Let us ignore the reason. On the day of the 2024 Lok Sabha election results in India, stocks and indices witnessed massive profit-booking, as not a single political party attained a majority. By end of day, there was political certainty of policy continuation, with talks of formation of a coalition government.

2. In the next 3 days, buyers rejected the downmove. 3 days of buying volume was far greater than the sell volume of 4 Jun '24. The price formed an RTEP pattern. Selling was completely absorbed in the next 3 days. (The RTEP pattern is discussed in detail in the chapter on chart patterns.)
3. The price broke out of the RTEP pattern with high volume at 428. The stop-loss of the trade is 20 EMA at 400. The risk on the trade is 28 points.
4. The price hit the trailing stop-loss at 494 in 23 days, resulting in a profit of 66 points.

- Risk = 28 points
- Profit = 66 points

Why did we choose a 20-period EMA for *initial* stop-loss? Because the stop-loss, according to the nearest low point, would have come at the low of the sell candle (i.e., 333). The initial risk on the trade would have been close to 95 points, which would have altered the risk/reward equation adversely. In such situations, the initial stop-loss can be taken as EMA(20) and can be trailed as such through EMA(20).

EMA(20) is not a set in stone method for a trailing stop-loss. This is just one example of how to define risk. As a trader, you can explore other methods that suits your trading psychology. Some of the other methods for setting a stop-loss or trailing stop-loss are Supertrend, average true range, parabolic stop and reverse, HH-HL or LH-LL structures, and Donchian Channels. Unless you try and test, you will not know what works best for you.

Case Study 3 – DIVISLAB

IMAGE 8.4: A weekly chart of DIVISLAB

1. DIVISLAB witnessed selling at the 4150 level three times, making this level a strong resistance.
2. On 20 May '24, the price broke the resistance line. The next candle witnessed a decisive breakout with increased volume. The entry for the trade is at 4300.
3. The stop-loss for the trade is at the recent candle low of 3700. The risk of the trade is 600 points.
4. The stop-loss can be trailed at EMA(20), currently at 4326, making it a breakeven trade at the current level.
5. The target for the trade is 5200 levels, which is an all-time high for DIVISLAB. The reward potential for the trade is 900 points.

How do we decide the target price for the trade? In fresh breakouts where the price is breaking out into all-time high territory, it is difficult to ascertain the target price because we never know how high a stock price can rise before consolidation begins. Therefore, it makes sense to trail the stop-loss. But when a recent high is already in place (as is the case with DIVISLAB), such a high price acts as a resistance and a good target to book profits for a buy trade.

For further reading into price targets when previous highs are not available, traders take help of tools called Fibonacci retracement and Fibonacci extension. I suggest you give them a read and decide for yourself if they suit your trading style.

Another point worth mentioning is the risk/reward ratio of this trade. When we started the trade, the trade with a 600-point risk and 900-point reward had a risk/reward ratio of 1:1.5, which is low. Once the price started moving in our favor, the trailing stop-loss moved above the cost, which makes the risk/reward equation of the trade better at 0:900. This is the benefit of a trailing stop-loss. If the stock moves in your direction, you can keep increasing your stop-loss as the price keeps moving in your direction. This further reduces your loss and increases profitability in the long run.

Case Study 4 – FINPIPE

IMAGE 8.5: A daily chart of FINPIPE

1. FINPIPE (Image 8.5) faced resistance at the 195 level twice, making it a strong resistance. On 27 Jul '23, the price broke the resistance and closed above the resistance level. The entry price for FINPIPE is 198.

2. The breakout was backed by heavy volumes.
3. The stop-loss for the trade is 189; i.e., 9 points.
4. The trailing stop-loss at EMA(20) is hit in one and a half months at 228, giving a profit of 30 points.

- Risk = 9 points
- Reward = 30 points

Case Study 5 – GRSE

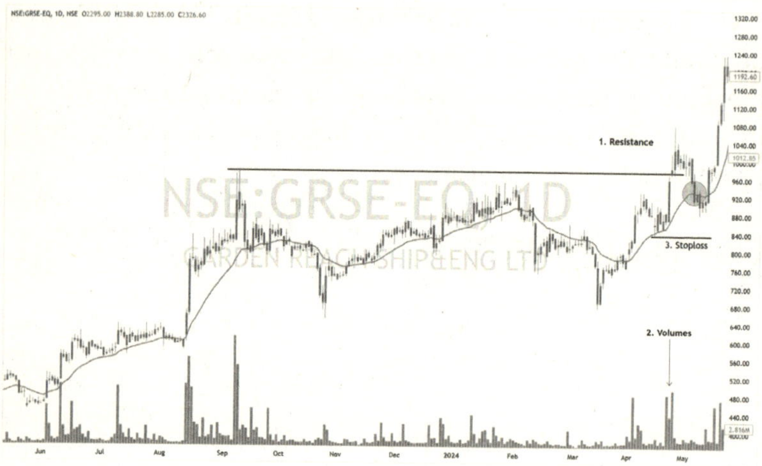

IMAGE 8.6: A daily chart of GRSE

1. The price of GRSE breaks the resistance line at 974.
2. The breakout is backed by heavy volumes.
3. The stop-loss for the trade is the recent low at 834. The risk of the trade is 140 points.
4. The trailing stop-loss on EMA(20) is hit at 933. The loss on the trade is 41 points.

- Loss = 41 points

How do you identify fake breakouts?

Even though the breakout volume is high, traders must also consider the candle formation. If we look closely, the breakout candles in GRSE (Image 8.6) were indecisive. By the end of day, sellers were able to push the price lower, showing some control, which could hint that the breakout was not strong. Therefore, traders must look for decisive bullish candles in a breakout where the price closes near the day's high.

But let us take another case study of GRSE (Image 8.7) and see what happens after our stop-loss is hit.

Case Study 6 – GRSE

IMAGE 8.7: A daily chart of GRSE

1. After hitting the stop-loss of 41 points, GRSE (Image 8.7) forms an RTEP pattern. The fake breakout was followed by hitting the stop-loss. Even though the price came down to hit the stop-loss, volumes were negligible compared to breakout volumes.
2. The whole selling is negated in 4 candles with heavy volumes, giving a breakout from the RTEP pattern with the entry price at 1082 (Image 8.8).

3. The stop-loss at EMA(20) is at 950. The risk of the trade is 132 points.
4. Trade hits the trailing stop-loss on EMA(20) at 1240. The profit of the trade is 152 points in 12 days.

- Risk = 130 points
- Reward = 152 points

Why are we taking a trade again, even when our first trade hit a stop-loss?

As a trader, we deal with winning probabilities and risk management, and we cannot be right 100% of the time. We will win some trades and lose some trades.

Secondly, technical analysis of stock prices is the study of human behavior, and it takes years of practice to master it, and even then, there are factors out of our control. We might make a mistake, or the price might fall due to some news or unforeseen reason, etc. That is why we follow proper risk management. If a trade is signalled by our system, as traders, we must take it. After that, we have to let the trade run systematically and let the probabilities, risk management, and position sizing work in our favor.

Remember, the journey to trading profits is not (1000 + 3000 + 2000 + 4000 + 1000 = 11,000), but rather (-2000 + 4000 + 1000 + 0 - 2000 + 6000 + 4000 = 11,000).

What happens when we let the trade run systematically? Let us look at Case Study 7 of GRSE (Image 8.8) and see what happens.

Case Study 7 – GRSE

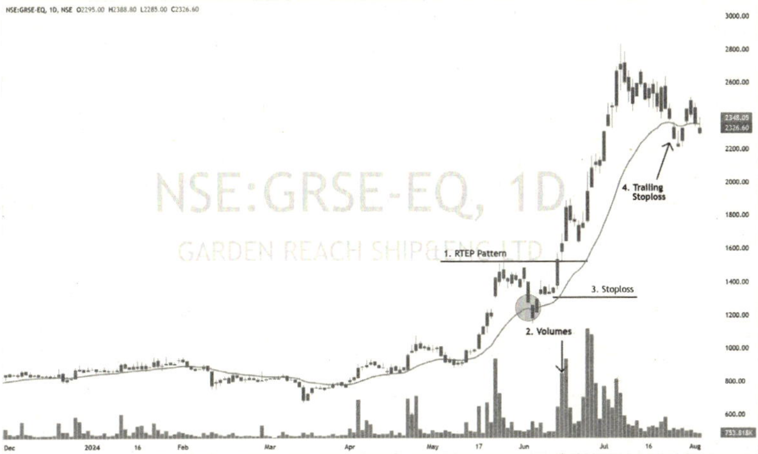

IMAGE 8.8: A daily chart of GRSE

1. In Case Study 6, we were stopped out with a profit of 152 points from the trade. GRSE (Image 8.8) formed an RTEP pattern once again. Even though we were stopped out in the previous trade, the selling volumes were negligible.
2. In the current RTEP pattern, observe how the selling that stopped us out is negated in 3-5 candles with heavy volumes, giving a breakout from the RTEP pattern with an entry price at 1515 once again.
3. The stop-loss at the recent low is at 1320. The risk of the trade is 195 points.
4. The trade hits the trailing stop-loss on EMA(20) at 2360. The profit of the trade is 840 points in 28 days.

- Risk = 195 points
- Reward = 840 points

What do case studies 5, 6, and 7 on GRSE tell us?

Case studies 5, 6, and 7 demonstrate the importance of following a trading system which, in this case, is breakout trading.

But along with that, we must understand that while, with experience, traders can learn to avoid fake breakouts to some extent, no trader can avoid 100% of all fake breakouts.

As a trader, we can only manage the risk. The reward is always unknown. We started the GRSE trade with a loss of 41 points, but following the system, our three trades resulted in a net profit of (-41 + 152 + 840) = 951 points.

The most effective breakouts are the ones that break out in the direction of the existing trend, or break out after an extended duration. Longer consolidation results in a much stronger breakout, just like a spring.

Regarding the timeframe, there is no ideal timeframe to trade breakouts. Breakouts work for both intraday and swing trading. It just alters the trade and target duration on the given timeframe. Every stock or instrument has a different way of moving, which can be understood from its past behavior. Only after getting some experience will you understand whether a specific stock is ideal for a breakout or not.

The concepts shared here are not set in stone. Trading is a multi-dimensional discipline with various tools available to traders. The method discussed here works across all timeframes and markets. Finally, while the fundamental concepts remain the same, the application of these concepts defines the success or failure of each trading style.

Lastly, there is a fine difference between breakout trading, trend-following, and momentum trading. While the fundamental concepts of the market discussed in earlier chapters remains the same, it is the way we understand and use these fundamental building blocks that defines the success or failure of each trading style.

CHAPTER 9

Trend Trading

Trade with the trend, unless it bends

If breakout trading is about capturing the sudden imbalance in equilibrium, trend trading is riding the long-term trend. Every stock market wizard has made most of their money by following the one golden rule of the market; i.e., "trade with the trend". In this chapter, I am going to share with you exactly how to trade with the trend using exact entry, stop-loss, and exit rules.

In price action analysis, we understood the 4 phases of the market cycle: accumulation, markup, distribution, and markdown. Trend trading is all about buying a stock when it is in markup and selling it when it enters the distribution phase. If you look at any investor who made big money in the stock market, you will notice that they made their biggest money during the markup phase.

But an obvious question arises: if trend trading is so lucrative, why do market participants often fail to profit from it? There are two main reasons:

1. **Obsession with low-priced stocks:** Many traders have a fixation on buying stocks below a certain price. For example, if a trader has Rs. 50,000 to invest, they might look for stocks priced under Rs. 100 or even Rs. 20 (penny stocks). However, they need to understand that the price per share is irrelevant to the

overall investment value. Whether you buy a stock at Rs. 100 or Rs. 2500, it is the total investment value that matters.

2. **Buying cheap stocks during a downtrend:** Many market participants buy stocks during a downtrend, considering them cheap. However, they fail to grasp that 'quality comes at a price'. If a stock is truly valuable, it generally won't be in a prolonged downtrend. Furthermore, if a stock is in a downtrend or its accumulation phase, it can remain in that zone for months or even years, delaying any potential profits. A strong-performing company is typically reflected in a higher stock price. If a stock price is significantly depressed, it often indicates underlying issues within the company that might not be publicly known but are impacting its price.

To illustrate my point, I'll share two examples with you:

SUZLON: In 2007, Suzlon (Image 9.1) was trading at an all-time high of ₹420. However, during the recession, the stock price plummeted and entered a prolonged markdown phase. By 2022, the stock had crashed to as low as ₹3. It was only after the central government's push for renewable energy from 2014 that the stock started to recover.

MRF: In 2000, the stock price of MRF (Image 9.2) was ₹2,000. Fast forward to 2024, and the stock is trading at ₹1,36,000.

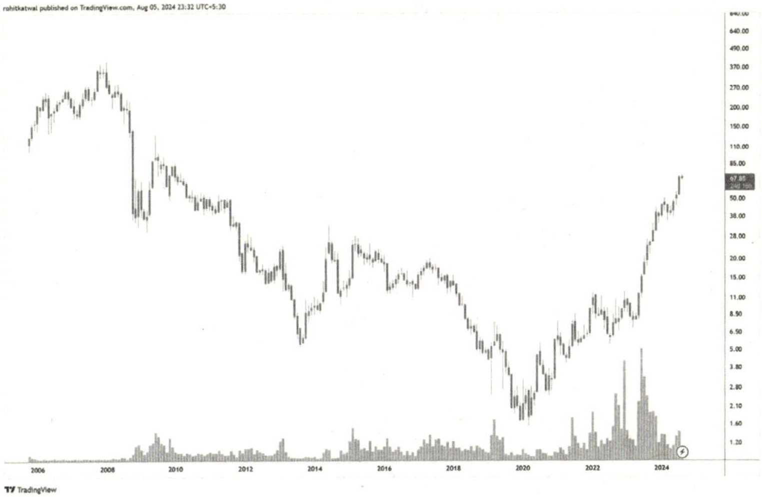

IMAGE 9.1: A monthly chart of SUZLON (log scale)

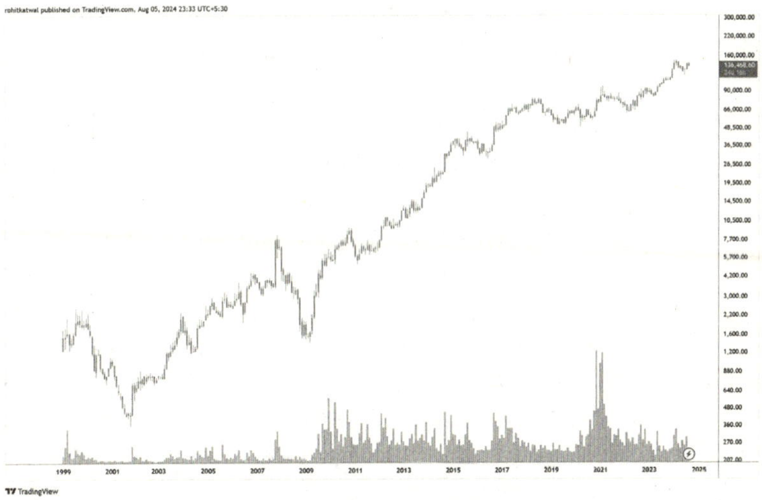

IMAGE 9.2: A monthly chart of MRF (log scale)

These two charts illustrate a fundamental concept that new traders often fail to grasp and struggle with in the markets: the importance of quality and trends. While SUZLON suffered a massive decline due to underlying issues and market conditions, MRF's stock consistently appreciated, reflecting the company's strong performance and market position. In a nutshell:

There is a limit to which a stock price can fall (i.e., 0), but there is no limit to what extent a stock price can rise.

Therefore, in trend-following, we buy the stock that is in an uptrend (markup phase) and exit when the trend ends (distribution phase). Trend-following is about buying stocks that perform for a longer duration, weathering the market volatility.

How to identify the markup phase

Stocks that have outperformed the market in the long term usually show a few common signs before a big trending move starts. Here are the key indicators:

1. **Price near 52-week high:** Stocks trading within 25% of their 52-week high are strong candidates. The nearer, the better.
2. **Significant price increase:** Stocks trading at least 30% above their 52-week low are worth considering.
3. **Above moving averages:** Stocks trading above major exponential moving averages (e.g., 20, 50, 100, 150, 200) show strong momentum.

This scanner helps identify potential stocks in a definite uptrend. However, identifying the long-term trend's actual start is crucial. One of our criteria is stocks near their 52-week high. But why does a 52-week breakout hold such significance in trading?

When a stock reaches a 52-week high, traders who bought at that price and have been stuck ever since may try to exit at breakeven prices. This selling pressure can hold the stock back temporarily. Once these weak holders are out, the price can finally break out and start a new long-term trend. We use price action analysis to identify the optimum entry point and stop-loss for trend trading.

Similarly, a significant price increase indicates that the stock has successfully bottomed out from the consolidation phase but is still within 25% of its 52-week high range. This condition ensures that the stock price has yet to reflect its true market value and will eventually catch up. Often, companies face hurdles around their 52-week high, causing the stock price to stagnate for several months despite the company continuing to operate, make profits, and expand. This growth and profitability are not immediately reflected in the stock price. However, once the 52-week high is broken, the stock price catches up to reflect the company's true value. Trading above a previously established 52-week high also suggests that the company has overcome the obstacles it faced when the price last reached this level and is back on a growth trajectory. Remember, it is the horizontal break of a price level that matters. An all-time high must be broken for the price to move further upward, and there is no limit to how high it can go.

The moving averages of 20, 50, 100, 150, and 200 days are essential for confirming a bullish trend across various timeframes. The 20-day moving average captures the short-term trend, reflecting price movements over the past month. The 50-day moving average offers insight into the trend over the past quarter, while the 100-day and 150-day moving averages cover six months and roughly three quarters, respectively. Finally, the 200-day moving average represents a full year of trading activity. As these moving averages increase in length, they provide a broader perspective on the trend's strength and sustainability. When shorter-term moving averages (e.g., 20-day) are above longer-term ones (e.g., 200-day), it confirms that the trend is bullish across all timeframes, with each successive moving average reinforcing the trend's strength and consistency.

Trade setup

1. **Price above moving averages**: The price should be above the 20, 50, 100, 150, and 200-day moving

averages, indicating a bullish trend across short to long-term perspectives.

2. **Sequential moving averages**: Ensure the moving averages are in a bullish sequence: 20-day > 50-day > 100-day > 150-day > 200-day. This alignment confirms a consistent upward trend through increasing timeframes.
3. **Chart pattern breakout with volume**: Look for a breakout from a chart pattern accompanied by increased trading volume. This combination signifies strong momentum and validates the trend's strength.
4. **Timeframe**: Focus on daily or weekly charts to ensure the trend is well-established and to avoid the noise of shorter timeframes.
5. **Stop-loss**: An aggressive stop-loss for a trade setup is a moving average of 50. Conservative traders can keep a stop-loss at MA(100).

For the purpose of these case studies, we will consider the stop-loss at a moving average of 100.

Case Study 1 – NESTLEIND

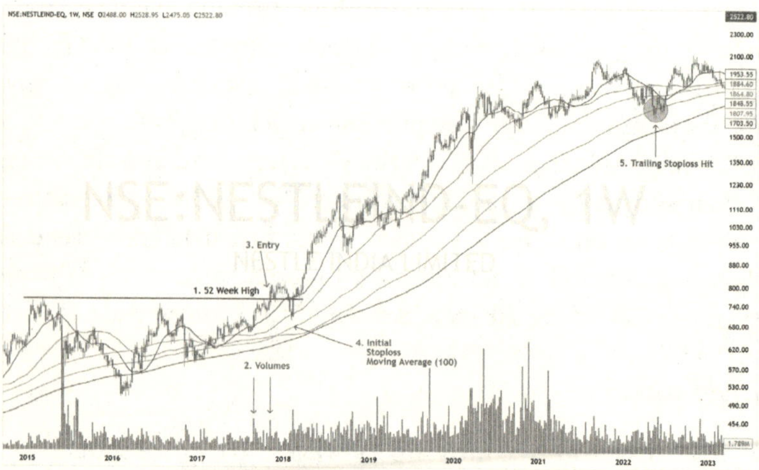

IMAGE 9.3: Weekly chart of NESTLEIND

1. In March 2015, NESTLEIND reached a high of ₹750.50. This level remained unbreached until October 2017.
2. Whenever the price approached the 52-week high of ₹750.50, it faced selling pressure, likely due to profit-booking or weak buyers trying to exit their positions.
3. In October 2017, the price decisively broke above the 52-week high with significant volume. (Refer to Image 9.3 for the weekly chart of NESTLEIND.)
4. For a long-term trend-following trade, a stop-loss was placed at the 100-day moving average (MA100) of ₹665.
5. Despite occasional pullbacks, NESTLEIND's price continued to rise, hitting the trailing stop-loss at ₹1670 in May 2022. Remarkably, NESTLEIND did not hit the stop-loss even during the COVID-19 crash. Traders benefited not only from the stock price appreciation but also from the dividends paid by the company.

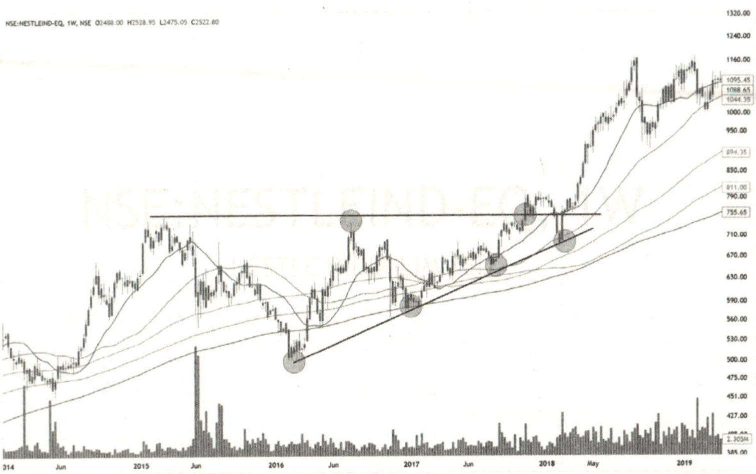

IMAGE 9.4: A volatility contraction pattern (VCP) on NESTLEIND

Volatility Contraction Pattern (VCP)

NESTLEIND's price action exemplifies the volatility contraction pattern (VCP). After reaching the 52-week high of ₹750.50, the stock repeatedly approached this level but faced selling pressure each time. Despite this, buying pressure negated the selling, resulting in a series of higher lows (HL) and a period of price consolidation.

This consolidation created a VCP, where the price contraction acted like a coiled spring. Patterns such as triangles (ascending, descending) and cup-and-handle formations are classic examples of VCPs. As the price contracts, it eventually breaks out with increased volume, indicating a strong bullish trend.

In NESTLEIND's case, this breakout was supported by heavy volumes, confirming the trend and validating the VCP as a reliable signal for identifying trending stocks. (Refer to Image 9.4 for the VCP on NESTLEIND.)

Case Study 2 – CUMMINSIND

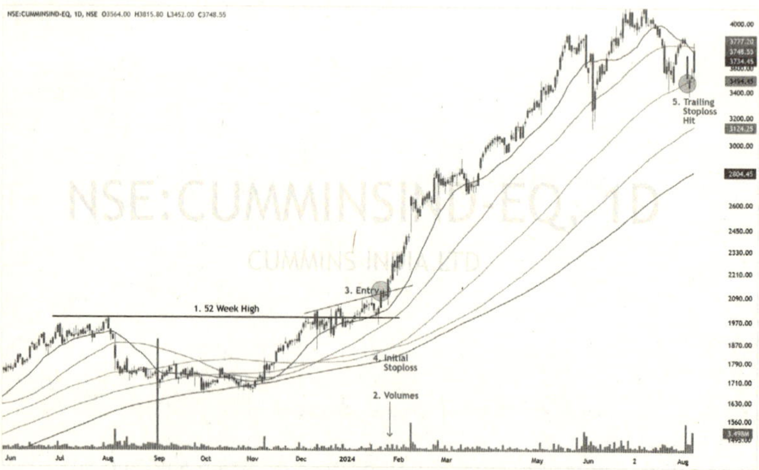

IMAGE 9.5: A daily chart of CUMMINSIND

1. CUMMINSIND traded sideways for 7 months, staying above its crucial moving averages but below the 52-week high. In January 2024, it started consolidating at this level.
2. The price began to break out above the 52-week high consolidation level at ₹2105.
3. Volumes increased significantly with the upward move.
4. The initial stop-loss for the bullish trend-following entry was set at the 100-day moving average (MA100) of ₹1830.
5. The price hit the trailing stop-loss in August 2024 after 7 months at ₹3400, resulting in a 60% gain.

Case Study 3 – BPCL

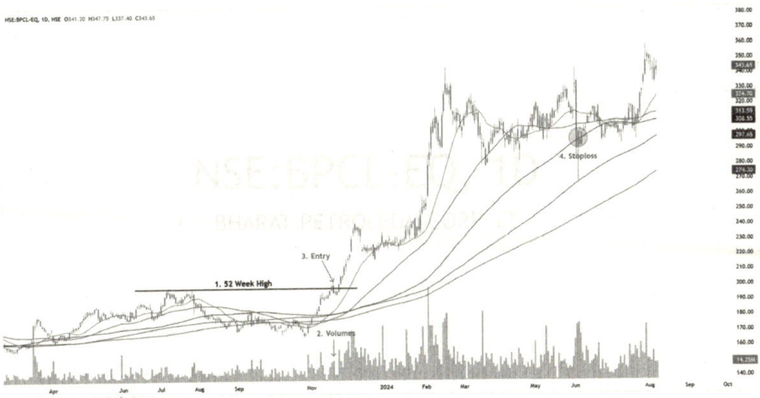

IMAGE 9.6: A daily chart of BPCL

1. BPCL (Image 9.6) started trading above its 20, 50, 100, 150, and 200-day moving averages, breaking its 52-week high in November 2023.
2. Volumes increased as the price moved up.
3. The entry for the trend trade was at ₹198, with an initial stop-loss at MA100 of ₹183.

4. BPCL hit the trailing stop-loss in June 2024 at ₹298, generating a 50% profit within 7 months.

Case Study 4 – NTPC

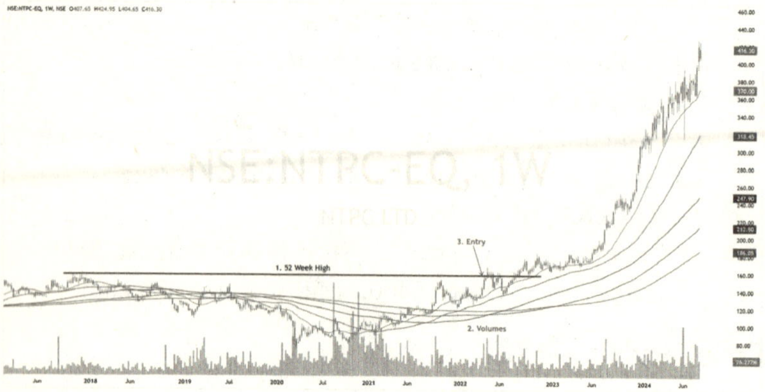

IMAGE 9.7: A weekly chart of NTPC

1. In April 2022, NTPC (Image 9.7) broke the 52-week high, trading above all crucial moving averages.
2. The breakout above the 52-week high was supported by heavy volumes at ₹158, with a stop-loss for the trade at ₹120 (MA100).
3. NTPC formed a proper volatility contraction pattern around the 52-week high (refer to Image 9.8).
4. The trend-following trade on NTPC is currently trading at ₹416 and hasn't hit a trailing stop-loss yet.

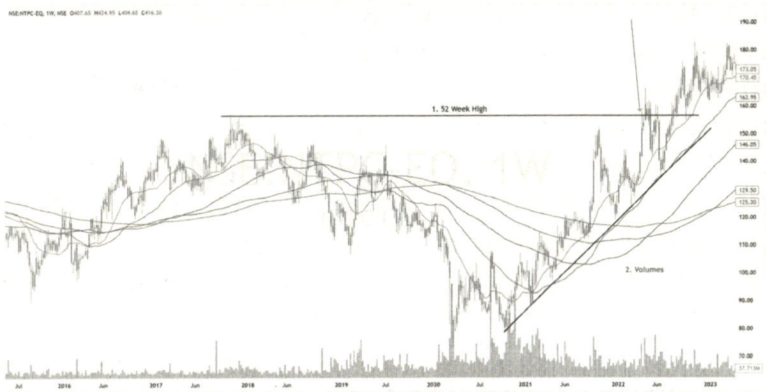

IMAGE 9.8: A volatility contraction pattern on NTPC at a 52-week high

Stop-Loss and Strategy Considerations

All these trades might have resulted in higher profits if the stop-loss was set at MA50. It's up to individual traders to decide which stop-loss method best suits their trading appetite. While different moving averages might seem to offer better returns at times, it's advisable to stick to one systematic approach. As traders, we cannot foresee which stop-loss method will be optimal for every situation. Each stop-loss method has its pros and cons, so maintaining a consistent strategy is the best decision.

This trend-following strategy is simple, time-tested, and its accuracy lies in trading larger timeframes. It is suitable for swing traders, working professionals, or investors seeking better returns from the market. However, it is not a holy grail strategy and might require tweaks based on individual preferences. It is not a blind buy-and-hold strategy. If the profit target is significant, then so is the stop-loss, which might require smaller position sizing. Diversification also plays a key role in overall profitability. I have used this strategy to allocate 3% to 5% of the total portfolio to a single stock, diversifying across 15 to 20 stocks.

The difficulty with the strategy is not in its execution but in adhering to it consistently day in and day out. When working with larger timeframes on daily or weekly charts, checking your portfolio daily might not show significant positive changes, and you might even see occasional losses. In worst-case scenarios, such as investing just before the housing market crash of 2009 or the COVID-19 crash of 2019, the strategy might give negative returns. Therefore, it is advised that traders thoroughly backtest the strategy to understand its risk management, winning probability, and whether it suits them or not.

The method that I have discussed for trend-following is one that I personally use, and this is not the only method that can be used for trend-following. I have seen traders who are following trend trading in a much better way through Bollinger Bands, Trend Lines, RSI, Darvas Boxes, etc. Ultimately, it will depend on the individual trader to decide the method best suitable for him/her. The best way to do that is experimentation, and that experimentation should be through paper trading, backtesting platforms, or with the least amount of money that keeps you engaged, and that you can afford to lose as a part of the learning process.

Remember, successful trend trading is not about predicting the future, but capitalizing on the present momentum. By understanding market cycles and employing disciplined strategies, traders can position themselves to ride the wave of market trends and achieve consistent profitability.

With that said, let's move to the next chapter and move away from breakout and trend trading towards momentum trading.

CHAPTER 10

Momentum Trading

Identify the trend early, capitalize on its momentum, and exit before it fades

Momentum trading is like attending a party. If the party starts at 7 p.m., you don't need to be the first one there, waiting around awkwardly before things get going. Instead, you can arrive around 8 p.m., when the music is playing, the drinks are flowing, and the energy is high. You'll enjoy yourself while the party is in full swing, and leave before it winds down.

Momentum trading works similarly. You enter a stock when its momentum has already begun, riding the wave as it gains strength, and exit before the momentum fades. For example, if a stock is rising from 100 to 200, it's not crucial to capture the initial rise from 100 to 120 or the final push from 180 to 200. Your goal is to catch the bulk of the move, from 125 to 175, when the trend is strong, and the 'party' is in full swing.

Catching the major swing has two main benefits:

1. You enter a stock when it has a higher probability of moving in your direction immediately.
2. You avoid the consolidation or accumulation phase, which can be lengthy and unproductive. By trading momentum, you can bypass the waiting period and allocate the same capital to other momentum opportunities.

When a stock is in a sideways zone, it might not be incurring a loss, but it isn't generating a profit either, which incurs an opportunity cost. With momentum trading, we capitalize on the immediate momentum and exit once it fades

Take GRANULES (Image 10.1), for example. It moved 40% in 33 trading days. This is what momentum looks like. The moment we enter a trade, it should either fail with a very small stop-loss or start moving up, giving constant profit. We exit the trade when the stop-loss is hit or the momentum fades.

In momentum trading, hitting a stop-loss is not a problem, but wasting time is. Don't get me wrong: losses are part of the game. But when we are specifically doing momentum trading, our trade should move, or hit a stop-loss, or we should exit at a breakeven.

IMAGE 10.1: Daily chart of GRANULES

In trend trading, we might have to endure sideways zones, and that's okay. When trend trading, our mindset is such that we're prepared for the occasional sideways days, which are inevitable. But the mechanics are different for a momentum trade.

Another thing traders must understand is that momentum trading is the toughest aspect of trading. The market is trending only 30% of the time and is sideways 70% of the time. Accurately predicting the 30% zone, when the market is in momentum, requires world-class trading skills and a lot of practice and experience. It will require a lot of backtesting and tweaks around risk management and position sizing before a trader can hit a sweet spot in momentum trading that works for them. Most of all, the fundamental idea behind any strategy, be it trend, breakout, or momentum, has to be conceptually strong. In my personal experience, momentum trading has a winning probability of around 45-55% with a 1:3 or 1:4 risk/reward ratio, which improves as we protect our profits with a trailing stop-loss.

IMAGE 10.2: A daily chart of BAJAJ-AUTO with strong momentum

Traders employ various methods to capitalize on momentum. My approach involves using daily or weekly charts and incorporates:

1. Price action
2. Williams Alligator
3. MACD indicator

Momentum trading is always conducted in the direction of the overall market trend. For instance, if major market indices are bearish, we should avoid looking for bullish momentum trades on stocks within those indices. For example, if the NIFTY PHARMA index is sideways or bearish, trades on PHARMA stocks with a bullish outlook should be avoided, as they go against the sector trend. Similarly, if NIFTY, BANKNIFTY, or SENSEX are bearish, then bullish momentum trades should be avoided. Remember the golden rule:

Trade with the trend.

To identify the market trend, use daily charts of major indices with a Williams Alligator plotted. The Alligator's 'jaws', 'teeth', and 'lips' provide insight into the trend's direction:

1. If the jaws, teeth, and lips are opening upwards and the price is above the Alligator, the trend is bullish.
2. If the jaws, teeth, and lips are opening downwards and the price is below the Alligator, the trend is bearish.
3. If the jaws, teeth, and lips are criss-crossing, the trend is sideways.

We can capitalize on momentum when a stock is in an established uptrend or emerging from a long consolidation with a strong move signalling a trend change.

IMAGE 10.3: A daily chart of NIFTY with a Williams Alligator

IMAGE 10.4: A daily chart of NIFTY with a Williams Alligator

The Williams Alligator is a modified version of moving averages, smoothed and extending slightly into the future. Essentially, it's a moving average indicator. When the price trades above the Alligator, it indicates that market participants are willing to pay above the average price, suggesting a bullish scenario. In a sideways market, prices tend to revert to the mean—prices go up and come down or vice versa, bringing the price back to equilibrium.

So, how do we identify high-probability momentum trades? Look for instances where the lowest price of a candle is completely outside the Williams Alligator—meaning the low of the candle does not even touch the lips line. This suggests buyers have taken control. If the following candles (let's say 6 in total) also remain completely outside the Alligator *and the price action shows that the closing price is consistently towards the higher end of the range for the last several candles,* it indicates strong bullish momentum.

Consider this: If the price remains completely outside the Williams Alligator for six consecutive candles (days or weeks), and each closing price is near the average high of those six candles, it signifies that buyers are exerting such strong control that they haven't allowed the price to revert to the mean. If volumes increase during this period, it further confirms the strength of the bullish momentum. Even if volumes are low, it suggests a lack of selling pressure.

This criterion satisfies three conditions for a momentum trade:

1. The price action is bullish.
2. The Williams Alligator is bullish.
3. Volume conditions are favorable.

We also check whether, based on our price action analysis, the price is already in an established uptrend, or the price is breaking out strongly from an extended consolidation.

Lastly, we check the MACD indicator. If the MACD line is greater than the signal line and the MACD is trading above the 0 line, our setup is complete. As already discussed in chapter on technical indicators, the price gets really bullish when the MACD line starts trading above the 0 line.

- **Stop-loss:** The initial and trailing stop-loss for the trade can be at the Alligator's teeth.

- **Target:** The target or exit for the trade shall be the price closing below the Alligator's teeth or the crossover of MACD line below the signal line.

Now that we understand the setup and the rationale behind it, let us see some case studies.

Case Study 1 – SHYAMMETL

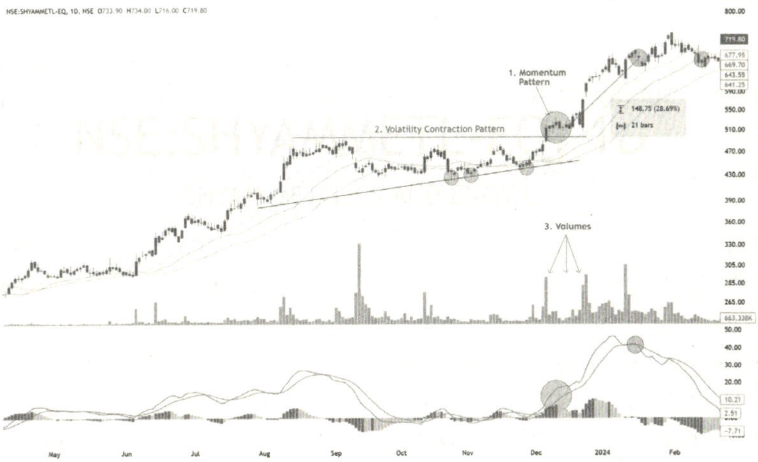

IMAGE 10.5: A daily chart of SHYAMMETL

1. On 12 December 2023, SHYAMMETL (Image 10.5) started forming a bullish candle pattern that was suitable for a momentum trade.
2. The bullish candle pattern coincides with the breakout of a volatility contraction pattern.
3. The breakout was confirmed by significant trading volumes, suggesting strong participation by market participants.
4. The initial stop-loss is placed at the teeth of the Alligator (a moving average line from the Williams Alligator indicator).

5. The trailing stop-loss is when the MACD line crosses below the signal line, signalling a potential reversal.

The trade resulted in a 28% gain in 21 trading days through momentum trading.

Traders must understand the psychology of the market participants at this point. The volatility contraction pattern was already forming, signalling a period of consolidation where price volatility decreases. As the breakout approached, market participants started buying in heavy volumes, showing strong conviction in the stock's upward potential. The price candles began trading continuously outside the Williams Alligator indicator, suggesting a strong, sustained trend. Additionally, the MACD started trading above the signal line and the 0 line, confirming bullish momentum and further supporting the case for a strong upward move.

Once the breakout occurred, small candles began to form with negligible volume, indicating a lack of participation from sellers. This suggested that the sellers were not actively involved, allowing buyers to dominate and push the price higher. Finally, market participants resumed buying SHYAMMETL with heavy volumes, driving the stock price further up.

There are two ways to exit the momentum trade. The first method is to exit when the MACD line crosses below the signal line. This type of exit is slightly aggressive and captures the bulk of the movement, providing a timely exit with a substantial profit. In the case of SHYAMMETL, this strategy resulted in a 28% gain over 21 trading days. The second method is to exit when the stop-loss hits the trailing stop-loss set at the Alligator's teeth, a moving average line from the Williams Alligator indicator. This method is more conservative and allows the trade to remain open longer, potentially capturing more extended trends. If used in the SHYAMMETL trade, it would have resulted in the same profit percentage but over a longer period (39 bars).

The key difference between these two exit strategies is the duration of the trade. The aggressive exit captured the profit in a shorter period, while the conservative exit took longer, representing an opportunity cost as the capital could have been deployed in other trades during this time. As traders cannot foresee future opportunities, it is wise to use one system consistently for exiting trades to avoid missed opportunities or prolonged holding periods. Understanding the psychology of market participants and recognizing the significance of volume surges and price patterns is essential for making informed trading decisions and achieving successful trades.

Case Study 2 – LICI

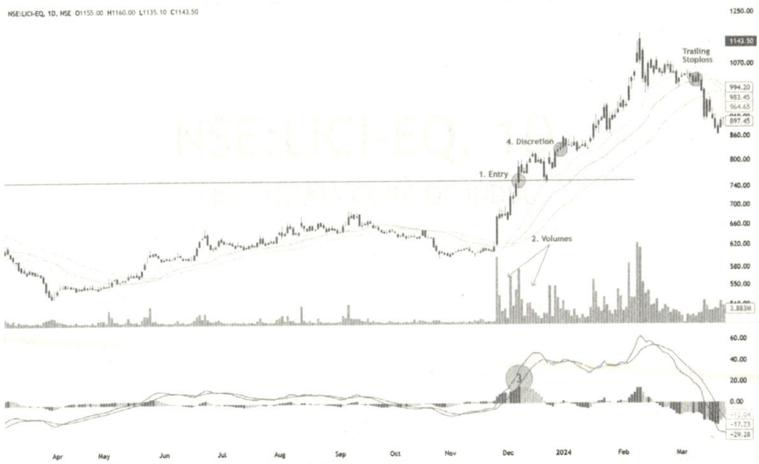

IMAGE 10.6: A daily chart of LICI

In December 2023, LICI (Image 10.6) started appearing on our momentum trading filter.

1. The price broke out from a 52-week high, with the last six candles completely above the Williams Alligator, and not a single low touching the lips.
2. The breakout was supported by significant heavy volumes.
3. The MACD line was trading above the signal line and above the 0 line, indicating a new trend.

4. Traders could either cover the trade when the MACD line crossed below the signal line or use a trailing stop-loss, which was hit in the first week of March 2024.

The trade resulted in a 6% gain using the MACD crossover as the stop-loss and a 28% gain using the trailing stop-loss at the Alligator's teeth.

Discretion defined: At times, the MACD crossover will generate an earlier exit, resulting in better profits, while other times the Alligator's teeth will provide better returns. This is why traders are advised to follow one system consistently.

That said, observe the pattern formed when the MACD line crossed below the signal line:

1. The price pulled back to the Alligator's lips and bounced back within three candles, indicating that buyers remain strong and that it's not a clear exit signal.
2. Except for one pullback candle, the other six candles were completely outside the Alligator, indicating continued strong price action.
3. The volume of the pullback was negligible, indicating a lack of selling pressure.

Experienced traders leverage their comprehensive understanding of price action to their advantage. Good trading results from following rules, but experience teaches when it might be wise to deviate from them.

Case Study 3 – MOTHERSON

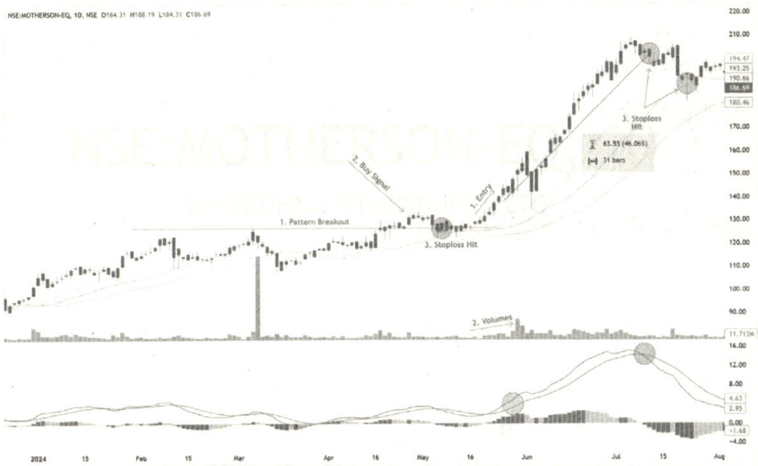

IMAGE 10.7: A daily chart of MOTHERSON

MOTHERSON (Image 10.7) exemplifies the importance of following a trading system without letting emotions interfere.

On 26 April 2024, MOTHERSON started appearing on our daily charts via the momentum filter. The stock met all the criteria for a momentum trade:

1. It broke an all-time high. Volumes were insignificant, indicating an absence of sellers.
2. The MACD line was crossing above the signal line and above the 0 line. The price was completely above the Williams Alligator.
3. Despite these positive signals, the trade resulted in a 5% loss.

On 23 May 2024, MOTHERSON reappeared on the momentum trading filter:

1. The stock had six consecutive bullish candles outside the Williams Alligator.

2. The MACD line crossed above the signal line and was trading above the 0 line with increasing volumes.

With a stop-loss at the MACD line crossover below the signal line, the trade resulted in a 50% profit in 25 days. With a trailing stop-loss at the Alligator's teeth, the trade resulted in a 46% profit in 31 days.

Case Study 4 – VEDL

If you examine the historical charts of VEDL (Image 10.8), you will see that it was consolidating for the last two years.

1. On April 3, 2024, the stock broke its 52-week high and started appearing on the momentum filter.
2. On April 3, 2024, VEDL broke out above its 52-week high. The entry candle, according to our momentum price action, where six candles outside the Williams Alligator never touched any of the lines, formed on April 8, 2024.
3. The breakout was supported by heavy volumes.

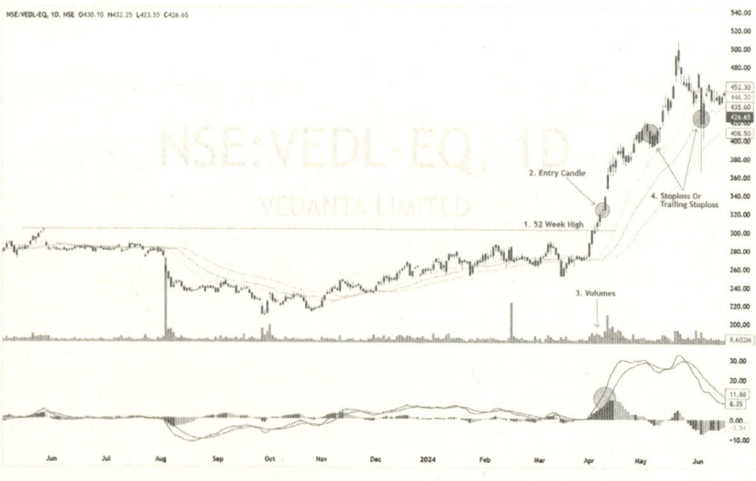

IMAGE 10.8: A daily chart of VEDL

With the MACD line crossing below the signal line as the stop-loss, VEDL gained 24% in 20 days. Using a trailing stop-loss at the Alligator's teeth, VEDL achieved a gain of 30% in 28 days.

Case Study 5 – INFIBEAM

Let's delve into another case study with INFIBEAM (Image 10.9) to highlight a crucial aspect of the momentum trading strategy.

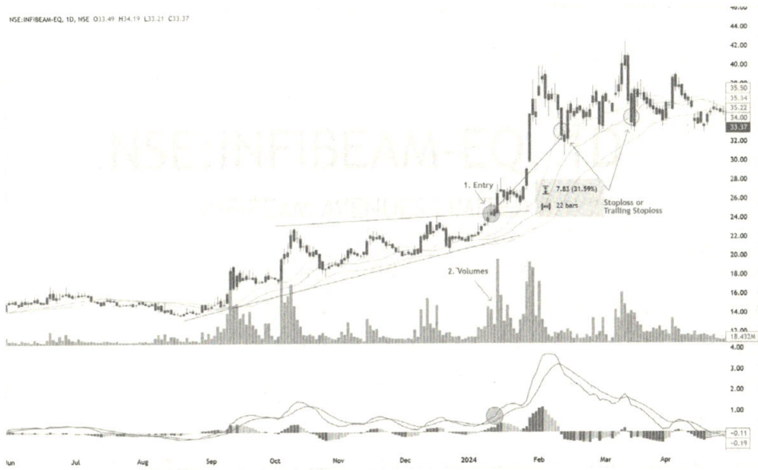

IMAGE 10.9: A daily chart of INFIBEAM

1. INFIBEAM formed a volatility contraction pattern above its 52-week high. From January 3 to January 10, it created a momentum price pattern where all six candles closed outside Williams Alligator and broke out of the volatility contraction pattern.
2. The breakout was supported by heavy volumes.
3. The MACD line was above the signal line and above the 0 line.

Within 22 days, INFIBEAM achieved a profit of 32% when considering the stop-loss according to the MACD condition. If the stop-loss was based on the Alligator's teeth, the gain would have been 39% in 43 trading days.

Important: One crucial aspect to observe in INFIBEAM is that before breaking out of the volatility contraction pattern and above the 52-week high, it formed a momentum trading pattern through six candles completely outside the Williams Alligator. However, it missed one essential condition: the closing prices of the six candles should be towards the average high of those six candles. This means that successive candles, if not closing at the high, should at least be near the average high of the six candles. This indicates that market participants are closing the price at a position of strength rather than weakness.

Many of the examples discussed in trend and momentum trading are trades taken in live markets on various platforms like YouTube and *The Economic Times.* During this time, major indices were trading above the Williams Alligator, satisfying the bullish condition for the market. Unlike trend-following, where the focus is on following the trend regardless of pullbacks, in momentum trading, it is essential to take bullish momentum trades only when the broader market is also bullish. If the broader indices are bearish or sideways, it is not advisable to take bullish momentum trades.

With that said, momentum trading is one of the most difficult forms of trading and requires experience and practice. Therefore, before applying these methods in the live market, do a comprehensive backtest and analyze what works for you. A system should be backtested in all market conditions to actually gauge whether it works or not. I have seen traders learn about strategies and directly implement them in the market, which is wrong. Apart from signals from price action or indicators, there are subconscious signals from the market, which comes with experience.

Practice is key.

CHAPTER 11

Case Studies

Real-life case studies

Trading is more than simply buying and selling stocks; it's about understanding the underlying psychology reflected in price movements. While strategy is crucial, the unpredictable nature of the market, influenced by countless known and unknown factors, highlights the importance of probability and risk management in achieving long-term success.

The principles outlined in previous chapters represent the foundation of my trading approach, honed over 15 years of experience. I'll now share several case studies of stocks I've analyzed and discussed publicly to illustrate how these principles are applied in real-world scenarios. You'll notice that each case study is a combination of the fundamental concepts we've covered.

Case Study 1 – DREDGECORP

DREDGECORP (Image 11.1) broke out of a volatility contraction pattern with high volumes. The MACD indicator confirmed a bullish trend, and a momentum trading pattern was also formed. As a result, the stock price rose by 38% over 38 trading days.

IMAGE 11.1: A daily chart of DREDGECORP

Cast Study 2 – TATAPOWER

TATAPOWER (Image 11.2) broke out to an all-time high with a momentum trading pattern supported by heavy volumes. The MACD line was above the signal line and the zero line, confirming the bullish trend. As a result, the price gained 23% in 46 days.

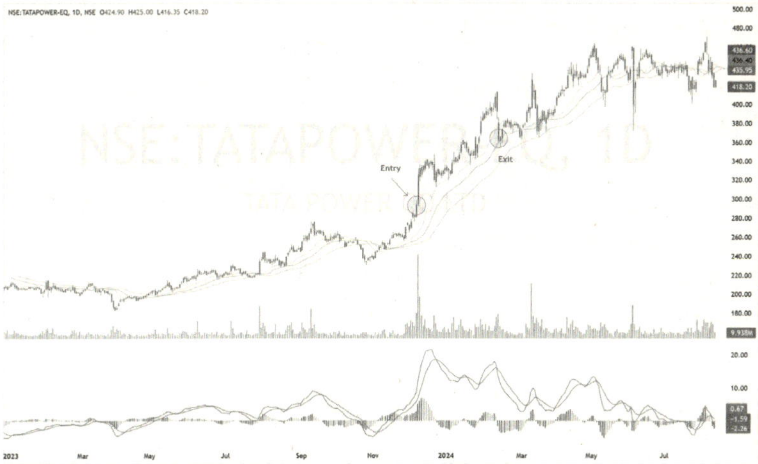

IMAGE 11.2: A daily chart of TATAPOWER

Case Study 3 – INDUSTOWER

INDUSTOWER (Image 11.3) broke out of its 52-week high with heavy volumes, indicating a strong move. The price is above all major moving averages, suggesting the beginning of a long-term trend. Over 150 days, the price has gained 103% and continues to trend upwards.

IMAGE 11.3: A daily chart of INDUSTOWER

Case Study 4 – JIOFIN

JIOFIN (Image 11.4) initially struggled to trade upward after its IPO, leading to a period of consolidation below its IPO price for 7 to 8 months. Eventually, it began to break its all-time high with a cup and handle pattern, which is a form of volatility contraction patterns. The price broke the all-time high with increased volume and was trading above all major moving averages. JIOFIN yielded a profit of 20% over 80 trading days before hitting a trailing stop-loss.

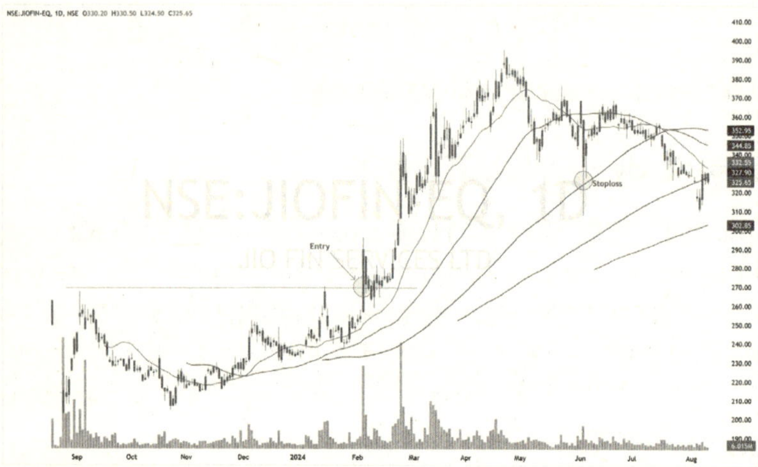

IMAGE 11.4: A daily chart of JIOFIN

Case Study 5 – POWERGRID

POWERGRID (Image 11.5) broke its 52-week high and initiated a new trend, with all major moving averages trending higher. Within 51 weeks, the stock gained 162%. The stock has not hit a trailing stop-loss yet.

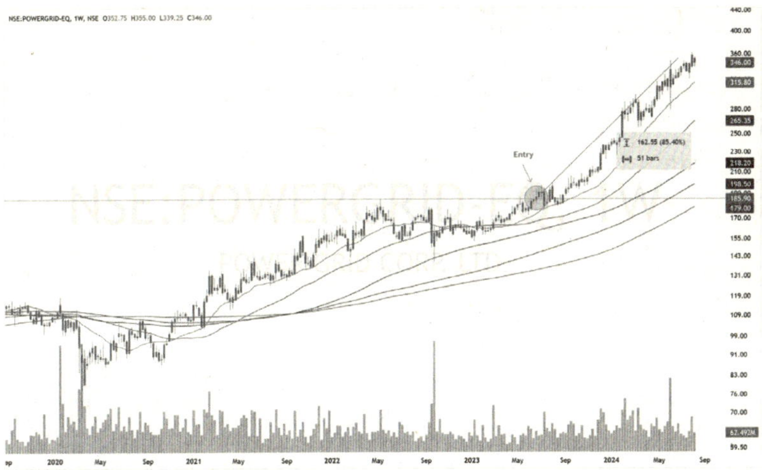

IMAGE 11.5: A weekly chart of POWERGRID

Case Study 6 – MGL

MGL (Image 11.6) broke out of its all-time high and a rectangle pattern, forming a momentum price pattern. The MACD line also crossed above the signal line and the 0 line. The breakout was backed by increased volume. In 60 trading days, the stock price gained 24%.

IMAGE 11.6: A daily chart of MGL

Case Study 7 – BASF

BASF (Image 11.7) broke out from its 52-week high with heavy volumes. All the major moving averages were trending higher, signifying a long-term trend. In 84 trading days, the stock gained 114%.

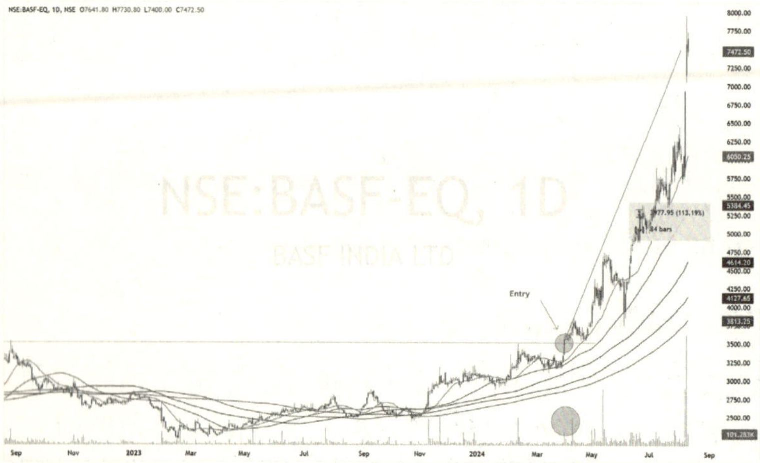

IMAGE 11.7: A daily chart of BASF

Case Study 8 – HAL

HAL (Image 11.8) broke out of its all-time high with heavy volumes following a period of low volume consolidation on weekly charts. All the major moving averages are trending higher. To date, the stock has not hit the trailing stop-loss, and in 136 weeks, HAL has risen by 534%. This exemplifies the power of trend-following.

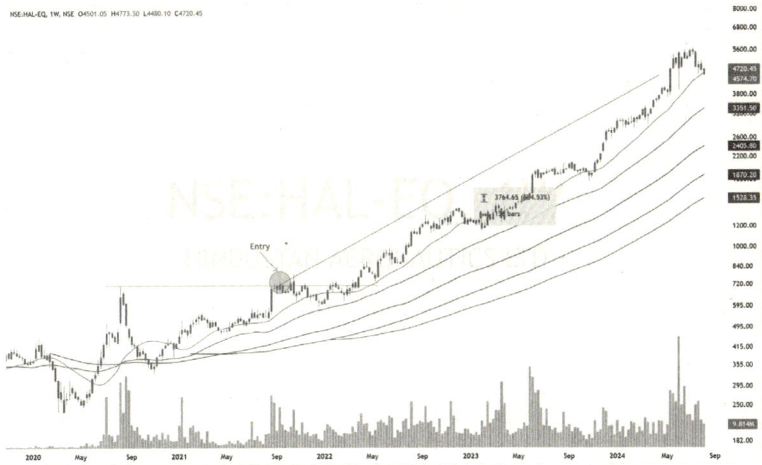

IMAGE 11.8: A weekly chart of HAL

These are just a few examples of trades that demonstrated the fundamentals shared in the previous chapters. Real money is not made in trading; real money is made in waiting for that perfect trade which matches all your trading criteria. When learning a new method, there is an urge to take a trade based on the new method; quench that urge and grasp the fundamentals discussed in this book patiently. Rome was not built in a day, but Hiroshima and Nagasaki were destroyed in a day. The same is true with trading. It is essential to learn and practice the strategies and ideas before implementation.

We have covered all the important topics of trading, but lastly, let's move on to the most important aspect of trading that you must follow:

Maintaining a trading journal.

CHAPTER 12

Trading Journal

Your trading journal is your biggest mentor

The trading journal is often the most underrated aspect of a trader's journey. While traders frequently seek mentors to guide them through their trading endeavours, what they truly need is a well-maintained trading journal.

In my own trading experience, I spent four years struggling with losses, jumping between various trading books and systems without much success. It wasn't until I began keeping a trading journal that I started to recognize and learn from my mistakes.

Just as you would log daily weights to track a weight-loss journey or document calorie intake while dieting, maintaining a trading journal is crucial for improving your trading performance. It's not about recording just a few trades here and there, but about diligently documenting every trade as it occurs.

By consistently noting down your trades, you'll begin to see patterns in your trading behavior. A trading journal doesn't require any specialized software; a simple Microsoft Excel spreadsheet can be highly effective. Before diving into live trading, consider starting with paper trading. This phase is challenging because the market's allure can tempt traders to deviate from their plans. However, resisting these temptations is what separates successful traders from the rest.

A well-maintained trading journal offers several benefits:

1. Identifying Trading Mistakes

Trading mistakes are inevitable, but a journal helps you pinpoint them and avoid repeating them. Many traders are unaware of their recurring errors until they review their documented trades. I've stressed this point before and will reiterate it here: many strategies that seem promising can turn out to be unprofitable. A trading journal helps you recognize and rectify these issues before they lead to real losses.

See Image 12.1 for a sample image of a trading journal.

	A	B	D	E	F	G	H	I	J	K	L	M	N	O	P	Q
1	NAME	:K	FUT/EQ/OPT	STRIKE	QTY	LOTS	B/S	ENTER	EXIT	BUY	SELL	BROK	P/L	Net Value	Day P/L	ROI
77																
78	SUN TV NETWORK LIMITED (XNSE:SUNTV)		SUNTV	EQ	184		BUY	13-Jun-24	08-Jul-24	759.55	₹ 772.85	648.51	1798.7	1,42,204.40		1.3
79	ADANI PORTS AND SPECIAL ECONOMIC ZONE LIMITEC		ADANIPORTS	EQ	100		BUY	14-May-24	13-Jun-24	1333.95	₹ 1,401.70	629.20	6145.8	1,40,170.00		4.4
80	MphasiS Limited (XNSE:MPHASIS)		MPHASIS	EQ	60		BUY	27-May-24	14-Jun-24	2434.95	₹ 2,445.60	673.52	-34.5	1,46,736.00		0.0
81	JIO FINANCIAL SERVICES LIMITED (XNSE:JIOFIN)		JIOFIN	EQ	554		BUY	27-May-24	21-Jun-24	360.85	₹ 364.40	924.11	1042.6	2,01,877.60		0.5
82	UNION BANK OF INDIA LIMITED (XNSE:UNIONBANK)		UNIONBANK	EQ	1243		BUY	03-Jun-24	21-Jun-24	160.9109	₹ 146.00	877.43	-19411.7	1,81,478.00		-10.7
83	AUROBINDO PHARMA LTD (XNSE:AUROPHARMA)		AUROPHARMA	EQ	162		BUY	23-May-24	24-Jun-24	1232.04	₹ 1,227.15	916.29	-1,708.47	1,98,798.30		-0.9
84	HINDUSTAN UNILEVER LIMITED (XNSE:HINDUNILVR)		HINDUNILVR	EQ	100		BUY	13-May-24	25-Jun-24	2361.418	₹ 2,438.15	1,103.90	6,569.30	2,43,815.00		2.7
85	ASIAN PAINTS LIMITED (XNSE:ASIANPAINT)		ASIANPAINT	EQ	100		BUY	03-May-24	27-Jun-24	2980	₹ 2,851.86	1,341.33	-14,155.33	2,85,186.00		-5.0
86	HINDALCO INDUSTRIES LIMITED (XNSE:HINDALCO)		HINDALCO	EQ	250		BUY	14-Jun-24	08-Jul-24	686.1	₹ 694.72	793.97	1,361.03	1,73,680.00		0.8
87	ASHOK LEYLAND LIMITED (XNSE:ASHOKLEY)		ASHOKLEY	EQ	1000		BUY	09-May-24	08-Jul-24	198.75	₹ 226.72	978.58	26,991.42	2,26,720.00		11.9
88	DR. LAL PATHLABS Limited (XNSE:LALPATHLAB)		LALPATHLAB	EQ	59		BUY	08-Jul-24	10-Jul-24	2929.55	₹ 2,910.55	792.50	-1,913.50	1,71,722.45		-1.1
89	Vedanta Limited (XNSE:VEDL)		VEDL	EQ	428		BUY	24-Jun-24	10-Jul-24	466.45	₹ 462.53	914.49	-2,592.25	1,97,962.84		-1.3
90	PIDILITE INDUSTRIES LIMITED (XNSE:PIDILITIND)		PIDILITIND	EQ	50		BUY	27-Jun-24	11-Jul-24	3154.06	₹ 3,160.25	726.15	-416.65	1,58,012.50		-0.3
91	BALKRISHNA INDUSTRIES LIMITED (XNSE:BALKRISIND)		BALKRISIND	EQ	60		BUY	28-May-24	12-Jul-24	3092.11	₹ 3,120.85	857.39	867.01	1,87,251.00		0.5
92	United Spirits Limited (XNSE:UNITDSPR)		UNITDSPR	EQ	160		BUY	09-May-24	16-Jul-24	1219.65	₹ 1,295.10	925.43	11,146.57	2,07,216.00		5.4
93	3M INDIA LIMITED (XNSE:3MINDIA)		3MINDIA	EQ	4		BUY	13-Jun-24	24-Jul-24	37913.75	₹ 38,444.55	702.50	1,420.70	1,53,778.20		0.9
94	ROUTE MOBILE LIMITED (XNSE:ROUTE)		ROUTE	EQ	143		BUY	25-Jun-24	24-Jul-24	1696	₹ 1,772.49	1,140.79	9,797.28	2,53,466.07		3.9
95	IVE GROUP LIMITED (XASX:IGL)		IGL	EQ	289		BUY	05-Jul-24	02-Aug-24	518.6	₹ 539.70	703.45	5,394.45	1,55,973.30		3.5
96																
97													32302.5			0.9

IMAGE 12.1: A sample trading journal

This is the minimum information that is needed in a trading journal. It includes the stock name, entry date, quantity, buy price, sell price, exit date, expected brokerage, net profit or loss, investment value, etc., but a trader can include any information that might be useful for analysis later.

For example, in the journal in Image 12.1, if I look at the profit figures, everything looks normal in column N, but rows 82 and 85 show losses of -19,411.7 and -14,155.33 respectively. This tells us that losses in these trades were quite significant and may prompt us to reflect on whether the losses were according to the trading system or not. Similarly, it also shows maximum profit figures, giving us feedback on what is working and what is not. This feedback mechanism helps the trader with their subsequent trading decisions.

2. Assessing Capital Requirements

Many traders misjudge the capital they need for their strategies. Paper trading can reveal whether you have sufficient capital for your strategies, whether your profits are adequate, and if your position sizing is correct.

If we observe column O in Image 12.1, our second-largest loss of -14,155.33 on ASIANPAINT in row 85 had the maximum investment value of Rs. 2,85,000, which can give us insight into whether the trade incurred the second-highest loss because the position sizing was wrong, or for some other reason.

3. Evaluating Winning Probability

By analyzing a sample of 100 or more trades, a journal helps you gauge the winning probability of your strategy. It will also reveal whether your risk management is effective.

In Image 12.1, 6 out of 18 trades are at a loss or a breakeven. This means our winning probability is just 66%. Out of the winning 12 trades, only 6 or 7 trades incurred a profit of more than 3%. Therefore, 33% of the trades are giving the maximum profit. The remaining 66% are either a breakeven or a loss. This is a wonderful insight into your trading method. It mentally prepares you for the fact that only 3 out of 10 trades will hit a good profit.

4. Measuring Return on Capital Deployed

A trading journal helps you determine if the returns on your invested capital align with your strategy's goals. It will show whether your strategy is financially viable. In Image 12.1, you can spot the return on capital deployed in column Q.

5. Understanding Loss on Capital Deployed

Your journal will reveal the extent of losses incurred and whether you can sustain a series of losses without depleting your capital.

6. Tracking Costs Incurred

Brokerage fees can significantly impact your profits, sometimes consuming up to 30% of them. Your trading journal will help you assess whether these costs are affecting your overall profitability and if you're overtrading. Many traders don't know that a significant expense of trading goes into brokerage.

Apart from brokerage fees, there are other hidden charges like GST, STT, education cess, etc., which need to be considered while calculating the net profit. If you buy a stock at Rs. 100 and sell it at Rs. 102, you still might see a loss in your ledger because you are not considering the brokerage fees and hidden costs in your trading. In column M in Image 12.1, we are specifically taking into account the expected brokerage fee for the trade to get a real picture of at what price our trade will be profitable.

7. Reviewing Position Sizing

The journal will indicate if your position sizing is appropriate. Uneven position sizing can contribute to losses even if you follow the same strategy consistently.

Maintaining a trading journal offers these and many more benefits, helping you refine your approach and enhance your trading performance. I have been trading for the last 15 years, and I have a trading journal of each and every trade that I have taken over the last 10 years. Even though I can see my position in the net positions or the back office, unless I work on my positions in an Excel sheet, it doesn't give me satisfaction. Excel allows me to do all types of calculations that I need to be better prepared for the markets. Money is not a by-product of the strategy that you deploy in the markets. Money is a by-product of how well you have done your homework the previous day for the market. A journal provides you with your practice book, where you can prepare for the day ahead.

A trading journal should ideally be able to tell you:

1. Stock that you purchased
2. Date on which you purchased the stock
3. Buy price of the stock
4. Quantity purchased
5. Sell price of the stock
6. Date on which you sold the stock
7. Instrument: whether it is stock, future, or option
8. Expected brokerage
9. Net profit or loss after brokerage
10. Investment value or margin blocked for the trade
11. Return on capital deployed
12. Stop-loss or initial stop-loss
13. Status or learning

This is sufficient for a good trading journal. As a trader, if you feel like some other information would be useful for you, feel free to incorporate it as per your preference.

CHAPTER 13

Don't Trade Just Yet

The stock market won't solve your problems—
it will amplify them

The stock market is undeniably seductive, especially for new traders. It lures people from all walks of life—retirees, professionals, students, married individuals, businesspeople—with the promise of making money from money. The idea of getting rich without the need for a traditional job, business, or factory seems within reach of anyone with just a laptop and an internet connection.

Many are drawn to trading as an escape from the difficulties of the job market, hoping to avoid starting a business or taking on a traditional career. People are motivated to trade for various reasons: low salaries, unpleasant bosses, insufficient savings, physical disabilities, divorce, or a highly competitive environment. While these reasons may seem valid, it's crucial to understand one thing before you start trading:

The stock market is not as easy as it looks.

The Reality of Trading

Making money in the stock market is one of the most challenging tasks in the world. It's a zero-sum game—your loss is someone else's gain, and vice versa. You're up against institutions with far more resources, high-speed computer algorithms, better information, and extensive research. If you believe you can simply start trading and outperform experienced traders and investors, you're mistaken.

What You Need Before You Start Trading

Before diving into trading, two things are essential:

1. Zero liabilities and responsibilities
2. Extensive paper trading

1. Zero liabilities and responsibilities

Even with all the knowledge, insight, and experience in the world, no trader or investor can guarantee profits from the stock market. There will be days, weeks, or even months where losses are inevitable. This period of loss can cause even the best traders to doubt their strategies and decisions.

I've been approached by many people with various backgrounds and motivations:

- Individuals leaving jobs to start trading
- Housewives seeking work-from-home opportunities
- Handicapped individuals looking for a job
- Newlyweds aiming to increase their income
- Recently resigned employees
- People with standing debts venturing into the stock market
- Retired individuals without a steady income
- Students unwilling to leave their hometowns
- Employees who aren't receiving raises
- Individuals with recurring medical bills

All of these scenarios represent poor starting points for learning the stock market.

If you're trading for an active income and relying on it for your livelihood, the pressure to make a profit can lead to desperation. Desperation, in turn, leads to poor trading decisions, forced entries, and eventually, the loss of your capital. Rational thinking only lasts as long as your survival isn't threatened. Once desperation sets in, it drives desperate decisions and ultimately wipes out your resources.

If fear isn't causing your losses, greed will. Many people enter the market with limited capital, expecting unrealistically high returns. For instance, I've seen people with Rs. 50,000 expecting to make Rs. 10,000 in a single day—a 20% return. Such expectations would translate to a 600% return in a month, and 7,200% in a year (without compounding). Ask yourself: would those kinds of returns be realistic in *any* business?

When losses start piling up, they affect your emotional and mental health. I've witnessed traders' personal lives fall apart, marriages end, and even suicides due to overwhelming debt burdens. The common factor in all these cases is unrealistic expectations.

If your trades are profitable, you'll feel happy. But when they're not, frustration sets in, often spilling over onto your relationships with those around you—people who might not even understand what you're going through.

As losses accumulate, you'll likely start to introspect, questioning what you're doing wrong. To find the answer, you may turn to new trading methods. If you run out of trading capital, you might dip into savings or take out loans, convincing yourself each time that you've finally found the perfect strategy. This cycle can continue until there's no money left.

Even with the perfect strategy, there's no guarantee that there will always be trades to make. As the end of the month approaches and bills come due, desperation can force you into mistakes, causing you to deviate from your trading system.

The conditions for profitable trading are:

1. Your life should not depend on profits from the stock market.

2. Your life should not be affected by losses in the stock market.

In essence, even if you invest money in the stock market, you shouldn't rely on the profits to sustain your lifestyle. And if you lose your capital, it should only be a small, manageable part of your net worth.

2. Extensive paper trading

One way or another, you *will* pay the market for your education—either through losses or through paper trading.

The biggest mistake new traders make is diving into the market with real money without understanding the fundamentals. This often results in losses, with your hard-earned money essentially serving as tuition for learning through experience.

Paper trading is simulated trading where you assume you have a certain sum of money and record your trades in a journal as if they were real. This practice allows you to learn the market without risking your actual capital. This is crucial, and easier said than done. The market has a certain pull, even when you are monitoring it for paper trading. Noting a trade in your journal without participating in it can be boring. If your trade turns out to be a loser, you feel good that it's just a paper trade. If your trade turns into a profit, you lament over missing out a real-world profitable opportunity. This is how fear and greed play with you in the stock market.

The stock market requires army soldier levels of discipline from a trader. Traders tend to make the habit of repeating the same mistakes and expecting different results. The stock market requires doing the same thing repeatedly. All these factors make paper trading very difficult, but even more necessary. Even sufficient paper trading cannot ensure that you are ready to handle the real trading. Paper trading is emotionless, because there is no real money involved. But once you start trading with real money, emotions (fear and greed) play a big part. Even after 3 years of backtesting, I was not ready to take a stop-loss on my first trade in the real world.

Why am I telling you all this? Because I have seen the same story play out over and over, all the time. Lured by the thought of extra income, people start out with buying options or intraday trading. Over time, they turn into swing traders, then investors, or their capital is wiped out. It is for you to decide whether you want to learn from practical experience, potentially losing your hard-earned money. Or you can paper trade and then start real trading by losing a little less, but shortening your learning curve. The market will take its tuition fees.

About the Author

I have presented my experience of 16 years in this book. Do share your feedback with me via rohit.katwal@gmail.com.

- **Twitter:** www.twitter.com/rohit_katwal
- **YouTube:** www.youtube.com/@rohit_katwal
- **Instagram:** www.instagram.com/rohitkatwal
- **Threads:** https://www.threads.net/@rohitkatwal

If you are looking to delve into options trading:

- http://amazon.in/dp/B087ZZMY9Z